KEN HAIGH

UNDER THE HOLY LAKE

A Memoir of Eastern Bhutan

THE UNIVERSITY
of ALBERTA PRESS

Published by
The University of Alberta Press
Ring House 2
Edmonton, Alberta, Canada T6G 2E1

**Library and Archives Canada
Cataloguing in Publication**

Haigh, Ken, 1962–
Under the holy lake : a memoir
    of eastern Bhutan / Ken Haigh.

(Wayfarer)
Includes bibliographical references.
ISBN 978–0–88864–492–3

    1. Haigh, Ken, 1962- 2. Bhutan—
Civilization. 3. Bhutan—Social life and
customs. 4. Bhutan—Description and travel.
5. Teachers—Bhutan—Biography. I. Title.
II. Series: Wayfarer (Edmonton, Alta.)

DS491.5.H34 2008
954.98   C2007–907548–7

The University of Alberta Press is committed
to protecting our natural environment. As
part of our efforts, this book is printed on
Enviro 100 Edition: it contains 100% post-
consumer recycled fibres and is acid- and
chlorine-free.

The University of Alberta Press gratefully
acknowledges the support received for
its publishing program from The Canada
Council for the Arts. The University of
Alberta Press also gratefully acknowledges
the financial support of the Government
of Canada through the Book Publishing
Industry Development Program (BPIDP)
and from the Alberta Foundation for the
Arts for its publishing activities.

Canadä Canada Council
for the Arts Conseil des Arts
du Canada

FOR NANCY

                                        Perhaps
I may love other hills yet more
Than this: the future and the maps
Hide something I was waiting for.

One thing I know, that love with chance
And use and time and necessity
Will grow, and louder the heart's dance
At parting than at meeting be.

—EDWARD THOMAS, "WHEN FIRST I CAME HERE"

CONTENTS

PREfACE

WHEN I RETURNED TO CANADA after two years in Bhutan, I was able to bring home a few souvenirs: an infection of giardia, head lice, some lovely flea bite scars, and a tapeworm. I had also lost a great deal of weight during my sojourn. When I left Canada I was a healthy 83.9 kilograms (185 pounds). When I returned, I weighed only 65.8 kilograms (145 pounds). My doctor was both alarmed and impressed.

"You're very underweight," he worried after a thorough physical examination, "but, on the other hand, you're very fit. You have the heart and lungs of a sixteen-year-old track star. What have you been doing?"

"Climbing mountains," I explained. Down the mountain in the morning with a stack of corrected essays under my arm on the way to work. Up the mountain at the end of the day with a new pile of papers to correct that evening.

My dentist was also very impressed.

"These are the healthiest teeth and gums I have ever seen," he exclaimed. "What sort of diet have you been following?"

"The rice diet," I said. "Rice for breakfast, rice for lunch, and..."

"...rice for dinner?" ventured the dentist.

"Yup."

"That would do it," he conceded.

If I am sounding remarkably glib now, I truly was not at the time. In fact, I found myself homesick for a place that had never really been my home; where, as much as I wanted to, I could never really fit in. In the years that have passed since my time in Bhutan, I have earned two (more) university degrees, have taught school in China and in the Canadian Arctic, have become the chief administrator of a small public library, have married and become a parent three times over, and have grown grey and stout. And not a day goes by that I don't think of Bhutan and wish I was twenty-five and could experience it all over again.

For many people, there are landscapes that obsess the memory, that provoke even the dullest of us to bad poetry: the white cone of Fuji rising from the sea, the morning's sunrise over the Ganga at Benares, the long blue shadows and green ice of the Baffinlands, Ayers Rock, rose-tinted in the tangerine of dawn. And yet, for me, there is only one place: a green narrow valley in the eastern Himalayas, resting under the influence of a holy lake and an ancient tree, a place that for two short years I called, however mistakenly, my home—a place called Khaling.

ONE

WELCOME TO KHALING

BUT IT WASN'T LOVE AT FIRST SIGHT. Love would come later. My initial feelings toward Khaling were more like apprehension, even dread.

"Is it much further to Khaling?" I asked the driver.

The driver of the bus wagged his head in a noncommittal fashion, eyes fixed on the treacherous road. I sighed and settled back onto my hard bench seat, looking out the window at the rounded green peaks slowly unwinding in the distance, careful not to look down, as there was nothing to see there but cloud. The road, a mere scratch in the mountainside, clung to the ridge tops, ensuring that one shoulder of the road was always a precipice over which a tired or unskilled driver could fling his charges to certain death. After four days of this I had become numbed to danger. We approached yet another in an unending series of blind corners and the driver began leaning on his horn to warn oncoming traffic of our approach. Not that there was much traffic. Hours went by and the only thing we seemed to share the narrow winding road with was the occasional herd of cows or sheep being moved to new pastures. When we did meet another vehicle, both drivers would brake with equal desperation, hurling passengers and luggage into the aisle, and then one driver would have the unenviable task of backing up until a place could be found where two vehicles might pass abreast.

We drove past a sign: "Accidental Area Ahead." I leaned across the aisle and nudged Michael, who seemed to be half asleep.

"Did you see that?"

He shook his head, and I explained. "What is an accidental area?" I asked, knowing the answer. The whole country of Bhutan was an accidental area, an

Chorten and prayer flags in monsoon.

unknown place, a place out of step with the rest of the world. That was its appeal. Our favourite sign had been at Thumsing-La, the highest pass the bus had crossed:

Welcome

Thumsing-La (12,465 feet)

You are crossing the highest pass

Bash on regardless!

At Thumsing-La there had literally been no middle distance; the earth dropped away at our feet, and, spanning the horizon, was a range of snow-capped peaks that resembled teeth. Bash on regardless, indeed. On this road, that imperative would become our mantra.

Four days before, when the bus had left Thimphu, the capital of Bhutan, it had been packed to the ceiling with foreign volunteer teachers and their luggage. Now it had only two passengers left, Michael, an English mathematics teacher, and me. We were heading to Jigme Sherubling High School in Khaling Valley. Before leaving Canada, I had not been able to find out very much about Khaling. I had searched in vain for it on maps of the area. Indeed, if you had been an astronaut heading to Mars, you would have known more of your final destination than I did of Khaling. Here is what I had been able to glean:

Khaling Valley was located in the district of Tashigang in Eastern Bhutan.

The people of Khaling were called the Sharchopa, or "people of the east,"

Thumsing-La.

and they spoke Tsangla, also known as Sharchopkha, sometimes shortened to "Sharchop" in ordinary conversation. The east of Bhutan was the most densely populated, least affluent, and, according to some, the least developed part of the country.

There you have it. Now you know as much as I did when I first arrived in Khaling. Well, almost as much. I had been able to gather a few more insights in the bar of the Druk Hotel during my brief stay in Thimphu. I had quizzed the returning volunteers, the old hands, about Khaling. Few had visited Khaling Valley, but they all knew something of its reputation. The answers I received were always qualified and hesitant.

"Ah, Khaling," one would say. "Well, you have a gymnasium at the school. That's a bonus, and it's a nice place to be when it rains. It rains a lot."

Another would add, "You would like Father John Perry..."

"Yeah, he's great."

"...but, of course, he's leaving."

"Oh, right. I forgot."

"Yeah, that's too bad. He was cool."

"Khaling is famous for its *ara*."

"Yes," someone would laugh, "they're great drinkers in Khaling. They once turned so much of their corn crop into moonshine that they nearly starved over the winter."

Then there would be a period of awkward silence until someone would mutter, "Leeches."

"Oh, yeah. Leeches. Lots of leeches"

"Monster leeches. Big as your thumb, some of them."

When they realized they weren't really helping matters any they would rein in their enthusiastic discussion of blood-sucking terrestrial annelids and say, "Still, leeches are no big deal."

"Sure, no big deal. You get used to them."

"Yeah, a bit of salt and they fall right off."

Someone would brighten up a little. "Well, there's the Holy Lake. Never been there, but it's supposed to be famous in Eastern Bhutan."

"Mind you," someone else would counter, "in this country, a pond is called a lake."

"Or a pool in a river," another would add.

Night after night people would struggle to be kind and to dredge up something that would make Khaling seem like an appealing place to be. But the picture that always emerged was of a dark gloomy place, where it rained all of the time, where people drank their livers away, and where armies of giant leeches lurked in the underbrush waiting to pounce. This did not help alleviate my growing sense of doom.

"Khaling," announced the bus driver, pointing ahead with his chin.

I leaned forward, eager for a first glimpse of my new home. But I was to be disappointed. As the bus rounded the last curve, we were confronted by a thick bank of fog. The bus was swallowed up in a world of damp murky greyness. The sun was blotted out. The air was so saturated with water vapour that the roadside foliage glistened and dripped. If this was winter, I asked myself, the dry season, what would Khaling look like three months from now in the monsoon?

The little bus left the road at Khaling Bazaar (a grim huddle of huts leaning together in the fog), passed under a half-finished arch that looked like something left over from an Armistice Day parade, and began a series of tortuous serpentine switchbacks up the mountainside. We were climbing through pastureland bounded on one side by a jutting mountain spur and on the other by a river that ran down the length of the valley. Soon we were passing little white cubes of concrete with red corrugated zinc roofs. The whitewash seemed grey and streaked in the gloom. These, I had to assume, were the teachers' quarters. The pastureland rose in broad steps. The first step was a soccer pitch. It didn't look like much, but I later learned that it was one of the best in the country, simply because such a broad flat space was a rarity. Most schools had to make do with something much smaller and more precarious, where a ball kicked out of bounds might take half an hour to retrieve. Above the field was the school gymnasium. It was constructed of whitewashed concrete, topped with steel roof trusses and a metal ceiling. Most of the windows, which formed a band just below the overhang of the roof, were broken. The school itself stood across the road from the gym on the same bench of land. It, like everything else, was made of concrete. It was long, rectangular, and two stories tall. All of the classrooms were entered by an outside two-storey verandah with a central staircase.

The driver continued up the hill, looking for some place to turn around, winding past more small teachers' cottages, past some wooden go-downs, and coming to a stop at a low building that turned out to be the dining hall. From here, I could see, you had to proceed on foot up broad concrete steps, which passed three lime-coloured dormitories resembling the school building in proportion. At the top of the steps was a handsome two-storey building, which I later learned was the residence of the Teaching Sisters. To the left of this was a small cottage where the Jesuit Fathers lived. That was our school—only ten years old and already crumbling to putty in the world's wettest valley.

The school appeared to be deserted. My introduction to Jigme Sherubling was dispiriting. Cold, damp, and foggy, Khaling had exceeded my worst expectations.

When the bus reached the foot of the concrete steps, the driver turned around and proceeded slowly down the hill again, coming to a stop on a gravel patch between the school and the gymnasium. He killed the engine. It was silent now except for the distant baying of hounds. Fog enshrouded everything. Michael and I decided to check out the school. Everything was locked up. We peered into the darkened and deserted classrooms. Each room was furnished with a cracked green chalkboard and rows of crudely-made desks and benches. Each desk seated two students. On the top floor there were two reasonably well-equipped science labs with appropriate rows of test tubes, Pyrex flasks, Petri dishes, Bunsen burners, and amphibians pickled in formaldehyde. The gymnasium also appeared to be locked up. I told Michael I was going to walk up the hill to the residences to see if anyone was home.

I was only partway up the first switchback, outside the first of the drab little cottages, when I became aware that the baying and snarling of hounds was drawing closer. Wisps of fog were swirling around me and much of the valley was lost to sight. I began to feel like the doomed heir in *The Hound of the Baskervilles*. The pack of dogs passed above me, unseen, moving from right to left. What were they chasing? I wondered. A deer, perhaps? The snarling faded. Then it seemed to turn a corner in the mist and began to grow louder again. Unless I was much mistaken, the pack of dogs was following the winding road and was now heading straight toward me.

"Mad dog!"

The door of the nearest cottage had opened a crack and a man's head and shoulders protruded.

"What?"

"Mad dog!" the man shrieked in terror and slammed the door in my face.

I turned and looked up the road. Emerging from the fog was The Hound, all fangs and foaming chops. I turned and sprinted down the hill toward the bus. Michael and the driver had seen me and were already on board. I launched myself through the open door and the driver slammed the accordion doors shut behind me. The Hound hit the bus so hard it rocked. He tried his best to eat the door, leaving a trail of saliva on the glass. The pack caught up with him and rolled him in the dust, circling and snapping. Then he was up and they vanished in pursuit.

I looked at Michael and the driver. Their faces registered the same shock and horror that I was feeling. I sat down heavily on the top step.

I swore silently and thought, "Welcome to Khaling."

TWO

TEACH THEM TO THINK!

A YEAR PREVIOUSLY I HAD BEEN A GRADUATE STUDENT in English literature, studying for a master's degree. I had fully intended to carry on to a Ph.D. and ultimately to a professorship, but three weeks into the program I realized it was not for me. At an introductory wine-and-cheese, the dean of the English department greeted the incoming grad students and made a little speech. It began with a shot to the solar plexus.

"None of you," she said, "should actually expect to find jobs when you graduate."

This was 1986. It was all about demographics, she explained. Most university professors were relatively young, and we would have to wait fifteen or twenty years for her generation to retire. I was not as disappointed by this news as you might expect. I was finding grad school dull and insular. The height of intellectual achievement seemed to be developing a conversancy in semiotics, deconstruction, or reader-response theory. I didn't care about these things.

A change of plan was called for. I wanted to travel, and I wanted a job worth doing, but I had no money and I quickly discovered that a degree in English literature didn't really qualify me to do anything. So, like so many young people of my generation, I decided to seek employment as a teacher overseas, preferably in some developing country where teachers were badly needed.

My roommates at this time were in the faculty of education. They told me of an information meeting to be held in the auditorium of the teachers' college for student teachers who might be interested in teaching overseas. I slipped into the darkened auditorium and listened as a number of returned teachers described their experiences and answered questions about the organizations for which they had worked. Most of the speakers had worked in well-funded international schools in large urban centres, but the speaker who impressed me most was a young woman who had worked in rural Africa under the auspices of the World University Service of Canada (WUSC). WUSC's candidates were called volunteers because they taught in local schools and shared the same living conditions and salaries as their local colleagues. This program appealed to me. I wanted to feel virtuous about what I was doing, and I liked the idea of a job that came with a hair shirt.

After the meeting I approached the speaker and asked her how I could apply to be part of the program. She handed me an application package and counselled patience. I filled in the application—about twenty-five pages long, if I remember correctly—and waited.

Almost a year passed, then one night, the phone rang. "Mr. Haigh," the voice said, "Are you still interested in teaching overseas?"

"Sure," I replied.

"Would you be interested in a posting in Bhutan?"

Bhutan? I wondered. Where's that? Somewhere in the Middle East?

"Okay. Sounds great."

"Good. Tomorrow morning, you will receive a sealed envelope by priority courier with instructions as to the time and place of your interview. Follow your instructions and I will see you in a couple of days."

I spent the next few days trying to find out as much as I could about Bhutan, which was surprisingly little. The public library had two very bad and dated travel books. The university library had some material, but most of it was about twenty years old. Even the university map library only had one map of the country, prepared by Indian Army surveyors, and this, as I learned later, was horribly inaccurate. Bhutan, it turned out, was in Asia, not in the Middle East as I had first assumed (that turned out to be Bahrain); and, according to statistics published in 1978 (which were all I could find at the time), was the poorest country in the world with the highest rate of infant mortality. Bhutan was a tiny landlocked Himalayan kingdom, ruled over by a benevolent monarch who smoked stogies and who was so beloved by his people that when he tried to introduce legislation limiting his own powers his offer was indignantly refused. Bhutan was a Buddhist country with strong cultural links to Tibet, which bordered it on the north. It was, in fact, after the Chinese "liberation" of Tibet in 1959 and Sikkim's absorption into India in 1975, the last country in the world to have Tantric Buddhism as the state religion. It was a predominantly agrarian society and most of the population earned their living through mixed farming in isolated mountain valleys. It was an extremely mountainous country. There were few roads, and people had remained so isolated for so many generations that, even though the country was only three hundred kilometres (one hundred eighty-seven miles) from east to west, twenty-four different language groups had formed with many regional dialects.[1] It was common, I read (and it proved to be the case), that people separated by a single mountain range could not understand one another.

As I read, I began to imagine how it might be. And as my experience of mountains at this time was limited to the Canadian Rockies, a picture formed in my mind of a land composed of similar jagged snow-capped and pine-clad peaks; except that here there were also elephants carrying princely riders in howdahs through terraced tea gardens where colourfully garbed women bent under the weight of baskets of tea leaves and where half-ruined marble palaces peeked out of the encroaching jungle. I pictured cobras and tigers, temple monkeys and lotus ponds, holy men and incense. Of course, I was completely wrong.

I arrived at my interview in Toronto with moments to spare. I straightened my tie, ran my fingers through my hair, knocked on the door, and entered the room. Two people, a man and a woman, were seated at the far end of a long birch conference table.

The woman was the elder of the two. Something about her sphinx-like manner, her bleached and brittle hair and the tiny network of wrinkles about her eyes, told me, without having to ask, that she had spent some considerable time under an African sun. The man was bearded, cheerful, and encouraging. His was the voice I had heard on the phone. His purpose, I decided, besides recording the statements I made in response to their questions, was to try and draw idiotic generalizations out of me. This he did with accomplished ease.

The woman had been knitting a large black web-like thing when I came in and, while the introductions were being made, she continued to work, needles clicking together like dry bones, scrutinizing me with hooded eyes. When she lay her knitting aside, I knew she had sized me up and the real interview had begun.

Most of the interview I don't remember, which is probably a reflection that it went very well, but toward the end of the hour I do remember very clearly one question being posed: "What do you feel is the role of a teacher in a developing country?"

I answered without pause, having anticipated this question. "A teacher's role is always to teach students to think for themselves, to develop a critical attitude in everything they do, so they can see their way through problems, and to enable them to learn and grow as individuals." This seemed to be just the sort of wrong answer they had been waiting for. They exchanged excited glances, and an unspoken signal was given. The young man leaned forward aggressively and wagged an authoritative finger in the air.

"That is *exactly* what a host government does *not* want you to do. In their minds, they are hiring people who can teach skills. Skills! In your case, written and spoken English skills. Teach them to think!" he chuckled, as if to say, what a naïve, liberal, nay, simple-minded, thing to do.

"Teach them to think, you say." He tapped his briefcase significantly. "I have in here a report prepared by the leaders of various African nations examining the question of popular discontent against their regimes. Do you know what they concluded?" I did not. "They concluded that the number one factor in every case of unrest was that these people had been taught how to think." He sat back in his chair with a broad smile and spread his hands expansively in such a way as to indicate that there was really nothing more to be said. The woman nodded in mute but enthusiastic agreement.

Despite my blunder, I was offered the job, and, strange as it may seem, I had cause to remember his words many times over the next two years.

A few weeks later, I arrived in Ottawa for my orientation. There were four other volunteers going to Bhutan. One, a young man named Tom, would not make it through orientation. A tearful phone conversation with his girlfriend in Vancouver convinced him that he was making a dreadful mistake, and he caught the night bus home. Knowing how profoundly the experience of working in Bhutan affected those of us who did go, I have often wondered if he regretted his decision. The other three would become good friends in time, but at first I found them a little intimidating. There was Jerry from Montreal, Catherine from the Eastern Townships of Quebec, and Sarah from Vancouver. All three were trained teachers. All three had travelled extensively. They were older than I and exuded a sophisticated confidence that I did not possess.

We were taken to a retreat centre in the Gatineau Hills. There, for three days, we were briefed on what to expect in a developing country and what sorts of problems we might encounter. Because our recruitment had been so hurried, none of us had had the time to get all of the inoculations that were required; so in between briefings, we would step into the hall and get jabbed. I remember walking back into the room after two massive gamma-globulin injections, one in each buttock, and passing out on the floor.

None of the people who were brought in to talk to us had been to Bhutan; most had worked in Africa, and so their information was maddeningly unspecific. There was a photo album that had been loaned to us by a couple who had returned from two years in Bhutan, but they were unavailable to talk to us. In between sessions, we poured over these snapshots, trying to extrapolate beyond the frames of the pictures. There was only one photograph in the album labelled "Khaling," and it was worse than useless; it was disturbing. It was overexposed and seemed to have been taken from a moving car. The foreground was a vast field of corn stubble, and in the distance, disappearing below the horizon, was a cluster of snot-green buildings, surrounded by what appeared to been a high barbed wire fence. I examined these buildings closely, trying to discern which of them might be the school. The image looked depressingly like a military encampment or a prison. There were lots of photographs of Jerry, Sarah, and Catherine's postings. These all looked suitably picturesque and inviting. What was so awful about Khaling, I wondered, that it didn't even warrant stopping the car to take a picture?

We left directly from the Gatineau Hills to the airport. There was no time to say goodbye, no time to make adjustments to our luggage (we were allowed just two bags). We felt like astronauts setting off into the unknown, scared and exhilarated. I would give anything to feel that way again.

The flight to India took two days with a stopover in Amsterdam. I knew we would have to spend several days in Calcutta before we flew on to Paro, Bhutan's only airport, so I had tried to prepare for the experience by reading City of Joy prior to boarding the plane. I can say now, in all honesty, that nothing prepares you for the reality of Calcutta. Most Westerners coming to Calcutta for the first time are strongly affected. I have known some who gave away most of their belongings to beggars on the street, others who broke down in tears.

Even though it was February in India, this was nothing like February in Canada. Stepping off the plane was like stepping into a warm shower. We had just left Amsterdam's snow-filled streets, we were still wearing winter clothing, and our bodies had not had time to adjust to the heat. The very air was unfamiliar. There were smells I could not identify at the time, like the fustiness of marigolds and the acrid scent of burning dung. These relatively pleasant smells overlaid the smells of rot, decay, and jet exhaust. Calcutta had the worst smog I had ever experienced and our eyes and lungs smarted from it.

Our field director, Howard Solverson, met us in the lobby of the airport. Howard was tall and slim and always seemed to lean hunched forward as if he were in a hurry even when he was standing still. His hair was long and streaked with grey, and he sported a Kiplingesque moustache.

Howard had lived in India for a time and offered to guide us around the city that evening. I was pretty jet-lagged but agreed to go. We set off on a long walk through the darkened post-apocalyptic streets. Tattered beggars loomed out of the shadows, holding out their bony arms, brushing their cupped hands against our chests and arms, quietly speaking unintelligible phrases in smiling singsong. Legless cripples on wheeled carts pursued us with curses. Whole families slept huddled together in doorways. We stepped around piles of garbage that spilled across the sidewalks, where pye-dogs and children fought for the scraps. At one point, looking up at a particularly gothic old mansion, I almost stepped on a woman who was sleeping on the sidewalk. I recoiled in horror from this desiccated thing crouched on the pavement, twisting under a dirty shroud. I lost control of my facial muscles. My cheek twitched spasmodically. I felt physically ill. I wanted to go back to the hotel but had no idea where I was, so I clung to the group like a drowning man while the night city spun around me, growing more lurid and horrific with each step.

When we returned to the hotel, I immediately excused myself and went to my room. As I lay in my bed, feigning sleep, I could hear the others as they sat on wicker armchairs in the lobby, sipping their gin and tonics.

"Did you see Ken?" said Jerry. "Man, he nearly lost it tonight. If he can't take this, he's never gonna last two years in Bhutan."

At that moment, I tended to agree with him.

Morning brought new perspective however. After breakfast I took a walk by myself, determined to put on a better show. I successfully haggled for a silk scarf in the New Market; I took a walk in the Maidan, Calcutta's central park, and watched the cricket matches; I saw the art treasures in the Indian Museum, taking particular note of the Bhutanese textiles; I visited the Victoria Memorial; and I ended my tour in St. Paul's Cathedral.

Tall and vaulted with cast-iron arches like the great railway stations of Europe, the cathedral was a bit of translated English gothic, an oasis of peace in this mad city. I sat down in the nearly empty church and caught my second wind. I noted with pleasure that the church was full of songbirds; indeed, their droppings littered the pews. It seemed fitting that they, too, should find sanctuary here. I walked around the church reading the memorials to the dead: soldiers, statesmen, clergy, lawyers, wives, and administrators of the Raj. Most had died young, I noted, either by act of war or by disease. It was a bit of a shock when I came across a particularly prominent memorial in the porch to those killed in the war in "Bootan." I was not even aware that there had been a war in Bhutan. It was both unsettling and intriguing. I returned to the hotel chastened but determined. I wasn't ready to throw in the towel just yet.

We flew from Calcutta to Paro in a twin-prop Dornier 228, a plane so small that every one of its seventeen passengers had a window seat, and the passenger sitting at the back, next to the toilet, had to double as flight attendant, handing cups of hot tea forward to the other passengers from the thermos beside her seat. In 1987 this homely broken-beaked aircraft was Druk Air, making its twice-weekly flight between India and Bhutan.

I was unprepared for the dramatic suddenness of the Himalayas. The land around Calcutta had been a lush patchwork of green and completely flat; but this plain ended abruptly as we approached the mountains. The small plane seemed to be flying straight toward a blank green wall. By a miracle, we managed to scrape over the top of this wall only to be met by another higher wall. Beyond that was another wall, slightly higher, and beyond that another, like giant steps leading to the plateaus of Tibet. The last step was the greatest and was marked by a line of snow-capped peaks.

As the plane struggled to ascend, shaving the treetops, cresting another of these green steps, we could see whitewashed houses, paddy fields, isolated temples, larger castle-like fortresses, and a network of trails leading in every direction. Occasionally, small figures would look up, shading their eyes. This was not what I had expected, having been raised in the shadow of the Rockies. The Himalayas are older mountains, smoothed by time and covered in trees right to their crests. They were more like the Appalachians in appearance, but then appearances were deceiving, since these were much higher. Many of the villagers we saw were living at elevations greater that the summits of most Canadian mountains. A fellow passenger pointed out Everest to the west, her snowy head and shoulders towering above the smaller peaks in the foreground.

The airplane circled Paro airfield several times before beginning to descend. The airstrip looked far too short, our approach far too steep. It was like trying to land in the bottom of a not particularly large soup bowl. The plane hit the runway and bounced, decelerated quickly, and taxied over to the customs shed. We descended from the plane to the tarmac and wrestled our own luggage from its cargo bay. I set my things down, paused for a moment and stretched my limbs. It was quiet. I took a deep breath of the clean mountain air, noted the neat whitewashed houses and the

Paro Dzong.

terraced hillsides. There was no smog. There were no crowds, no touts, no beggars. No one was in a rush to do anything. Our passage through Customs was unhurried, the people friendly and courteous. We boarded a small bus and drove along a winding road above a sparkling river. There were huge long-tailed monkeys grooming on the riverbank. After Calcutta, things were beginning to look up.

In Thimphu, Howard put us up at the Druk Hotel and organized two weeks of further orientation. Each day we would listen to lectures on history, culture, health, and nutrition. We had daily lessons in Sharchopkha. We also were encouraged to purchase all of the supplies we would need for two years in the east, since as difficult as things were to find in Thimphu, they were almost impossible to locate in the Eastern Bhutan. I was told to think of my sojourn in Bhutan as a two-year camping trip and to buy accordingly. So, I purchased a kerosene stove, a kerosene storm lantern, a water filter, a wok, a couple of pots, some cutlery, a tin plate and bowl, an enamelled mug, some powdered milk, and a crate of rolled oats for my morning meal. Most important, however, I bought as much toilet paper as I could lay my hands on—two rolls in one shop, one roll in another. We would learn to dole out our TP a square at a time and, when this ran out, to cut up newspapers and magazines.

Much of my shopping was done in mime. I had learned a few words by this time. I knew that kading-chhe meant "thank you" and that kuzu zangpo was a polite form of "hello." I had also learned several useful suffixes, like ka (language of), pa (people of), and la, which could be added to a word or phrase as a sign of respect for someone of superior rank. It was even used in English. It was not unusual to hear "Good morning-la" or "Hello-la." "La" was also the word for a mountain pass, a lofty place, so there was a certain logic at work here. It was customary, I discovered, to address strangers by their familial roles, relative to one's own age. For example, older persons were addressed as Ama (Mother) or Apa (Father)—and much older people were called Abi (Grandmother) or Meme (Grandfather). Similarly, those younger than oneself were politely called Kota (Brother) or Usen (Sister).

There was no Sharchop equivalent to the English "yes" or "no." One could say "it is" or "it isn't," but in response to most questions, one replied by simply repeating the verb in the question. For example, if someone asked you, "Ara jamsho-mo?" (Would you like a drink of alcohol?), you could respond, "Jamsho" (Drink) or "Ma-jamsho" (Not drink), as the case might be. The simplest way to phrase a question was to tack the suffix mo on the end of the sentence, if it was an open question (Tashigang-ga dencha-mo? "Are you going to Tashigang?"), or the suffix ya if it was an open sentence containing an interrogative word like "when," "who," or "where" (Tashigang-ga iti dencha-ya? "When are you going to Tashigang?"). Also, as far as I could tell, there were no words for "evil" or "bad" or "ugly," or any of the other negative adjectives one finds in English. A Sharchopa would simply say "not virtuous," "not good," or "not pretty."

I also learned a bit of body language from the more experienced volunteers. There was a method of counting on your knuckles that was useful for bargaining with shopkeepers with whom you did not share a common language. There was also a way of signifying assent, which I learned the hard way.

One of the items I needed to purchase for my new home was a mattress. I wanted something that would not harbour mould or bugs, so I rejected the less expensive cotton and coir (coconut husk) palettes and opted instead for a ten-centimetre (four-inch) foam rubber mattress that I had found in one of the shops. In Bhutan, as in most of the world, it is necessary to discuss a price before purchasing anything, and a foreigner haggling tends to draw a crowd. I was, therefore, a little nervous at my first attempt to buy something in a Bhutanese shop. I approached the shopkeeper and asked him for a price on his foam mattress.

He sized me up and made his opening bid: "Four hundred rupees."

"Two hundred," I countered.

He looked thoughtful, perhaps even a little stern, and tipped his head slightly toward his left shoulder. People were beginning to gather to observe our transaction. I was worried. Clearly this shopkeeper was a tough customer. I felt like a rube in a high-stakes poker game.

"Okay," I said. "Two hundred and twenty rupees."

The shopkeeper looked slightly surprised, even amused. Once again, he tipped his head to one side.

"All right. Two-fifty." There was some nervous giggling at this. The crowd looked to the shopkeeper to gauge his response. Once again, he silently tipped his head.

"Two seventy-five." The onlookers seemed aghast. There was a great deal of background chatter. All eyes were on the shopkeeper. He was openly smiling now, savouring my defeat. Once again, he tipped his head. Damn, this guy was good. He knew I wanted the mattress badly and he was playing me. I was sweating, but I put on my best game face.

"Three hundred rupees," I said, trying to look like Clint Eastwood, "but no higher." At some point Catherine had entered the shop behind me.

"Ken, what *are* you doing?"

I turned to face her. She, like the shopkeeper, looked both amused and alarmed.

"Trying to buy a mattress, but this guy is really tough. I can't get him to agree on a price."

"But he did agree to a price."

"What? When did he do that?"

She was laughing out loud now, as was everyone else in the shop. "What was your first price?" she asked, gasping for air.

"Two hundred. Why?"

She put her hands on my shoulders and looked me straight in the eye. "Because this," she said, tipping her head to one side, "means 'yes.'"

The national sport of Bhutan is archery, and while we were in Thimphu we had a chance to watch our first archery tournament. Archery, as it is practised in Bhutan, is unlike archery anywhere else in the world. In Bhutan, archery is played much like horseshoes, where teams of archers shoot arrows at posts set a football field's distance from each other. When a player strikes the post, the game pauses while the players form a circle, sing, and perform a victory dance to celebrate the shot. The interesting twist on the game is that once a player has shot his quiver, he can run the length of the field and stand beside the target and wave his arms and legs in an attempt to break his opponent's concentration. It was said (and I saw it attempted) that a good player could deflect his opponent's arrows using parts of his own body. This was perfectly legal, but understandably dangerous, given that large amounts of alcohol were frequently consumed during the course of a match.

The traditional Bhutanese bow was unique and required a special technique to fire. It was a fairly short bow made of two pieces of tapered bamboo, overlapped and joined at the handle. The bow was stiff and brittle and, hence, could not be held at full draw for any length of time. Archers would, therefore, nock their arrow, draw the bowstring back halfway, sight the target, and then with one swift motion, raise the bow, pull back the bowstring to full draw, and release the arrow. The trajectory was high, and you could actually follow the progress of the arrow through the air toward the target. Here and there on the field I saw wealthy Bhutanese with modern archery equipment. Modern compound bows were status symbols and were greatly admired both for their ease of use and their accuracy, but I could see that they gave their owners an unfair advantage over their more traditionally equipped opponents.

On my third day in Thimphu I fell down the hotel stairs and twisted my ankle. To give me some credit, they were *very* uneven stairs. I missed the program that morning. In the afternoon, however, we were expected at the hospital for a lecture on health by a volunteer doctor from Italy named Dr. Paolo Marisco. The Thimphu hospital was small and clean with only a few wards and no private rooms. The place was full of

Archery tournament, Thimphu.

people coming and going, and I soon learned that in Bhutan, as in most hospitals in the developing world, families were expected to do much of the caregiving. The doctors made their rounds, examined the patients, gave the nurses and orderlies instructions, but it was the family members who fed the patients, bathed the patients, and emptied the bedpans.

Dr. Marisco met us in his office and then led us on a whirlwind tour of the hospital. The idea was that he could show us some of the problems to be avoided. He led us into the first ward, drew back the curtain, and we were confronted by an emaciated woman of uncertain age who slobbered and grinned and nodded at us in a friendly if simple manner. We stood around like young interns and stared at her. It was uncomfortable for us, but she did not seem to mind. Her skin was covered in lesions that had been stained purple with a solution of gentian violet. I saw with horror that her nose was missing. In its place was a yawning purple cavity. She looked like Lon Chaney in *The Phantom of the Opera*.

"Advanced syphilis," said Paolo in a matter-of-fact manner, "characterized by partial paralysis, deterioration of the septum and palate, and severe brain damage. There is not much I can do for her at this stage. She is not yet thirty years old." We shrunk back, for we had placed her age at fifty at the very least. "Let this be a lesson to you. Venereal disease is rampant in this country. The wealthy keep asking me for penicillin. They think that if they take a pill a day, they can avoid this fate. I have tried to explain to them that overusing antibiotics actually decreases the effectiveness of the medication, but they don't believe me." He sighed. "So far, there is only one confirmed case of AIDS in the country: a young monk who picked it up while travelling in India. If AIDS ever gets a foothold in Bhutan..." He left the rest unsaid. "Follow me."

The next bed held a genial old man with an enormous growth about his neck like a leather horse collar. "Goitre," said Paolo. "Caused by the lack of iodine in his diet. Normally iodine is transmitted through the soil to the vegetables you eat. There simply isn't enough iodine in the environment in most of these valleys. This isn't anything you need to worry about, however. As long as you eat iodized salt you will never get like this. Cases like this, while common once, are fairly rare these days."

The next bed was the worst yet. The young boy's nose was carbuncled, his lip fattened, his hands battered claws. I knew what this was. As a child I had nightmares about this disease. Paolo smiled at the boy and patted his shoulder. "Leprosy," he said sadly. "Is anyone here being posted to Wamrong? Khaling?" I nodded. "The valleys south and east of you have some of the highest concentrations of leprosy in the world. Or I should say had some of the highest concentrations. The Scandinavian missions have done some remarkable work there. Still, it is not something you need to worry about."

Great, I thought. Khaling was sounding better and better: rain that never ends, monster leeches and, now, the highest concentration of lepers in the world living right next door.

In the next bed, a middle-aged man was resting, his leg slightly elevated and bandaged. "What happened to him?" asked Jerry.

Paolo snorted. "Arrow wound. Bloody idiot."

He continued to lecture us as we walked around the hospital. The number of patients was clearly overwhelming. It was evident that there were not enough medical personnel to treat them all. Paolo warned us that the most serious threat we were likely to face was gastrointestinal. "Tapeworm, roundworm, pinworm, giardia, dysentery, not to mention a host of related viruses gathered under the generic title 'Calcutta Syndrome.'" He warned us to boil all of our drinking water and then to filter it. Never eat uncooked vegetables. Be wary of pork. All of these warnings, he acknowledged, only worked in an ideal world. "You are going to be in a village, visiting someone's house, and they will offer you a cup of tea. Where did the water come from? Did they bring it to a rolling boil?" He shrugged. "You will have to make up your own mind about things like that. Use your common sense."

Throughout the tour, I should mention, an albino orderly pushed me about in the hospital's only wheelchair. I felt uncomfortable with this special treatment and offered to push the wheels myself, but he refused. I learned a quick lesson. Pushing me was his job. Just because I could do it myself did not give me the right to put him out of work. By this point, my right ankle was swollen up to the size of a grapefruit, turning a lovely shade of purple, and quite painful. The others went off for lunch and I was left to sit in a chair in a crowded hallway with other patients, until Paolo could examine my ankle.

I had been sitting quite some time, lost in thought, when I became aware that someone was standing right in front of me, pushing a crumpled slip of paper under my nose. I took the paper and examined it. It was a hospital form of some kind, but the alphabet was unfamiliar. It might as well have been written in Chinese or Greek for all that I could understand. I looked up. Standing before me was a Nepali man dressed in blue plastic sandals, ragged polyester trousers, and a patterned acrylic sweater that was parting at one shoulder. His one arm was roughly bandaged in a dirty towel, and he cradled it across his chest. He smiled ingratiatingly and raised his good hand vertically in front of his face, making half of the salute one sees so often in South Asia. "Namaste, namaste," he said.

I nodded and smiled in reply and held the paper toward him. He frowned and pushed it back at me. Then he rooted around in his pocket and held out a grubby ten rupee note. Now I was alarmed. I felt helplessly lost. "I'm sorry, I don't understand," I said and I shrugged in an exaggerated manner, thinking that large gestures might help. He persisted, beginning to look upset, as if to say: Look, I have been standing here bleeding all day and you will not brush me off. "I don't know what you want. I don't know what this paper says. I..." and then it dawned on me: He thought I was a doctor. I looked around for help, but of course everyone was far too busy to hail from where I was sitting. Just when it looked like things might get ugly, I was rescued.

"Ah, there you are, Ken. Let's look at that ankle."

It was Paolo. I explained about the man and his piece of paper. Paolo spoke to an orderly, who took the unfortunate aside and gave him a dressing down right there in the hallway. I don't know what was said, but I felt terrible. First of all, I felt responsible for the poor man's predicament. Secondly, it was quite clear in everyone's eyes that I was jumping the queue. And finally, after the orderly had finished publicly humiliating the poor man for bothering me, there was a hushed conversation, a promise made, and the orderly slipped the money into his pocket.

"Well, you are in luck. It's not broken. Just a bad sprain. Try to stay off it for a while. You should be able to walk in a couple of days, but it will take a very long time before you are ready for any serious hiking. Remember, too, that it is weakened. It would be very easy to re-injure yourself. So no basketball, okay? Also, if you can find one, wrap your ankle in an elastic bandage to give it some support."

"Don't you have any elastic bandages here?"

"Elastic bandage, are you kidding?" He stood up and looked around, his gaze taking in the general chaos. He laughed. "Where do you think you are? Canada?"

THREE

NOT EXACTLY AN APARTMENT

THE HIGH SCHOOL IN KHALING was not nearly as deserted as it first appeared. The support staff was there—the kitchen and cleaning staff—as was a skeleton staff of teachers. After the dogs had cleared off, a man approached the bus. He was Indian. He was short and well-dressed—although, as a concession to the cold, he was wearing a striped sweater under his black suit jacket, which made the jacket fit a little tight under the arms. He was balding but had dark hair that curled up over his collar. This aureole of hair combined with a bow mouth and apple cheeks gave him a cherubic expression, like one of Dickens's Cheeryble brothers.

He introduced himself, but it was clear that he was not exactly sure who we were.

"I'm Father Cherion," he said extending his hand. "I'm the new principal of Jigme Sherubling. Or, I will be, after Father Perry leaves."

"Father Perry is still here, then?"

"Well, not exactly. He is in Samdrup Jongkhar on school business—ordering supplies, settling accounts, picking up the teachers' wages. He should be back tomorrow."

We introduced ourselves. We chatted for a bit and then gently suggested that we were tired and enquired where we could put our things.

"Ah, yes," he sighed. "I guess we should find you some place to stay." He cupped his right elbow in his left hand, stroked his chin with his right, rocked up and down on the balls of his feet, and looked around the campus. "Most of the teachers' quarters have already been spoken for, and I think you will realize that, as bachelor gentlemen, the teachers with families will have first dibs. There is one bungalow just below the school that is still vacant and that will perhaps suit Mr. Michael. And Mr. Ken..." he paused and looked up the hill, "there is an empty box room in the boys' dormitory..." The look of horror on my face must have given him pause, for he made a sudden decision, "...no, I think the apartment in the gymnasium will serve better. Yes," he nodded emphatically. "I think you will be quite comfortable there."

"There's an apartment in the gymnasium?"

He looked pensive. "Well, not exactly an apartment..."

"Can I see it?"

"Not right now. The students are writing their Class 10 examinations. Later, perhaps, when they have finished."

The driver was anxious to get going, so Michael offered to put me up in his bungalow that first night. We thanked Father Cherion and obtained a key for Michael's new residence. We unloaded the bus, said goodbye to our driver, and shifted our things into Michael's very basic little concrete bungalow.

I was just trying to decide where to unroll my sleeping bag on the floor of the cold, unfurnished room, when the campus was invaded. Military jeeps roared up the school driveway and fanned out on the gravel plain beside the school. Intimidating men in army fatigues, wearing sidearms and red berets, jumped out of the vehicles and formed a perimeter. Then a more luxurious 4-wheel drive Toyota Hi-Lux with tinted windows swept up the drive, flying the flag of Bhutan, and stopped. It was His Majesty, King Jigme Singye Wangchuck.

I called to Michael and together we peered cautiously over the windowsill in my room. We had a good vantage point, but we were too far away to hear anything. The king got out of his vehicle and looked around sharply. Even from where we stood, we could see that he was not pleased. He was a handsome man, but he looked older and heavier than he did in his pictures, more careworn. He was dressed in a beautiful *gho* of raw silk with broad brocade-like stripes in chrysanthemum colours of yellow, orange, and red. He barked at a soldier, who saluted and ran off. The king paced impatiently. Father Cherion emerged from the school office, visibly nervous, escorted by the bodyguard. Watching the scene that followed gave me cause to truly understand the term "tongue lashing" for the first time; for even though we were too far away to hear what was said, we could see the principal-in-waiting flinch under each well-directed lash of the king's tongue. Poor Father Cherion. No one had warned him of the king's visit. The king, who had expected a dignified reception and an audience to address, had arrived to find no one was expecting him at all, and he took out his displeasure on the diminutive Jesuit.

"Do you think we ought to go help him?" I said.

Michael looked at me thoughtfully, taking time to consider how best to reply.

"No," he said.

Almost as soon as they had arrived, the king and his entourage departed. I would see the king three times during my two years in Bhutan, each time he seemed grave and hurried. And yet, I found it encouraging that, despite the social divide, the average person in Bhutan had such close and frequent contact with the head of state. I have never met the prime minister of Canada.

Later, when I had judged that Father Cherion had recovered from his ordeal, I was able to track down a key and see my apartment. I entered the gymnasium by a door nearest the classroom wing. It was a door set in an enormous whitewashed wall and approached by a set of concrete steps that stood shoulder-high. The reason for this rise was made clear when I stepped into the gloom of the gymnasium. For when I passed through the door, I stepped, not onto a concrete playing surface, but onto a wooden stage. The stage was quite large and separated from the rest of the gymnasium by heavy dark curtains. Beyond the curtains was the polished concrete floor of the basketball court, now occupied with rows of boxy wooden desks and benches for the Class 10 students' final exams. I was accompanied by the school's handyman, a Nepali named Ramgi. I asked him where the apartment was and he pointed to a solid wooden door at one side of the stage.

Ramgi was slight, as thin as a whippet, and about as highly strung. He had a pencil moustache and wore his black hair slicked back with Brilliantine. He always looked worried and smiled nervously when addressed. As he tried to fit the key in the lock, his hand shook so badly that I offered to do it for him.

We entered a small whitewashed room with a three-metre (ten-foot) high ceiling and floorboards that matched the stage outside. The far wall was solid glass—tall narrow windows that extended from about waist height to the ceiling. There were a few sticks of furniture—a bench, a chair, a table, a bed frame, and a crude armoire. There was an empty light bracket above the door and one electrical outlet on the wall to my right as I entered. All of the wiring was exposed, fastened to thin strips of wood that were tacked to the concrete. (The school had a diesel generator, I was told, an antique workhorse, which would supply us with a few hours of unreliable electricity each evening.) There was a door on my left and I peered inside. It was a washroom of bare unfinished concrete, a long narrow room about half the size of the room I had first entered, with a squat toilet at the far end and a white porcelain sink attached to the wall about halfway along on my right. There was another empty light bracket above the sink.

My "apartment," I realized, was the change room for the gymnasium.

I stepped into the bathroom. There was a single window high above the toilet, hinged at the top and open a few inches. I tried to close it. It was jammed. I indicated this to Ramgi. He smiled and shrugged. I pulled the chain on the toilet reservoir, which was fastened to the wall above my head. A shower of rust trickled down. Otherwise, nothing happened. I looked at Ramgi and he pointed to a faucet protruding from the wall next to the toilet. I turned the tap and cold water came out, spilling across the floor and running down the cracked porcelain bowl. Oh well, I thought, I could fill a bucket to flush the toilet. There was a small wooden table, the size of a card table, in the corner between the sink and the door. It had burn marks and food rings on its surface and the wall around it was soiled with grease. Clearly, the last tenant had used this table to cook his meals. It seemed a reasonable arrangement. I could do the same.

We went back to the main room. Already my initial disappointment was wearing off and I was beginning to see the possibilities of the place. The wooden floors, for example, though ill-fitting and warped, would be warmer than concrete. The enormous windows and the bright whitewashed walls meant that the room would never be gloomy. After several weeks of travel and living out of a backpack, I realized that any place I could call my own seemed appealing.

We did a quick inventory of the room. I noted that one of the windows was broken and that one of the floorboards needed replacing. It was rotten and a one-metre (three-foot) section had collapsed. I knelt down and peered through the hole to an earthen floor about four feet below. I noted that the room was not square and that there was a gap along one wall, only a few inches at one end, but opening to about eight inches at the other end. Ramgi cheerfully agreed to address each of these items, wagging his head from side to side and jerking his right hand up spasmodically in a partial salute. And he was as good as his word. A few days later he returned with an assistant, an enormous plank, and an ancient handsaw and he cut that plank to fill the gap against the wall, stopping frequently to re-sharpen the saw with a triangular file.

I noticed that only two of the tall windows opened and that these were covered with iron bars stapled horizontally into the window frames. I questioned Ramgi about this. He just shrugged and smiled. As we were leaving, I emptied my pockets onto the table by the window. I had brought a few tools from home: a pair of pliers, a multi-blade screwdriver, and a horn-handled pocketknife—the last was an heirloom and had belonged to my grandfather. I felt that there was no point in carrying these things back to Michael's house, as I would be back the next morning to move my stuff in.

The next morning, when I returned with my banjo, backpack, and trunk, the tools were gone. I realized then why there were iron bars on the windows and why the windows in traditional Bhutanese homes were rows of narrow gothic slits banded by wooden cross-members rather than one large opening. Anything not nailed down, it seemed, was fair game. I would miss my grandfather's pocketknife most of all.

As I was cursing my luck and unpacking my few belongings, there was a knock on the door. I opened the door and there stood the man who had warned me of the mad dog the day before. His name was Bhola and he was the school's sweeper or janitor. He was a tall handsome man, wearing blue plastic sandals and dressed in a strange combination of second-hand clothing—tight-fitting blue polyester trousers, two acrylic sweaters with patterned horizontal stripes and frayed cuffs, one worn over the other, and a toque that looked like a tea cosy. Bhola was from Bihar, a poor man by birth, but, as I soon discovered, a man with an eye for the main chance.

I invited him in. He asked me questions about myself—where I was from, was I married, what did my father do, how much money did a teacher in Canada make— and proceeded to poke through my belongings, which were scattered over my bed and table. His eye was caught by the combination cassette player/shortwave radio sitting on the bench.

"How much?" he inquired.

"Sorry?"

"How much do you want for this two-in-one?"

I was dumbstruck. Why would I want to sell my radio? I explained that I had only just purchased it and that I really didn't want to sell it.

He laughed. "No, no. You do not understand. Not now. *When you leave.* I will pay you now, and you give it to me when you leave Bhutan."

"But I will be here for two years."

"Okay."

It took me a while to digest his strange proposition. It was my first morning in Khaling and two years seemed like such a long time. But he was very persuasive and, to my surprise, I found myself agreeing to his proposal. After all, he said, do you really want to take this two-in-one home with you to Canada? You will have no room in your luggage, and you can use the extra money to buy a souvenir of Bhutan, some weaving perhaps, that will fold up small and fit in your bag.

And so it was settled. We agreed upon a price, which was about half what I had just paid for it in Amsterdam. He would return the next day with a deposit and would pay me a little each month until I was paid in full.

As he was leaving, still very pleased with the transaction, he turned to me, looking concerned. "We have a deal, yes? If anyone asks, you will tell them that you are selling the two-in-one to Bhola?"

Yes, I reassured him. After all, how likely was it that someone else would make me an offer for my radio?

A few minutes after Bhola left, there was another knock on the door. It was Wangpo, Ramgi's assistant, a cheerful young man of about my own age. He greeted me warmly and entered the room, looking around curiously until his eyes fell on the radio.

He smiled, showing lots of gum. "Ramgi told me you had a good two-in-one." He looked it over longingly. "Indian two-in-ones are no good," he sniffed dismissively, "but this is very good, yes?"

"I suppose."

"It is American?"

"Japanese."

"Ah, Japanese. Yes, very good. How much do you want?"

I had a sinking feeling. I explained that I had just sold it to Bhola. Wangpo asked how much and quickly offered me double. I had to apologize and say that I had given Bhola my word. Wangpo seemed much put out, and he left cursing Bhola under his breath.

A few minutes later, there was another knock on the door. It was one of the Dzongkha teachers. He entered the room making small talk, asking me how I liked Khaling. His gaze swept the room, coming to rest on my radio.

"Ah," he said, "I see that you have a Japanese two-in-one..."

Father Perry returned the next day. He stayed for only two days, doing his best to prepare Father Cherion for his new role as chief administrator. Father Perry was very busy, but I desperately wanted to talk to him about my classes. I finally caught up with him in his office, as he was cleaning out his desk and packing up his books and files. The door was open. The room looked like a typhoon had struck. I knocked on the doorframe.

"Excuse me, sir. I was wondering if I could possibly see the curriculum for the Class 9 and 10 English?"

"Ah," he said turning around and peering at me carefully through Buddy Holly-style spectacles. "It's Ken, isn't it? You'll be taking over my English classes. Good. You'll enjoy the students. Hard workers. Yes, lovely children really. Now, the curriculum...where did I put that?" He scratched his head and began lifting piles of papers, folders, and books stacked on his desk. Then he turned to a row of filing cabinets, began opening drawers, and flipping through folders. "Ah," he pulled a single sheet of white paper from a file folder. "Here it is."

He handed me the paper. It was a list of books, a very short list, about half a dozen in all. I turned the page over. It was blank.

"But..." I began. He had returned to sorting and packing.

He looked up affably. "Yes?"

I did not know what to say. Was this all there was? How was I going to fill two years with this? I had a class to teach tomorrow, and I did not know where to begin.

"Yes?"

I knew his time was short, but I really needed his help. I had been made the head of the English department—Father Perry's replacement, in fact—but I had never been to teacher's college or taught a day in my life. I did not know how to plan a lesson, grade a seminar, or mark a test. I was terrified at my own inexperience and the enormous responsibility that the school was confidently handing to me on the assumption that I was the Foreign Expert. He raised his eyebrows.

"I...I guess I was expecting something a little more...a little more...well, just a little more."

He laughed. "It's easy. You have each section for three classes in each rotation. Teach one class of grammar and composition to two classes of literature. Just dip into your old teaching bag of tricks. You'll be fine."

But that was the problem. There was no bag of tricks for me to dip into, and I was feeling very far from fine. I was far more worried about being an incompetent teacher than I was about coping with a new culture.

"Thank you, sir. Safe journey tomorrow."

I left him to his last minute packing and started to panic. Okay, I told myself, calm down. First things, first. Let's track down these books. The books I learned were stored in the school go-down, and I had to see a man with the oddly redundant name of Matthew Matthew to gain access to that. Mr. Matthew was a science teacher; he was also the school's quartermaster. All requests for supplies had to be made through him. I found Mr. Matthew in the staff room, deathly ill with a cold.

"Mr. Matthew?"

He sat huddled in his greying white polyester sport jacket, thin neck protruding out of a tatty wool scarf, dark bitter eyes staring out over a beaked nose, looking for all the world like an ailing vulture. He sat alone at the head of the table.

"Mr. Matthew?" I reiterated.

"Hm," he awoke from his meditation, turning his black eyes upon me, malevolent at being disturbed in his sickness.

"Excuse me, sir, but I need a few things from the school's store."

"You need a chit," he muttered, turning away.

"A chit?"

"A chit. A chit. A piece of paper signed by the principal." He waved me away. It was my first brush with Indian-style bureaucracy. I tracked down Father Cherion and asked him to notarize my chit. Then I returned to Matthew Matthew and handed him my slip of paper. He surveyed the page, irritated, but at least giving it his full attention.

"These books," he noted, making xs beside three of the titles on my list. "We do not have these books. You do not need them."

I looked on in horror. Not need them. What did he mean, not need them? Of course, I needed them.

"Could we order them?"

He snorted in amusement. Then he looked carefully at me for the first time and smiled gently. "Mr. Ken, believe me, that would be a wasting of much time, hmm. I am telling you that this will not happen. Besides of which, Father Perry was never needing these books. Isn't it, Mr. Ken?"

I was downcast at this news and at the implied criticism of my teaching skills. He waved me away with an underhanded flip of his wrist.

"Send a boy with the chit to the go-down at twelve o'clock to pick these things up."

I had been dismissed.

We were handed a class schedule the day before school opened. By the end of the first day, it had changed. Two days later, it had changed again. By the end of the first two weeks, it had changed five times. I found myself standing in front of the same class again and again, until Class 9B was a full week ahead of its peers, and I was trying to develop new ways of stalling.

I decided that, as a new teacher, the first thing I needed to do was to find some way to gauge my students' fluency in English, so I assigned lots of writing assignments. The downside to this strategy, and I discovered it immediately, was that I had to mark all this stuff. I had a two-metre (six-foot) bench along one wall of my room and I started stacking my marking on top of it in neat piles to be corrected in turn. Over the next two years, I never saw the top of that bench. If I was not sleeping or working, I was marking—often late into the night by storm lantern or before breakfast or while eating dinner. I frequently marked the same composition more than once, since I believed, and still do, that students will not learn to write well unless you force them to rewrite.

I did manage to obtain some copies of old Indian Central School Examination (ICSE) papers, so that I could have some idea of what my students were working toward. The marks on these exams at the end of Class 10 were all anybody worried about anyway, for they decided whether the student proceeded to college or went back to the farm, and a college graduate in this country was virtually guaranteed a lucrative position in the civil service, so most teachers taught to the exam. It was more coaching than teaching. The Indian teachers tended to lecture, giving the students copious notes to copy from the blackboard, and they would give them sample questions and then sample answers to memorize and regurgitate. Despite my insecurity, I felt uneasy with this sort of instruction. I still felt my role was to teach my students to think for themselves. I refused to give them predigested answers. Instead, I would teach them to do research, to construct an argument, and to write a formal essay.

After the first week, my students were clearly uneasy. By the end of the second, their unease had become panic, verging on revolt. This was unusual, for teachers commanded a great deal of respect in Bhutanese culture. The students addressed me as "Mr. Ken Sir," or sometimes just as "Sir Ken." When I entered the class each morning, they would rise in unison and say, "Good morning, Sir!" and would remain on their feet until I had said, "Good morning, class. You may be seated." At the end of the lesson, they would rise once again and chant, "Thank you, Sir!" and would remain standing until I gave them permission to leave the room. The students never questioned that this should be the order of things. They grew up in a Buddhist tradition where teachers were automatically given respect and revered as repositories of hard-won wisdom. I was called *lopen*, the same title used for teachers in the Lamaist tradition. I never had to carry anything. If a student saw me struggling with a stack of textbooks, he would be at my side in a flash, protesting, "No, Sir. Let me. You should not be carrying this, Sir." So it was rather unusual for students to demonstrate the sort of behaviour I began to experience in the second week of studies. Not that there was anything overt—they wouldn't dare challenge me—but there was a murmur of unrest in the class all the same. It was not revolt exactly. It was more like worry or alarm. Finally, I confronted the class.

"What is the matter?" I asked in exasperation. "Why are you all so fidgety?"

After an uncomfortable length of time, one student bravely rose from his seat and, looking timidly at the floor, whispered, "Sir is not teaching us correctly."

I knew I was green and I was very insecure about my teaching skills, being fresh out of university, but *not teaching them correctly*? That seemed a bit extreme.

"How do you mean, Sonam?" I asked, and with excruciating shyness, an explanation slowly emerged. Because I hadn't given them a lecture with carefully prepared notes that they could copy from the blackboard into their notebooks, they were under the impression that they hadn't learned a thing. And if Sir intended to continue teaching in this style, expecting them to come up with the answers to his questions instead of him supplying them with knowledge, they were going to fare very poorly indeed on their final exams.

I took a deep breath, crossed my fingers behind my back, and addressed the class, trying to sound older than my twenty-five years. "I understand your concern. I know how important scoring well on the ICSE is to you all. But I am asking you to trust me. When your government asked me to come here and teach you, they had your best interests at heart. I will prepare you for the final exam. I will. But for the next two years, we will do things my way and, when we get to the exam, I promise, you will be ready. I will not let you down. Please, trust me."

The tension slowly left the room and although nothing was said, I knew that my request had been granted. They had given me their trust. Now it was up to me.

Because of the distances between settlements and the lack of driveable roads, most schools in Bhutan were boarding schools. Ours was no exception. This meant that, in addition to the teaching staff, there was a large support staff of cooks, sweepers, handymen, and, in our case, a driver, who was in charge of the school's battered Jeep. The teaching staff, for the most part, was recruited in India. Since some of the best educational institutions in India are run by the Roman Catholic Church, six of our staff members were in religious orders. The principal and two of the teachers were Jesuits and three of the teachers were nuns, Sisters of the order of St. Joseph of Cluny. There were also eight other Indians on staff, all men, most of whom came from southern India. There were eight Bhutanese men on staff. Three taught the national language (Dzongkha), two taught science, one taught physical education, one taught folk dance, and the last taught art. Finally, there was Michael and me. That was our staff and we were responsible for approximately three hundred students in Classes 7 through 10.

The student body at Jigme Sherubling reflected Bhutan's regional variety, since students came to the school from all across the country. A dozen different language groups were represented each morning at assembly. While most of the students came from northern Bhutan and followed the Drukpa or Nyingmapa sects of Buddhism, a significant proportion, about a third, came from the more tropical south. These southern students, or Lhotsampa, had sharper features than their northern counterparts, generally followed Hinduism, and were the descendents of Nepali immigrants to the country. Perhaps a quarter of the student population was female. This imbalance reflected an imbalance in the country as a whole. For while Bhutan had an excellent record for women's rights—there was, for example, no purdah, no dowry system, and women could own property and marry whom they wished—there were still very few women in the professions. Girls were simply too valuable in the home to be sent to school. They worked on the farm, cooked, cleaned, fetched firewood, and looked after younger siblings. Most women married very young, raised large families, and aged incredibly quickly. And while many of my male students were already fathers, if a girl became pregnant, that was the end of her school career.

I spent the first two weeks teaching in a shirt and tie. It was not until the beginning of April that I worked up the nerve to dress in my gho.

In Thimphu, we had been encouraged to have ourselves fitted for the national costume. Seeing foreign teachers instructing while wearing Bhutanese dress, it was felt, would help the students to understand that, while we were introducing new ideas, we were not trying to replace their culture with our own.

For a woman, the national costume was a kira, a blanket-sized rectangle of woven cloth that she folded in an elegant sheath about her body, pinning it over each shoulder with a brooch and cinching it at her waist with a colourful cloth belt. The brooches used at the shoulder of the kira were the Bhutanese woman's chief item of jewellery and were often as large as belt buckles and made of chased silver and inlaid with precious stones, particularly coral and turquoise. Often, a woman would join the two pins by several strands of linked coins that would fall across her chest like a necklace. Over the kira, a short plain jacket of silk or cotton would be worn.

The man's dress, a robe called a gho, was somewhat more complicated. Undone, it resembled an oversized bathrobe that dragged on the floor. Properly assembled, the hem had to be drawn up to just below the knees, all the excess material had to be folded into neat pleats behind his back and a cloth belt was wrapped about the man's waist and cinched up as tight as a tourniquet. The excess cloth above the belt was allowed to billow down, forming a capacious pocket. It was necessary to keep the belt as tight as possible in order to insure that all of the folds and seams remained perfectly straight. Otherwise, in the course of the day—what with all of the walking and lifting and bending that a farmer was required to do—it would come all askew and would look an awful mess. I had ordered two *ghos* for myself, one of plain blue cotton for summer and one of winter-weight wool in a plaid pattern called Bumthang *matha* after its place of origin, a valley in central Bhutan.

It took half an hour of fiddling in front of a ridiculously small shaving mirror before I was satisfied with the result. I knew that I would get quite a reaction—the Indian teachers did not wear local dress and Michael refused to—but I was determined to do it to make a statement to the students and to the Bhutanese teachers. It was not fancy dress or "going Native" or being more comfortable—in fact, the *gho* is perhaps the most uncomfortable form of dress ever invented—but a statement that I respected local traditions and culture. I had dreaded this day, but I felt that I had put it off long enough. I steeled myself, took one last look in the mirror to make sure all of the folds and pleats were in order, and then strode off toward the assembly ground with a determined step.

Halfway to the school, four boys from my Home Form ran forward and stopped me.

"No, Sir," they said, clucking their tongues, and without a by-your-leave, they began undressing me in public to the great amusement of the other students. I had expected a severe reaction but not this. I was spun around, the belt was unwound, and the hem of my robe dropped to the ground. Hands began plucking and pinching. Quite a crowd of experts gathered round to watch. Orders were shouted and countermanded. I was spun this way and that and trussed up tightly. They cinched the belt so tightly that all circulation below my waist ceased. Then, when they were finished, the four boys stood back, holding their respective chins, and pronounced me satisfactory. One boy said, "You look very handsome, Sir." Another said, "Sir looks very handsome *and* very dangerous." The handsome part I understood, they were being polite, but *dangerous*? Why dangerous? So I pushed the boy to explain himself.

He said, "It is the beard, Sir. It makes you look like a very dangerous fellow. You should cut it off. Then very handsome, very handsome."

No, I thought, thanks anyway, but I need an edge, even a very pathetic one like facial hair. I think I will leave it on and be very dangerous, very dangerous indeed.

FOUR

LEARNING THE ROPES

A FEW DAYS AFTER FATHER PERRY'S DEPARTURE, Father William Mackey arrived at the high school to continue Father Cherion's orientation and to ensure a smooth transition of the administration. Father Mackey, a Canadian Jesuit, was the founder of our school and is generally acknowledged to be the father of the modern education system in Bhutan. As it happened, I had already met Father Mackey.

Back in Thimphu, Father Mackey had invited me and the other new Canadian teachers to his house for an evening meal. He lived in a small stone cottage just outside of town. A low stone wall surrounded the property to keep out the cattle. Father Mackey met us at the door and invited us into his home. The house was a modest bungalow, the furnishings simple and spare. Unseen in the kitchen we could hear dinner preparations underway where Mindu, Father Mackey's driver, and Mindu's wife were busy chopping and frying. Mindu's family lived in the back part of the house and took care of the elderly but still active Jesuit.

He greeted us warmly, dressed in a traditional *gho*. He was tall and clean-shaven, and he stood with an erect military bearing. His hair, what was left of it, was white and cut short. He peered at us with bright enquiring eyes through incredibly thick glasses. There was something of the tortoise in the way his balding head thrust forward from his square shoulders on a thin ropy neck. Father Mackey was a legend in Bhutan, one of the few foreigners to be given citizenship.

Father Mackey was invited to the country in 1963 by the previous monarch, Jigme Dorje Wangchuck, to set up the country's first secular high school. Mackey, even when I met him at seventy-one, was a man of incredible energy. In his youth, as he never tired of telling me, he had been a remarkable athlete, a championship hockey and lacrosse player. At the age of seventeen, he was forced to make the difficult decision between Junior 'A' Hockey and the religious life. He chose the Society of Jesus. Upon graduation, his order sent him to India, first as a teacher in Kurseong and later as the headmaster of one of the best schools in Darjeeling. Many of the wealthier Bhutanese had sent their children to this school for a Western-style education, and so Father Mackey had befriended several Bhutanese families whose sons would later become influential in the Bhutanese government.

In 1962, political troubles in Darjeeling were blamed, in part, on the teachings of the Jesuits, who were seen as sympathetic to the Ghurka separatists. Father Mackey and several of his colleagues found themselves relieved of their teaching positions and in professional limbo. It seemed certain they would not be allowed to teach in India again. For a time he served as secretary to the Bishop of Jamshedpur and as a liaison officer to Mother Teresa of Calcutta. Then a call came from the sympathetic prime minister of Bhutan, Jigmie Dorji, inviting Father Mackey to work for the Bhutanese Department of Education. The prime minister knew of Mackey's excellent work in Darjeeling, and so India's loss became Bhutan's gain.

Most of the development work in Bhutan had been in the western part of the country. It was decided, therefore, that the country's first high school should be in the more remote, more impoverished, and more densely populated east, as a means to encourage development in that part of the country. His trek across Eastern Bhutan, searching for a suitable location for the new school, is now the stuff of legend.

"There were no roads," he told us, "and money was useless, so I travelled by mule, and we paid for things with handfuls of salt."

The location he chose for the new school was the favoured plateau of Kanglung. The school was a great success, both academically and architecturally. By the late 1970s, however, it was decided that the country needed a junior college, and so the facilities were expanded and converted to this purpose. The high school would be moved thirty-two kilometres (twenty miles) south to Khaling. Father Mackey was not too happy about this decision. Kanglung was favoured with a mild climate, a lovely view of the northern mountain ranges, and a wide flat plateau. Khaling, in contrast, because of its topography, was one of the wettest and coldest valleys in Bhutan.

Nevertheless, Father Mackey was pleased to hear where I was to be posted. He had fond memories of his years in Khaling. "The school is called Jigme Sherubling, which means, 'fearless place of learning.' Before we built the school, the site had been sheep pasture. The grass was full of leeches. It was so wet that I insisted they build us a covered gymnasium—the only one in the country." Because he had been the founding principal of my school, he knew everyone up and down the valley.

We sat around his living room and had some real Bhutanese food by lantern light. We started the meal with *ara*, a homebrewed moonshine made of distilled corn mash. Into the glass of *ara* was slid a fried egg. "This is the preferred way to drink it," said Father Mackey as he opened his throat, tilted back his head and let the egg slide down. We followed suit. The *ara* was harsh and greasy with a metallic aftertaste. Father immediately topped our glasses. We watched in panic. "You should know that they drink a lot of this stuff in the East and that it is polite to drink three glasses before you refuse."

My head was ready to explode. "Three glasses?"

"Ah," he said, "but there's a trick." He demonstrated. He took a sip from his glass. The cook topped it up. He took another sip and the pantomime was repeated once more. "Now," he said, "I can leave that glass alone for the rest of the evening and propriety has been satisfied."

The meal, I should add, was delicious. We ate the nutty red rice of the Paro Valley, nothing like the rice I had eaten at home. Rice that, I now understand, is being exported in small quantities for those with discerning palates and deep pockets in the West. I had my first taste of *imadatsi*, a dish of fried chilis and soft cheese—hot as blazes but delicious, nonetheless. We also had smoked pork rind with the hair still on, also a delicacy, but one I never grew to appreciate. I think Father Mackey was trying to prepare us for what lay ahead. For dessert, he served us slices of cheese, quite good and reminiscent of something I had eaten before.

"Edam? Gouda?" we asked.

"Bumthang," he replied with a laugh and explained that a Swiss NGO had set up a cheese making plant in Bumthang District. "They also make a fine pear brandy and apple cider. Be sure to stock up on your way through."

As we settled back to drink more *ara*, it developed into one of the most pleasant evenings I have ever spent. There was no electricity and the room was lit by candlelight and kerosene. Life lived by candlelight, the intimacy of candlelight, is something I miss. Father Mackey was quite a storyteller and regaled us with tales of his life and his adventures in the Himalayas.

As the evening drew to a close, I questioned him about his own religious beliefs and how he squared them with living in a Buddhist country. "Oh, I know my superiors would be shocked, but I have no trouble reconciling Buddhism with Catholicism." To illustrate his point, he pulled a dog-eared and much-underlined book from his shelf and proceeded to read choice bits to me. The book was called *Christianity and the World Religions*. It was my first introduction to the Catholic theologian, Hans Küng.

"Listen to this," he said and began to read, jumping from point to point in the text, quoting passages that illustrated the similarities between the teachings of Christianity and Buddhism.

"Yes," I countered, "but Christians can't dismiss the world as illusory, the way Buddhists can."

Father Mackey grew excited. "Of course. And Küng is aware of that. Listen: 'The world, for Jesus, was not something futile and empty you withdrew from, seeing through its nothingness in the act of concentration. Still less was it to be identified with the Absolute. It was, instead, creation, good in itself, although continuously spoiled by human beings.'"

"Doesn't this cause you any problems?"

"Not as much as you might think. For the goal of the Buddhist is Nirvana and the goal of the Christian, eternal life. These states of being are less different than you might suppose." Again he dipped into the theology of Küng. "'For it seems to me, there need not be any contradiction between the Christian notion of a positive final state ['eternal life'] and the notion, supported by most Buddhist schools, of a positive final state [Nirvana].' He goes on to argue that, since both of these states cannot be described intellectually, there is no way to prove that they are not one and the same thing. The Buddha achieved Nirvana and then came back to tell us about it, but, like Christ, he speaks through metaphor. In the Christian tradition we have mystics who have experienced God, but clearly from their written accounts, their encounters took place in a state that was outside our intellectual ability to describe. One thing I so admire about my Buddhist friends is their acceptance of this possibility—their tolerance of the possibilities of other paths to God."

"But, as I understand it, a Buddhist would not use that word, 'God.'"

"True, I am being sloppy. Call it 'reality.' The idea of a loving personal God is alien to Buddhism. Buddhism is more of an intellectual than a feeling enterprise, and I think that is why Buddhism is currently in vogue in the West. We distrust our feelings."

I would like to have continued this discussion all evening, but I was not his only guest. Father Mackey was aware of the need of the others to have some of his time. He shared this freely. When we left and were driving back into Thimphu in the darkness, I realized that I had been blessed to meet, even for so short a time, such a remarkable man. Before he died in October 1995, Father Mackey received many honours from his adopted country, not least of which was the title "Son of Bhutan."

"Now I'm a real SOB," he loved to remark.

The opening of the year 1987 found Father Mackey once more back at the school he had founded, bustling about in his grey *gho*, chivvying and encouraging staff and students, and preparing Father Cherion for his role as the new principal of Jigme Sherubling High School. In addition to whipping the school into shape, Father Mackey also organized a Foundation Day to celebrate the school's tenth anniversary. All of the villagers were invited to attend, as were all of the important local dignitaries. The day's ceremonies began with what Father Mackey called Mass Drill.

Mass Drill involved the entire student body. They all assembled on the football field in neat lines facing the bleachers. Each student was dressed in their school uniform—newly washed and pressed—and held a brightly coloured plastic pom-pom in each hand. With the blast of a whistle, they began to move in perfect synchronous order. The movements were stiff, the children like little militaristic marionettes: turn to the left, squat on your heels, arms straight in front, turn to the right, rise smartly, bring your arms above your head, one step forward and snap arms down to the side, and so on. It was a very impressive display and it lasted for about five minutes. The students hated this, but they performed very well. I could not help reflecting that you would never get a group of Canadian high-school students to do this. It was too perfect, too uniform, too much the sort of thing you might have seen performed by the Hitler Youth for the party members at Nuremburg.

Following the Mass Drill there was a display of gymnastics by a few of the boys. They were dressed in white T-shirts and white trousers, with a red sash tied around their waists. Father Mackey had run a gymnastics program when he had been principal, and the school possessed some crudely made vaulting horses and a springboard. The vaulters landed on a thick foam mat, but the tumbling was done on the bare ground.

Following the gymnastics demonstration, there was an exhibition of Bhutanese folk dancing. This was the part of the day I enjoyed the most. The school had a dancing master who instructed all of the students in folk dance, though most of the students had picked up social dances in their home communities before they attended our school. The dancing was divided into three groups: Nepali dances, northern Bhutanese folk dances, and masked dances.

Father Mackey with gymnasts. The gym is in the background.

The Nepali dances were very energetic. There was a lot of hand movement, rolling of shoulders, wiggling of hips, and, for the men at least, a great deal of Cossack-like hopping up and down with bent knees. It looked very difficult. The star performers were allowed to come forward and dance solo for a time, improvising, to the great delight of the crowd. It was very sinuous and erotic, but the boys and girls never danced together.

The northern Bhutanese folk dances on the other hand were never erotic, even when the sexes danced together. The movements were stiffer, more formal and ritualized. Everyone moved in unison. Dancers generally formed a circle and performed to music that they sung themselves. The girls' movements were hampered by their long *kiras*, but the effect was very graceful and fluid. There was one dance performed by the boys holding long bamboo staves that was quite exciting. As they danced and sang, the boys slashed the air with the staves, bringing them together sharply in rhythmic claps. It was a bit frightening to watch, but it was so closely choreographed that no one ever got hurt. I wondered at the origin of this dance. Were these vestigial swords and was this a warriors' dance? Or did the staves represent flails and celebrate the harvest? None of the students could enlighten me on this point.

My favourite were the masked dances. These were generally performed at religious festivals, usually by monks, and always by men. The dancers disguised

Student dancers at Foundation Day.

themselves under layers of bright silk and wore hand-carved wooden masks that represented the character they were portraying in the dance. The choreography for these dances was often hundreds of years old, passed down from one generation of dancers to the next. Arms were held straight out from the body for balance and the dancers leapt and twisted in the air with enormous energy, tossing their heads this way and that, sometimes in imitation of the animal spirit each was portraying. The student masked dancers at our Foundation Day celebration were accompanied by a small orchestra. The dance master was on cymbals, beating time, and two of the Dzongkha lopens, their cheeks inflated like Dizzy Gillespie's, were blowing on long telescoping brass horns, shaped like Swiss alpenhorns, called dungchen.

Foundation Day ended with a few speeches and the singing of the national anthem. After the festivities, I was invited by one of the spectators to her home for coffee. In this crowd, she was not a woman you could overlook. Even though she was wearing a kira, like the other female spectators, she stood almost 183 centimetres (six feet) tall and had creamy skin, hazel eyes, and long red hair. Her name was Karin, and she was a teacher at the Zangley Muenselling School for the Blind.

Karin was one of a colony of Scandinavian missionaries found in Eastern Bhutan. Most were medical people. There were hospitals in Mongar and south of Khaling in Riserboo. There were also small clinics, one here in the valley near the village of

Karin near Dowzor.

Dowzor, where a registered nurse named Sven lived with his wife and three small children, and an isolated one in Thrimshing, which was the centre of the mission's leprosy work.

At the far end of Khaling there was also a weaving project sponsored by the Santal Mission and run by a young woman named Ruth. The project was an attempt to preserve local skills while at the same time providing a source of income for the valley's women. Ruth provided the commissions and the raw material. She provided the yarn to insure that the dyes were colourfast. The weavers were paid upon the completion of their projects. While the skills and patterns were traditional, the products and the colour schemes often were not. Ruth preferred shades of purple and pink as opposed to the primary colours favoured by local weavers, or the earth tones that could be produced with home-made dyes. And instead of kiras and ghos, the women made handbags, table runners, and cushion covers. Still it was a valiant attempt to give these women some purchase in the slippery modern world and to make them financially independent.

Karin worked at the other mission project in the valley: a residential school for the blind. In addition to the normal academic subjects, her students also had an excellent music program. The school was situated a few hundred metres below the bazaar, but Karin lived some distance away. After the Foundation Day celebrations, we left the high school, deep in conversation, entered the bazaar, turned right, and headed north on the road to Tashigang. We followed the road for perhaps half a kilometre, rounded a rocky spur, and entered a wedge-shaped valley at its narrower end. In a compact pocket above the paved road was the health clinic, which consisted of a hospital building, an Indian-style bungalow for Sven's family, and a few smaller outbuildings for the servants and assistants. Karin and I turned the other way, however, leaving the road, and heading down the small valley. We soon came to a chest-high wall of stone, which we crossed on stone steps set diagonally into the wall.

The high wall guarded a sloping compound that compassed two small stone cottages, also whitewashed. Karin's was nearest. As we entered through the brightly painted door, I realized that, though the building materials were local, there was nothing Bhutanese about this house. The dwelling spoke of Scandinavian summers at the seaside—it was an eremitical oasis of comfort. The walls gleamed with white paint, the linen curtains were white with woven bands of colour, the sofas and chairs of wicker had plump cushions, and the sitting room was dominated by a cast iron stove enamelled in forest green. Karin bade me sit down and set a kettle on the gas range in the modern kitchen. She fed me slices of sweet brown goat cheese on Ryvita crackers and a large mug of real coffee from beans she had ground herself. Heaven.

We talked late into the night. Talk, for Karin, was life. She loved to chat, but it was also, she confessed, painful. Talk gave her a headache. All day long she conversed in English, in Sharchopkha, in Swedish, but never in Norwegian, her native tongue. Sometimes, she said, she became so tired of conversation in other languages that she locked herself away, just to give her brain a rest. But she loved people, so her gregarious nature soon drove her out again to engage the world. Karin was one of the loveliest people I have ever met. She was able to combine the contrary qualities of selfless Christianity with an ability to talk about herself for hours on end. We became fast friends and spent hours in each other's company, walking, talking, and laughing about nothing at all. In two years, there was never an awkward moment between us.

The second cottage in Karin's compound was the dormitory for the senior girls at her school. It was a touching sight to see these young women, smartly dressed in their school uniforms, their hair neatly combed and faces scrubbed, walking in line through paddy fields, over stiles and bridges, through the muddy lanes of Dowzor, and down to the bottom of their valley where it joined the larger valley of Khaling, and then threading the last few hundred metres or so to the school for the blind, completely unassisted: the blind demurely leading the blind.

Only a few weeks after our arrival, Michael was asked to give up his comfortable bungalow. A new accountant had arrived at Jigme Sherubling, and his family was soon to follow. They would need a place to live. The new man, Mr. Muhkerjee, was from West Bengal. He was a slight bespectacled man with a pencil mustache and a penchant for sweater vests and corny jokes. Strangely enough, Michael did not mind. He had been contemplating a move anyway, somewhere off campus, where he could walk away from work at the end of each day.

Michael was not tall, but he was fit and he held himself very upright. With his short red hair and jutting beard, he reminded me of an old sea captain. It was an apt comparison, for in the classroom he ran a very tight ship. He did not joke, he did not smile, he assigned a lot of homework, and he expected it to be done to a very high standard. It was from Michael that I first heard the old teaching maxim: "Never smile till Christmas" (or perhaps Blessed Rainy Day, in our case). The students were a little afraid of him, but they respected him. He was, I suppose, the teacher I wanted myself to be.

Michael was a remarkable person in many ways, but two things about him stand out in my memory. The first was that he was complete unto himself. And by this I mean, that while most of us require, if not crave, human contact—someone to kibitz with or to vent one's spleen to—Michael seemed to require none of this. He did not often seek out human companionship. He did not socialize with the other teachers. His private life was truly private. I have no idea how he passed most of his time.

Over the next year, whenever I needed to talk, I would seek Michael out, and he would always welcome me, make me some of his dreadful instant coffee, and listen to my tales of woe. But it was never reciprocal. Michael had been a teacher for a very long time in troubled urban schools in England and in poorly funded community schools in the Caribbean. He was confident in his craft in a way that I envied. He had worked in the developing world before. Perhaps this gave him a certain grace. He did not require my company, but he seemed to be aware that I frequently needed his, and he never made me feel awkward about this.

The second remarkable thing about Michael was his terrible wardrobe. I don't think he really cared about his appearance. Don't get me wrong. His clothes were always clean and mended, his beard and hair neatly trimmed, for he was too professional to do otherwise, but his entire wardrobe consisted of only this: two shirts with collars, one tie, a pair of good Oxford dress shoes, a pair of sneakers, one pair of dress pants, one pair of stretchy nylon track pants, and one wool sweater. All of his clothes were pale blue or, if they were patterned, blue was the predominant colour, so that they could be worn together. Michael donned some combination of this wardrobe every day of the year I knew him. At first I found this amusing, but in time I saw the wisdom of his choice. Why own more than you need? None of my Bhutanese neighbours had more than this. Why should I require more?

Michael soon found new quarters in two rooms above a shop in the bazaar. The rooms had no running water, no electricity, and no doors. I helped him make some doors with broken-up crates from the school go-down. He slept on the floor, cooked on a little kerosene burner, fetched his water in a bucket from his landlady downstairs, and hung his few clothes on nails on the wall. I thought he was crazy.

Michael and I soon made a fast friend in Chogyal Tenzin. Chogyal was a science teacher, a young man, and recent college graduate. He was the only truly caffeinated personality I met among the Bhutanese. He simply could not sit still. During staff meetings, he was always nervously drumming his fingers on the conference table or jigging his knee up and down, or twisting in his seat from side to side. He was handsome and quick to laugh. In his youth he had gained a reputation as a ladies' man, but he had recently settled down and was now happily married. As bachelors, Michael and I were a little jealous, for Karma was lovely and she had a calming comforting presence that perfectly complimented Chogyal's excess energy. They were expecting their first child. While Chogyal was from Punakha Valley in the west, Karma was a local girl. Karma and Chogyal often invited Michael and me on family outings, and walks down the valley quickly turned into serial house parties—the Bhutanese equivalent of a pub crawl. Oddly enough, neither Karma nor Chogyal drank on these occasions, for as Chogyal wisely pointed out, the only exception to the three-drink rule was total abstinence. Bhutanese hosts understood one or the other, but there was no middle ground when it came to drinking.

While Michael was content with his own society most of the time, aside from the occasional binge with Chogyal and me, I craved companionship. Fortunately, the school was very accommodating in this regard. It was very social. I was frequently invited to other teachers' homes for dinner. At breaks, I would often sit with Mr. Mukherjee in his office and sip milky tea and joke. Sometimes Wangpo and Bhola, after they had served all of the teaching staff their tea, would join us. Mukherjee shared his office with the school typist, Tandin Zangmo.

Tandin was a single mother, raising four children, one of whom was an infant and another the daughter of her deceased sister. She had been married to the school's physical education instructor before I arrived, but when he was transferred to another school, he quickly abandoned her and remarried. Tandin's case was a good example of how traditional marriage customs in this country did not always favour women. Tandin was living with her parents in Khaling Gompa, a village located on a small plateau above the school. Her niece, Nangsi, stayed with the children during the day and carried the baby down to the school on her back when it was time to feed. I must say that the school administration was very good about this. They did not mind small children underfoot, as long as the work was getting done, though I think Father Cherion always looked a little uncomfortable if he walked into the office when Tandin was suckling the baby.

Tandin was good company. She was clever, funny, and very pretty. She was also the only unattached woman in the school. The male staff, even the married men, took to dropping in for a chat. They always had some good excuse to interrupt her—some exam that needed typing perhaps or a quiz that had to be copied on the Gestetner machine—and they would strive to make the occasion memorable with a clever remark. ("Ah, Miss Tandin, you are looking damned fine today. Is that a new kira? I am thinking you must be having a new boyfriend, is it not?") It was fun to watch. They all tried to impress her, but it was done awkwardly, and she was scornful of their attempts. ("Men! Useless, the lot of you! Here, give me that. Go on. Get out. It will be ready at five.") I rarely teased Tandin—for even at five-foot nothing she was too formidable—and in time we became good friends. School gossip linked us romantically, but it was never true.

At the beginning of my second week, I was disturbed at night by a tremendous racket in the gymnasium. I set down my pen, opened the door to my room and strode out angrily to the centre of the darkened stage. I could hear the sound of boys' voices, shrieking and howling. They seemed to be coming from the gymnasium and yet the basketball floor was empty. There was another room, under the same roof, a long narrow room that ran parallel to the basketball court, but it was quite separate and was entered by a separate door. The noise seemed to be coming from over there. I went outside. It was raining, and there was an ominous rumble of thunder in the distance. I squelched through the mud and ducked into a lighted doorway. All of the yelling instantly stopped. The long room was full of desks and each desk held a pair of boys. I had been in this room before, the entrance to the library was through here, but I had assumed that all of these battered desks were in storage.

"What are you doing here?" I demanded.

The boys looked at each other. "Evening study, Sir."

I paused to digest this. "Isn't someone supposed to be supervising you?"

The students looked at each other and shrugged. "Maybe you are supervising us, Sir."

I did not know what to say to this, so I began asking questions. It appeared that students had study hall twice a day, and that, yes, in past years a teacher had always been present to supervise them, but so far—and a week had gone by—no one had shown up. It seemed that in all the confusion, no one had bothered to draw up a schedule for study duty.

"So you boys have been coming here twice a day for a week, and no one has supervised you?"

They nodded. "Yes, Sir."

I could not very well turn around and walk away, even though I had plenty of marking to do back in my room, so I said that I would stay and supervise. "Well, get out your notebooks. Let's get some work done."

"We are not having any work at this time, Sir."

I looked around and realized that it was true; only a handful of the boys had notebooks with them.

"Well, what are we to do?"

One mischievous little boy piped up, "I think Sir is having a guitar, is it not?" The other faces gleamed with delight and anticipation. "Yes, Sir. Yes."

"It's a banjo, not a guitar and...well," I looked at the eager faces, "all right. I'll be right back."

So I played them "Cripple Creek," "Salty Dog," and an old fiddle tune called "Blackberry Blossom." Then I asked for requests. I was surprised. They asked for "Mary's Little Boy Child," "My Darling Clementine," and "Red River Valley," songs that Father Perry must have taught them. Then they asked for "disco," but I had to plead ignorance on that score. I continued to supervise study for the rest of the week. After that, Father Mackey decided to relocate the study hall to the boys' dormitory to prevent the boys from ranging far and wide in the dark on their way home each evening.

Study hall, I learned, was just one of the many duties teachers were expected to perform. We also had to supervise meals, campus clean-up, and gardening (for schools were expected to be as self-sufficient as possible, and all had large kitchen gardens). My favourite duty was prayer hall. The prayer hall was a small room attached to the dining hall. Every evening after dinner, all of the students, regardless of religious affiliation, filed into the prayer hall and sat in neat rows on the floor facing the altar. When everyone had settled and was quiet, I would look at one of the senior boys and nod my head. He would begin by ringing a hand bell, holding the bell cupped in his hand to muffle the sound, and the students would begin chanting, keeping time with the clack of the bell. The prayers could go on for twenty minutes, and I had no idea what was being said. My job was simply to sit cross-legged at the back of the room and look stern. It was a hard pose to maintain for long though, because the music of the prayer was so soothing and so repetitive that I frequently found myself drifting off and had to pinch myself to stay alert.

Meanwhile, in my English composition classes I had decided to begin with letter writing. It seemed a safe place to start. The lessons were easy to plan and I felt that the skills acquired would be useful to my pupils. So I taught them about the basic structure of a letter and about the differences between a business letter and a personal letter, their different purposes and tones. When I began correcting my first pile of assignments, however, I realized that my students had done this before. The same sentences and phrases kept recurring:

Dear Kind Sirs and Madams:

With due respect and humble submission, I would like to drip a few golden words from my pen onto this white paper, and submit a few sentences under your kind consideration and sympathetic action please. As we are telling you this last time, we are needing some moneys to satisfy our desires and to reach our zenith of glory. But since last time, we are not hearing from your good end. Please write soon. I am fine here with all my mates and beloved teachers. This much only. I will pen off here.

Yours sincerely,

Etc.

Clearly, they were using a different stylebook than I.

One evening, while I was sitting on the hill above the football field, admiring the view, and waiting for study hall to begin, a parcel of boys wandered up, greeted me, and flung themselves down at my side in a lethargic heap.

"We are feeling so boring, Sir," said one.

"Wery boring, Sir," affirmed another.

"Bored," I corrected them. "You are feeling *bored*."

They sat up and looked blankly at me.

"You cannot be feeling 'boring.' You can only be feeling 'bored.'"

I sighed in exasperation.

"You cannot say that someone is 'boring'—well, you can, but it would be impolite—you can only say that they are 'bored.' 'Boring' is an adjective; it applies to a thing—like, say, basketball. So you can say that *basketball is boring*, and that *you are bored* by playing basketball."

"But playing basketball is not making us feeling boring, Sir."

"No, perhaps that was a bad example. What about gardening? Is Socially Useful Productive Work boring?"

"Yarr, wery much boring, Sir."

"There! So you can say that doing supw makes you bored."

"Yes, Sir. supw is making us all of the time feeling very much boring."

I gave up.

We sat there, as before, contemplating the view in silence. One boy flopped back on the grass and flung his arms behind his head.

"Oh! I am so bored with feeling so very much boring."

Better, I thought, encouraged by this small success.

After a month of teaching, I was still unsure of my methods. Even though I seemed to be marking all of the time, I was not certain I was giving my students enough homework. Then one day, between classes, I stopped in at the staff room for a cup of tea. The battered aluminum tea kettle and the tea cups were arranged on the table, but the room was deserted. A stack of English composition notebooks was sitting on a corner of the table, nearest the door, looking as if they had just been set there the moment before by one of my colleagues. I told myself I shouldn't do this, that it was not collegial, but the temptation was too great. I sidled over to the table, looked back over my shoulder, and then quietly flipped open the first notebook on the top of the pile. There were two pages of written work. That was all. I quickly looked at the second notebook and the third. Two pages. They were all the same. Even the compositions were identical, neatly copied from the blackboard. Then something about the first sentence caught my eye.

"Dear Kind Sirs and Madams," it began, "With due respect and humble submission, I would like to drip a few golden words onto this white paper..."

Well, well, I thought and burst into laughter.

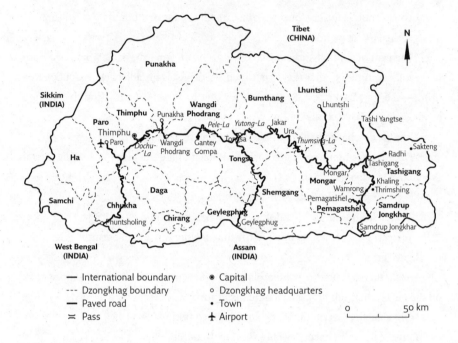

Tibet
(CHINA)

N

Sikkim
(INDIA)

Punakha

Lhuntshi

Bumthang

Lhuntshi

Thimphu   Punakha
Paro   Wangdi
Thimphu   Phodrang
Paro   Yutong-La   Jakar   Tashi Yangtse
Pele-La   Ura
Ha   Dochu-   Wangdi   Gantey   Tongsa   Thumsing-La
La   Phodrang   Gompa
Radhi   Sakteng
Tongsa   Tashigang
Samchi   Daga   Shemgang   Tashigang
Mongar   Khaling
Chhukha   Mongar   Thrimshing
Wamrong
Chirang   Geylegphug   Pemagatshel   Samdrup
Phuntsholing   Pemagatshel   Jongkhar
Geylegphug   Samdrup Jongkhar

West Bengal   Assam
(INDIA)   (INDIA)

— International boundary   ◉ Capital
--- Dzongkhag boundary   ○ Dzongkhag headquarters
— Paved road   • Town
≍ Pass   ✈ Airport

0   50 km

FIVE

AN ACCIDENTAL AREA

BY NOW, YOU PROBABLY HAVE A FEW QUESTIONS, like: "Where exactly is Bhutan?" or "If King Jigme Singye Wangchuck is only the fourth king, what form of government did Bhutan follow before it became a monarchy?" or "Why is it that your students speak English?" Perhaps this is the place in the narrative to try and answer a few of those questions.

If you have an atlas, go to it now. Open to the page or pages that show you the Indian subcontinent. See the triangle jutting into the Indian Ocean separating the Arabian Sea from the Bay of Bengal? Good, now travel up the page until you come to the northernmost fringes of the Indian Empire. You should notice the colour change if yours is a topographic map. On my map there is a lot of white fringed with grey. That means height and plenty of it, for this is the meeting place of two great tectonic plates, where the triangle of India butts up against the larger land mass of Asia and folds the earth into the highest mountain range in the world: the Himalayas. And look, the mountains sweep down from west to east like a great scimitar. From the Karakoram Range in Kashmir, this great mountain barrier sweeps southeast through Nepal, the once independent state of Sikkim, and then through a tiny hump-backed oval, called the Royal Kingdom of Bhutan, before it passes into the Indian state of Arunachal Pradesh. Now take a closer look at Bhutan. You have probably looked at a globe or a map of the world a thousand times and never even noticed it was there. Don't be ashamed; history has passed it by, as well. While the rest of the world was convulsed with various revolutions—political, social, and economic—Bhutan remained isolated, locked in a feudal society. While Europe, Africa, and India trembled under the heel of Napoleon, Bhutan quarrelled internally, each faction striving for supremacy with short bows, straight swords, lances, and bucklers of rhinoceros hide. The reason for this isolation is evident from a close look at your map; for Bhutan is not simply a mountainous country, it is, as Samuel Davis, the nineteenth-century British explorer, once remarked in his diary, "a country of mountains."

Bhutan's southern border rises with startling suddenness from the flat green plains of Assam, rising like a wall, only penetrated here and there by mighty rivers punching through from the interior. These riverine openings create doorways, or *duars*, into the interior and contain the only flat land in the country. From these *duars* the country quickly rises, one mountain range following upon another, each a little higher than that which preceded it, like a series of lush green steps that terminate at the northern boundary of the country in a range of mountains that is the highest in the world, the Greater Himalayas, perpetually snow-covered abode of the gods, the same chain that includes Everest, Annapurna, Kangchenjunga, and in Bhutan, Jhomo Lhari and Kula Kangri. Once over this formidable barrier and you reach the high, clear, and cold places of Tibet. Though the elevation is high throughout Bhutan, the vegetation for the most part is lush, for every year the country catches the edge of the summer monsoon that sweeps up the Bay of Bengal and, rebuffed by the Greater Himalayas, dumps its load of rain in the many narrow valleys. However, this is not a hard-and-fast rule; as with any mountain environment, each valley has its own microclimate and while one valley may grow as thick and lush as a jungle, its neighbour, standing in the rain shadow of a larger mountain peak, may be as arid as a desert and indeed display cactus along its mountain folds and ravines. Even within an individual valley there may be some variations: one wall may receive more sunshine, another more rain, and so you will see settlements along one side of a valley but not on the other.

Bhutan's geographic variety extends also to its people. Historically, each valley remained so isolated that the country developed a veritable Babel of dialects. As I've mentioned previously, there are more than twenty different languages spoken in Bhutan, a country roughly the size of Switzerland. A Bhutanese man leaving his isolated valley and travelling over one mountain range to the next will find a people who look like him, dress like him, live in similar quarters, worship in the same way, but who are virtually unintelligible. Why, you might ask yourself, is the culture so uniform if there are such language barriers? The answer, I believe, lies in the religion; for Bhutanese culture, at least in the north, is inseparable from Buddhism.

Buddhism first reached Bhutan from Tibet in the seventh century AD, but it was a missionary from Swat (in present-day Pakistan) in the eighth century, named

Taktsang temple.

Padmasambhava, who had the greatest impact. Padmasambhava is called Guru Rinpoche, or "Precious Master," in Bhutan and his image is encountered in religious art all across the country. He flew to Bhutan on the back of a tiger, and wherever he stopped in his travels to convert the local population or to subdue a troublesome demon, a temple or monastery may be found today. The most famous of these is the spectacular Takstang, or the "Tiger's Nest," Monastery in Paro Valley. Padmasambhava's legacy is the Nyingmapa school of Buddhism found mostly in Eastern and Central Bhutan.

At the time of Padmasambhava's ministry, Bhutan was not a unified country but a rough geographical area, known by many colourful names, such as "The Southern Valleys of Medicinal Herbs," or "The Southern Mon Valleys Where the Sandalwood Grows." Each valley or group of connected valleys had its own ruler.

It was not until the seventeenth century that Bhutan became a unified country under the leadership of one man, Ngawang Namgyel, known by the title of Shabdrung, which means "At Whose Feet One Submits." Fleeing religious persecution in Tibet in 1616, the Shabdrung, who was the prince-abbot of Ralung Monastery in the Tibetan province of Tsang and head of the Drukpa order, entered Bhutan and over the next thirty years succeeded in conquering most of the country. The Drukpa school, a sub-order of the Kagyupa sect, got its name because it was founded at the monastery of Druk, or "Thunder-Dragon," so named because thunder was heard during its consecration. The Bhutanese call their country, Druk Yul, or "The Land of the Drukpa Order," sometimes romantically (and mistakenly) translated as "The Land of the Thunder Dragon."[2] With the supremacy of the Shabdrung came a unified system of government and law—also, a written language, Choekey (Classical Tibetan), which was the language of the monasteries in which records were kept, histories written, and prayers said. It was a language, it should be noted, which would have been as unintelligible to the average farmer in Bhutan as Latin would have been to the peasant of medieval Europe.

As the Shabdrung's conquering armies marched east, they constructed massive fortresses, called *dzongs*. The idea of a *dzong*, an edifice that combined the dual roles of religious house and armed garrison, was invented as a way of consolidating political and religious control over the country. Today these fortresses are far less sinister, no longer symbols of conquest but treasured historical monuments, housing both monks and civil servants. This admixture of church and state only serves to emphasize how integral religion is to the average Bhutanese citizen. The sort of secular society we take for granted in the West has made small inroads in Bhutan.

Under the Shabdrung's leadership, a dual form of government was initiated. A head abbot, called the Je Khenpo, was appointed to rule over the state monk body, and a regent, called the Druk Desi, was appointed to handle secular affairs. Events were to prove that it was a poor design for government. In theory, after the Shabdrung's death, his mind incarnation would become the new head of state and take the title of Shabdrung. But in practice, the real political power lay in the hands of the district governors or *penlops*. The Shabdrung's followers must have sensed this weakness, for when the Shabdrung died in 1651, his death was kept a secret for over fifty years and the Druk Desi ruled in his name and carried on his work of unifying the country. After the Shabdrung's death was finally acknowledged, a long period of instability ensued, as each of the *penlops* fought for supremacy. The senior monks withdrew from politics for the most part, coming forward only in times of need to act as peacemakers or mediators, and the Druk Desi became the pawn of whichever governor had engineered his appointment. This power vacuum was finally filled in 1885, when Ugyen Wangchuck, the *penlop* of Tongsa District, through a series of military victories and diplomatic alliances begun by his father, became the leader of a united Bhutan in all but name.

In 1907, with British approval—for it was also in their best interest to see a stable government on India's northern border—Ugyen Wangchuck was declared the first hereditary monarch of Bhutan by a council of state. There was no opposition. People were heartily sick of bloody discord and yearned for stability.

It was Ugyen Wangchuck's grandson, the third king, Jigme Dorje Wangchuck, who made the decision that Bhutan must end its history of isolationism and join the world community. A down-to-earth monarch, Jigme Dorje Wangchuck was greatly beloved by his people and greatly lamented when he died in 1972 of cancer at the relatively young age of forty-four. He initiated a series of cautious social and economic reforms, which included land reform, the abolishment of slavery and the emancipation of women, the country's first five-year economic plan, and Bhutan's entry into the United Nations. He realized that if Bhutan was to survive in the modern world, she had to catch up. The first development projects started at this time. One of the first steps on the road to development was, well, the building of roads, for surprisingly, until 1961, there were no vehicle roads in the whole kingdom and wheeled traffic was unknown. Even today, the word for road, *lam*, is the same word for footpath, and you frequently hear the phrase *gharry lam*, used to designate a vehicle road from a traditional walking one.[3]

The first road began at Phuntsholing, a trading centre on the border with Cooch Behar, and travelled north to the capital at Thimphu. Road building progressed very slowly. There was no heavy equipment and roads were built with dynamite and large gangs of bonded labourers imported from the poorer corners of the subcontinent, the landless poor of India and Nepal. There are still very few kilometres of road in Bhutan even forty years later. The great lateral road, linking east to west was only completed in 1986. The unstable nature of the rock, frequent earthquakes and, of course, the yearly ravages of the monsoon rains, mean that road maintenance is constant and costly. The road system as it existed in 1987 resembled the letter "E" fallen on its side, ᗰ, with numerous subsidiary roads under construction.

The third king also introduced a modern education system to Bhutan. Previous to this there had been monastic schools and the presence of a few private tutors for the country's elite, but the king decided that if his country was to catch up to the rest of the world and enter the twentieth century on equal terms he needed a modern education system. But there was a problem. There are more than twenty languages spoken in Bhutan and, if one were to remove all of the recently introduced tongues—languages such as Hindi, Nepali, Tibetan, and English—then one would be left with a list of indigenous languages that possessed no written script.

In 1961 the government decided to rectify this problem by choosing a national language and creating a written script for it. The language they chose was Dzongkha, "the language of the *dzong*," a language spoken by the Ngalong people of Western Bhutan. The written form of the language was based on Tibetan characters, a language to which it was akin. A school for Dzongkha instructors was created. However, when the government of Bhutan decided to introduce a modern secular education system, Dzongkha was not ready to be the language of instruction; there were not enough Dzongkha speakers in the country, nor enough instructors to fill the schools, nor were there enough textbooks in that language. The government experimented briefly with Hindi as the medium of instruction but finally settled on English—a politically neutral language—as the language of secular education. (Monks are still educated in Classical Tibetan.) Thus, children across Bhutan, regardless of their native tongue, received their schooling, from kindergarten to college, in English. And so it was that I, as an English-speaking foreigner, was able to find employment as an English instructor in a small high school in the eastern part of that country.

The man who helped pioneer this system was, of course, Father William Mackey. Teachers had to come from someplace. Most were recruited in India, many from the sunny state of Kerala in the far south. A small number of teachers also came from the West. There were fifteen Canadians in Bhutan at the time I was there. There were also volunteer teachers from England, Ireland, Scotland, and New Zealand. The establishment of hospitals and medical facilities, at least in the east where I was posted, was largely done by medical missionaries from Scandinavia, like Sven. There were also lots of United Nations consultants in agriculture, irrigation, forestry, business, medicine, education, and even map-making. In Thimphu we joked that the UN offices were larger than those of the government of Bhutan, and it was not far from the truth.

When I first arrived in Thimphu, I was told that Bhutan had more aid workers per capita than any other developing country in the world. Strictly speaking, I do not know if this was true, but it felt true. The capital was crawling with foreigners. The suburbs of Thimphu were littered with lovely little cottages, each with a brand-new SUV parked in the driveway. I suppose that in the 1980s Bhutan was the place to be in the developing world. And there were good reasons why this should be so. To begin with, it was safe. At no time in the two years that I lived in Bhutan did I ever feel uneasy or threatened. Women, in particular, appreciated this and could live and travel quite comfortably and safely by themselves. The climate was healthy. Because of the elevation, we did not have to worry about malaria or many of the other tropical diseases common in South Asia. The scenery was spectacular, the surroundings idyllic. There was no urban sprawl, no air pollution, no noise pollution. The traditional culture was fascinating and vibrant. The temples I visited were living, breathing places, not cultural relics or historic sites.

There were also more practical reasons why aid organizations were eager to help Bhutan. To begin with, the government was stable, and support for development came from the top, from the king, where it counted most. The bureaucracy was honest and reasonably efficient. There was none of the "skimming off the top" so frequently encountered in the developing world; so aid projects had a fair chance of success, since the aid went to the people for whom it was intended, instead of lining the pocket of some corrupt bureaucrat. The people one worked with were intelligent and motivated. They really believed in what they were doing and had no desire to be anywhere else. That is not to say that there was no opposition to modernization—there was a great deal of opposition, particularly from religious leaders, who saw open doors as the first step toward the erosion of cultural values—but, at the time, the policy of modernization had the seal of approval from the king, whose father began the process by inviting in the first foreign advisors.

The presence of so many expatriates led to a fairly insular cocktail scene. The same faces were always present. The stories became tired. The situation was occasionally enlivened by the presence of foreign celebrities. Sarah met Pierre Trudeau at a reception in 1988, and, more recently, there have been well-publicized visits by Prince Charles, Joanna Lumley, Robert Bateman, Peter Matthiessen, Robert Thurman, and Michael Palin, to name a few. My favourite celebrity story involved a newly arrived volunteer attending her first cocktail party. Unsure of herself, she quietly nursed her drink in a corner. A grey-haired but obviously fit gentleman approached her, thrust out his hand, and barked, "Heinrich Harrer—*Seven Years in Tibet*." To which she replied:

"Uh, hello. Molly Jones—two weeks in Bhutan."

SIX

LOOKING FOR DEWA

I HAD BEEN WORKING STEADILY FOR SIX WEEKS before I took my first break. There was a lot to learn, and when I was not teaching or supervising the students, there was always plenty of marking to do, so my days were pretty full. But, by the Saturday of the sixth week, I'd had enough. Saturdays were half days at the school, but I had no classes scheduled, so I spent that morning pretending to mark essays. But it was no good; I couldn't concentrate. I needed a holiday and, despite the fact that the mercury was falling and the slate-grey clouds were threatening rain, I felt that I just had to get out of my room and off the campus. I grabbed my rucksack, stuffed in my windbreaker and a water bottle, and headed out the door. I was going to explore Khaling Valley; but it was not idle exploration, for I had a definite object in mind. I was going to discover the remains of King Dewa's Palace.

Back in Thimphu, we had been given a lecture on Bhutanese history by Françoise Pommaret. Françoise was a Tibetologist studying and working in Bhutan. She was developing a history of the country for the department of education and, at the same time, pursuing her own research. Knowing we were all to reside in Eastern Bhutan, she told us something of the history of that region.

At the time of Ngawang Namgyel's unification drive in the seventeenth century, the eastern part of Bhutan and parts of present day Arunachal Pradesh were ruled by a small group of independent kings. These clan kings, or "one-valley kings" as they were known, to indicate the size of their tiny demesnes, all claimed to be descended from the same man, a Tibetan prince named Tsangma who had been banished to Eastern Bhutan, possibly by the anti-Buddhist monarch, Lang Dharma, in the ninth century. The kings ruled their lands from palaces, which in reality were not much more than fortified watchtowers, called *khars*. I saw the ruins of one of these stone towers (the palace of Tshenkharla) above the school where Catherine worked in Rangtangwoong. Françoise noted that the last person to succumb to the westward expansion of Drukpa rule was King Dewa of Khaling. She said that not much was known of him, but he was mentioned in two obscure chronicles discovered in the archives of Tashigang Dzong, the seat of government for much of Eastern Bhutan. Dewa had defied the Shabdrung, until he had been forced to submit to the authority of Lama Namsay, the leader of the Shabdrung's forces. Françoise had noted the name of the place where the last confrontation took place but said that this village did not seem to exist anymore and that its exact location was a bit of a mystery. Later, after I had returned to Canada, I was able to locate transcriptions of these chronicles and fill in the details for myself. [4]

I found King Dewa's story highly appealing. I liked the idea that Khaling was the site of a heroic last stand, where Dewa, like some highland clan chief, resisted the tide of history, if but for a short time. So I set myself a task. I would seek solid evidence of this elusive historical figure; I would discover the ruins of King Dewa's Palace.

Khaling Valley is wedge shaped—twisting, narrow at the top, and open at the bottom. The Jeri River runs the length of the valley and is bridged near the narrow end, where the bazaar and all three schools were found (the high school above the bazaar, and the primary school and the school for the blind below). The new road, coming from the north in Tashigang, enters the valley at the lower end, at its widest part, and then travels up the valley (upstream that is), along one steep green wall, slowly descending, until it reaches Khaling Bazaar. There it leaps the river and then reverses its course, slowly ascending, following another steep forested slope, until it reaches the far end, opposite from where it had entered, and passes over a ridge, out of sight, on its journey south. This picture is complicated somewhat by a sharp mountain ridge that bisects the narrow end of the valley, separating the high school and the bazaar on the south side of this ridge from the village of Dowzor and the Scandinavian mission clinic on the north side. On the ridge rests the village of Khaling Gompa (which will feature prominently later in my story).

The bazaar itself was new when I was there, only as old as the high school and the paved road. Most of the buildings that comprise the municipality of Khaling Bazaar were still in the progress of completion, their construction proceeding in fits and starts as the shop owners acquired a little cash to add a wall here or a window there or perhaps remove a temporary roof of bamboo thatch and erect a solid second

Khaling Bazaar.

storey. One would have expected the appearance of a frontier town, but the sad truth is that surviving even one monsoon season makes a structure look as if it has stood there since the beginning of time. The ubiquitous whitewash turns grey and the mud mortar between the limestone blocks shrinks and cracks. The winter roofs of split woven bamboo lose their golden sun-polished lustre after the first spring rain, fade to brown, then grey, and finally to black as the monsoon season progresses and mould coats the flattened fibres. The buildings in the town, when completed, were usually two storeys tall—shop on the main floor and living quarters above—with a capacious attic for storage. Doors and window frames were painted a dull rust red and the eaves were intricately carved with brightly painted Buddhist symbols. There were no panes of glass in the windows, only sliding wooden shutters to keep out the driving monsoon rains and bitter winter winds, nor were there any nails to bind the structure together. The fabric of the building was woven together as tightly as a Chinese puzzle with wooden pegs and clever joinery.

There was a post office at one end of the bazaar, closest to the bridge. There was a hotel at the far end of the street with a restaurant/lobby on the ground floor and three roughly partitioned bedrooms upstairs. It was a hotel, I might add, where no one ever seemed to stay and with only two items on its restaurant menu: tukpa, a Nepali noodle soup, and mo-mos, a Tibetan ravioli similar to Chinese New Year's

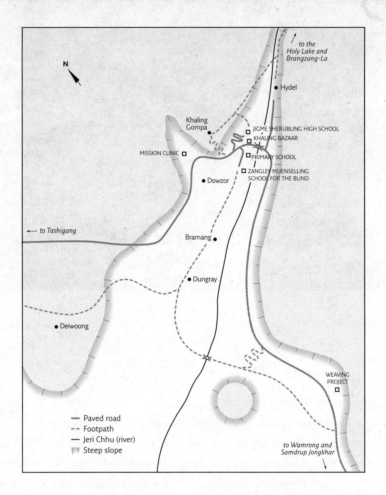

to the
Holy Lake and
Brangzung-La

● Hydel

Khaling
Gompa
☐ JIGME SHERUBLING HIGH SCHOOL
☐ KHALING BAZAAR
MISSION CLINIC ☐
☐ PRIMARY SCHOOL
☐ ZANGLEY MUENSELLING
SCHOOL FOR THE BLIND
● Dowzor

← to Tashigang

Bramang ●

● Dungray

● Deiwoong

WEAVING
PROJECT
☐

— Paved road
-- Footpath
— Jeri Chhu (river)
▓ Steep slope

to Wamrong and
Samdrup Jongkhar

jiaotze. That is not to say that the lobby was empty, for there were always the same four
old men present, seated on a wooden bed frame playing a complicated game of dice
on a marked blanket, using small pebbles for counters and loudly shouting "Shh-
Ping!" as they rolled the bones.

Ranged between the post office on the one end and the hotel on the other were six
shops on both sides of the street that kept going in and out of business, according to
the vagaries of the youthful economy, and all of which sold exactly the same things: six
varieties of bar soap, toothbrushes (these didn't sell well), tooth powder, dry biscuits
from large tins that required a chisel to open, mustard oil, sacks of dried lentils, two
grades of rice (bad and not-so-bad—one had more bugs, the other fewer stones), a
few withered vegetables for sale to the teachers (available according to the season
and the state of the roads), bunches of plantains, hair oil in dusty bottles (also for the
Indian teachers), plastic combs, small pocket mirrors, kerosene, bottles of ink for
the students' fountain pens, fountain pens (of course), bolts of cheap Indian cloth,
Chinese sneakers and thermoses (these were smuggled over the border), blue plastic

beach sandals known locally as *chappals* (standard footwear throughout the country, especially in the summer monsoon), and candy, lots of candy. In fact, one suspects that storekeepers in Khaling made the bulk of their profits from two things: candy and booze. For every store was also a tavern. Every shop served alcohol in chipped tumblers across the same counters where you purchased your bolts of cloth. Anyone who ever grew up in a small town and is old enough to remember the country general store would have felt at home in a shop in Khaling, except that here the loiterers sitting on the benches along the walls held glasses of alcohol, not lemonade.

It was, and perhaps still is, customary for the male teachers, most of whom were expatriates recruited in India, to come down to the bazaar after school for a "peg." They would take a seat on these plain wooden butt-polished benches, cut their rum from a pitcher of dirty water on the counter, and noisily get drunk. Dapper Keralans and Bengalis, scholars from New Delhi or Madras, would help each other to peg after peg of Apsoo rum or Changta whisky, and their voices would grow shrill with imagined wrongs and with the frustrations of work and life in Khaling; for Bhutan, to a well-educated Indian from sunny Kerala or Tamil Nadu, was akin to Siberia. Wages were high, but most longed for the dusty streets and crowded bazaars of home.

That particular day, I stepped into Nima's crowded shop and approached the counter to purchase a package of Gluco biscuits. Someone called my name. It was Ray, one of the teachers in my department, who was sitting on a bench by the window, nursing a peg of rum, flanked by two young Bhutanese men in Western-style clothing.

Ray was a handsome Bengali from Calcutta. An orphan, he was raised by Catholic Brothers, and they had done a good job on his education. His English was impeccable. His accent, if it could be classified at all, was vaguely North American. Father Mackey had recruited Ray when he was young and heading for trouble, had given him a vocation and a career, and Ray had not let him down. He had a good job at Jigme Sherubling, but Ray lacked the advanced education that he would have needed to teach in India.

"Ken," he shouted, "come and join me for a peg." I took a seat on the bench and he introduced me to his two companions, ex-students who were visiting from the college at Kanglung. Ray called for another round and I drank my shot of rotgut straight, declining the offer of cloudy water from the shopkeeper. "What are you up to?" he asked, and I outlined my plan to go for a walk and search for the ruins of King Dewa's Palace. I was not stumbling around completely in the dark. I had questioned a few people for the whereabouts of the ruins and everyone had heard of them, though no one could place them exactly. Father Mackey had thought that the temple at Dungray and the palace were one and the same; at least that is what he had been told. Others I questioned offered other possibilities for the palace's location, and I was determined to canvass them all. The only trouble was I had never ventured down the valley before. I did not know where these places were and my command of Sharchopkha was so poor that I had little hope of gathering more than the most rudimentary information.

"Well, what are we waiting for?" shouted Ray, lurching to his feet. "We'll come with you. Won't we, boys? It'll be fun." He called for two more shot glasses of whisky, and then, almost as an afterthought, bought two large bottles of beer and slipped one in each jacket pocket, balancing himself with alcohol.

We strolled, arm in arm, like a pair of inebriated sailors, supported by Ray's stalwart ex-students, down a muddy lane that led from the bazaar. This crude road took us first to the primary school and then to the school for the blind. After the blind school, the road narrowed to a muddy path, which continued down the length of the valley linking up with other villages as it progressed parallel to the river.

When we reached the primary school, we met a friend of Ray's who insisted on taking us to his quarters and giving us another drink to fortify us on our journey. As this was my first visit to the school, I asked if I could look around. Ray's friend, pleased at my interest, offered to give me a tour.

The primary school was a smaller version of the high school—a cluster of decaying buildings surrounded by a fenced enclosure to keep the livestock out: a two-storey school building, separate boys' and girls' dormitories, a kitchen, and a small collection of teachers' bungalows. It was, if possible, a bit sadder-looking than the high school. We poked our head in one of the ground-floor classrooms where a lesson was in progress. The room was large and gloomy. The only light came from the waist-high windows along the back wall and from the open door. The first grade students were seated in neat rows, cross-legged on the floor, in navy ghos and kiras. A young female teacher stood at the front of the room beating out time on a small cracked chalkboard with a bamboo cane. As we entered, the class was chanting their math lesson in unison: "One and one ees two; two and two ees four; four and four ees eight; eight and eight ees seeksteen, etc." Our entrance caused everyone to go silent. The teacher looked up nervously.

"Carry on. Carry on," said our guide affably, but the teacher seemed suddenly stricken of speech. As the silence lengthened, our new friend laughed uncomfortably,

Primary girls skipping with a rope made of tree bark.

and then, to save an awkward situation, moved to the front of the room and took charge. "Let us see what our students have learned," he said.

"Karma Dorje, stand up," barked our guide. A small bare-footed boy rose to his feet. His head was shaven and he wore a *gho* that was so faded it had probably been through several members of his family.

"Karma Dorje. Two and two is...?"

The boy looked startled. "Sir?"

Our guide looked annoyed now. "It is not a difficult question, Karma. I will repeat myself: Two and two is...?"

The boy looked at his dirty toes and whispered something into his cupped hand.

"What? What is that? Speak up boy!"

"Three?" ventured Karma Dorje.

"Three!" barked his examiner angrily. "What do you think, class? Is two and two, three?"

"Yes, Sir," shouted some. "No, Sir," shouted an equal number.

"Hmff!" sniffed our guide angrily. "Two and two is most definitely *not* three! Isn't it, class?"

"No, Sir," cried some lustily. "Yes, Sir," cried the others.

"Try again, Karma Dorje: Two and two is...?"

"Six?" said the alarmed child timidly.

"six! Six!" sputtered our guide, now thoroughly aroused. "What do I do to a student who does not know what two and two is, class?"

"Beat him nicely, Sir," came the reply.

"That is correct." Our guide appropriated the instructor's bamboo switch. "Hold out your hand, Karma Dorje. Now let us try again. Two and two is...?"

"Five?"

"No!" Down came the cane. *Twhack!* "Again: Two and two is...?"

"Eight?"

"No!" *Twhack!*

"Four?"

The bamboo cane seemed to hesitate in the air for a moment. Then it relaxed. The examiner smiled. "That is correct. Two and two is four. Very good, Karma Dorje. You may sit down. Now, let us see. Who shall we call upon next?"

I cleared my throat. "Excuse me, sir. I want to thank you for the trouble you have taken in giving me a tour of your excellent institution and for this wonderful demonstration of your pedagogical methods, but I am afraid that my friends and I must carry on. We have much to do." Then I turned to the teacher. "And thank you for allowing me to visit your classroom today. I only hope you will excuse this interruption." Everyone smiled at the compliment and assured me I was welcome to return at anytime. As we left the school, I whispered to Ray, "Is it always like this?"

He grinned impishly, "Yup."

We stumbled down the valley along the rutted path, past stony cornfields not much larger than basketball courts, past small copses of willow and alder, over streams, past a small walled orchard in which a mastiff was chained, until we came to the next village: Bramang. Our arrival basically stopped whatever work was going on. People stopped slopping their swine in mid-slop, stopped plucking chickens mid-pluck, stopped weaving kiras mid-weft, and gawked. The students canvassed the villagers, asking if anyone knew the whereabouts of King Dewa's Palace. The consensus was that the ruins were in the next village, but the problem obviously needed some consideration. In fact, it called for a drink. We were invited into a smoky kitchen and seated on a braided rug on the floor while the discussion swirled around us. Two wooden drinking bowls appeared before us and were magically filled. And refilled. And filled again.

Thus fortified, we waved our thanks and continued on our merry way. As we stumbled into the next village, Dungray, I noticed an abandoned house in the centre of the community, a nice home in a favoured location, but the roof was sagging, the thatch was ragged, the door hung askew, and it needed paint. Obviously, no one was living there. I asked one of the students why it was abandoned.

"It is haunted, Sir," he replied. "Someone died there—in a fire, I think. No one will live there now or they will get the same bad luck. Some houses are just unhappy, Sir."

We asked directions to the village temple—so far the best candidate for the location of the ruined palace—and were directed along another path. The temple at Dungray stood just outside the village in a small field enclosed by a low wall of white-washed stone. The temple was a white cube with a peaked red roof. A broad wooden stairway led to a recessed entranceway on the second floor. The windows were small, high up, and shuttered. It would have made a good blockhouse in a pinch, I thought, but it didn't look like the fortress of a king.

A man was walking by with a short-handled mattock on his shoulder. We called out. "Would it be possible to see the inside of the temple?"

The man considered. "The caretaker has just had a baby," we were informed, "but perhaps I can borrow the key."

One of the college students went off with the man while the other helped Ray to a seat on the bottom step of the temple. I climbed the steps and entered the darkened porch. The short walls on my right and left were decorated with frescoes representing the Guardian Gods of the Four Directions, also called the Gyelchen Shi or the "Four Great Kings." I had seen such representations at the entrance to just about every building of importance I had visited since I arrived in Bhutan, but I had no way of judging just how old these paintings might be or even if they were any good. Each of the guardians is painted a different colour: north is yellow, south is green, west is red, and east is white. Each of the figures is fierce looking, with bared teeth and bulging red-rimmed eyes, and each carries his traditional symbol: a banner and jewel-spitting mongoose for the north, a sword for the south, a chorten, or cube-shaped stone funerary monument, for the west, and a lute for the east.

The farmer returned with the key and released the giant padlock on the great studded door and heaved it open. We left our shoes in the vestibule and stepped over the massive doorsill. Our guide entered the room ahead of us and began throwing open shutters until the gloomy room was stabbed with dusty beams of light. The wall murals were smoke obscured but fascinating. Unlike most temples I had visited hitherto, these were all of a piece, like a giant cartoon, and traced the journey (we were told) of a many-faced yellow goddess on her flight from Tibet to Bhutan on the back of a tiger. Each vignette was sepa-rated from the others by a frame of stylized clouds and figured the same goddess in a new location meeting other creatures, both human and divine, and performing some notable act. What I found most interesting were not the doings of the goddess but the little slices of real life hidden in the margins of the pictures: wrestlers testing their strength, archers holding contests, elderly women bathing, guards sleeping in palace gateways, and men drinking and laughing. There were also about fifty gold-painted wooden statues in niches along the wall, each with its own door to hide behind.

As we were examining the murals, our guide disappeared for a moment, only to reappear a few moments later with a stack of wooden drinking bowls and a large black cylindrical flask bound with meticulously worked brass hoops. He bade us sit on the floor and despite our protests, proceeded to fill us with *ara*. As we drank, we quizzed him on the age and origins of the *lha-kang*. Was it, we wondered, the fortress of King Dewa? Our guide shrugged. Some people said so, but he had no opinion on the matter. He seemed vaguely amused that we should trouble ourselves over such a small thing and topped up our *gorbus*—"Jai, jai." We finished our drinks, offered our thanks, left a small offering on the altar, and continued on our way.

A short way below the village we had to pause and catch our breath. Despite the chill in the air, we were sweating, probably straight alcohol by this time. I broke out the biscuits and passed them around. I took a swig from my water bottle and offered the rest to the boys. They drank like Greek raki swillers, out of politeness, pouring the water into their throats from a distance so that their lips did not touch my bottle.

"I need a drink," Ray announced and opened one of his beers on the rim of a sharp boulder with a smack of his open palm against the top of the bottle. Beer gushed down the side of the bottle, and he laughed, shaking the foam off his wrist. "Cheers," he said and offered me the bottle. I took a swig, imitating the boys, and passed it back.

"Sir," said one of the boys, pointing to a cliff above us. "Up there is a cave that runs under the ground," he traced the route in the air with his finger, "and comes out over there, on the other side, in another cave." He pointed to the far side of the valley.

"Have you seen this cave?" I asked.

"No, but some people were telling me of this thing."

"Have they been in the cave?"

"No," he said, "but I am knowing this to be true. Some years ago, to find out where the cave went, they made an experiment. They put a cock in the cave and sealed that place with stones. Three days later, the cock came out on the other side."

We expressed our amazement and passed the bottle. Just ahead of us was a fork in the trail, and we would have to make a decision. One path angled up the side of the hill to a plateau called Deiwoong. *Deiwoong* meant "place of spirits" and that in itself was encouraging. The other path continued along the floor of the valley and eventually met the river again. Near this place, we had been told, there were some "old things." What these old things might be was left very vague. While we were interviewing the villagers, I had the sense that people were telling me what they thought I wanted to hear. While they had no personal interest in things that had happened hundreds of years ago, they did not want me to be disappointed. We decided to continue down the valley, leaving Deiwoong for another afternoon.

Soon we came to a place like a sheepfold. We entered through one of the gaps in the crumbling stone wall. In the tall grass were several weathered *chortens* and a long prayer wall inset with darkened slates. Each slate was incised with a sacred text. Everything had a neglected air, and the monuments were overgrown with ferns. I stumbled and fell into a shallow rectangular pit. As the students helped me out, they looked worried.

"Nasty hole," I joked. "A tiger trap?"

No, they replied, as they helped to brush the ashes off my clothes, a crematorium.

Our "old things" turned out to be a cremation ground and a few crumbling monuments to the dearly departed. I was disappointed: no palace here.

"Where now?" I asked.

We looked around. Below us, the path sloped down to the river where it crossed a covered wooden bridge. On the far side of the river, a sharp ridge came down the mountainside, dipping to a shallow saddle and ending in cone-shaped hill. After crossing the bridge, our path went over the saddle and disappeared.

"That is the old road to Wamrong," said one of the boys. "Before the *gharry lam*. That is how the people went from Tashigang to Samdrup Jongkhar in the old days."

I looked at the vista before us again. "If I was a king and wanted to guard the main road and exact tolls, I would build my palace on that hill," I said, pointing to the cone-shaped hill to the right of the saddleback.

Accordingly, we filed down the slope, crossed the bridge, and began to climb the hill in search of ruins. My plan was to spread out and search the hilltop methodically, but it was not to be. The hill was a jungle of thick underbrush and fallen trees, all knit together with thick vines. Ray was sweating profusely and was falling down every ten minutes or so. The boys were constantly rushing to his aid, and soon the three of them were sitting on a fallen log and resting. I was not much better. The alcohol was really beginning to hit me now. I crashed around in the underbrush a bit longer, but soon I, too, had to admit defeat. Not only was I done in, but it was clear that there were no ruins here—at least none that could be seen without removing the jungle and several tons of topsoil. We stumbled back down to the saddleback and the main path.

I did not relish the idea of retracing our steps up the valley, and I must have said something to that effect, for one of the students pointed to a narrow path that zigzagged up the ridge.

"We don't have to, Sir," he said. "That road goes to the *gharry lam.*"

I nodded. "Lead on, Macduff."

The journey up the ridge was arduous, but I remember very little. I was too nauseous. It was all I could do to place one foot in front of another without throwing up. Ray was in worse shape. The boys each grasped an elbow and basically lifted him up the mountain. When we reached the road, however, things got easier. We were walking on a level paved surface now that sloped down gently all the way to the bazaar several miles away. Despite the pounding in my head, I could not help but notice just how beautiful the valley was from this vantage point. Just twenty minutes' walk from the school and it was paradise. When we reached the school, I said farewell to my companions, entered my room, drank the tepid contents of my water filter in its entirety, and crawled into bed.

The next morning was Easter Sunday.

I rose. I poured a bucket of cold water over my head and looked at my tongue in the mirror. I had promised the Sisters that I would join them in celebrating the Resurrection, so I dressed in my Sunday best and climbed the thousands and thousands and thousands of concrete steps to their residence. I joined the Sisters, the Jesuits, a few of the Scandinavian missionaries, and a handful of teachers from the three schools, mostly Keralans, in the tiny and exceedingly bright chapel on the main floor of the Sisters' home. I partook of the body and blood of Our Lord and marvelled at hymns I had known since childhood, which had become completely unrecognizable when led by Sister Raymond on the wheezy harmonium. I joined them for tea and fellowship after the service, feeling somewhat human again by this time.

Coming down the steps I breathed deeply and looked around. The sun was resplendent on the hillside. A great glorious golden haze, like the light on the road to Damascus at Saul's conversion, enveloped the monastery on the ridge above the school. There were bright green highlights on the pasture, almost yellow, and deeper green in the shadows of the ravines. A lone white cow ambled down the hillside and onto the road where it was struck dead by a passing truck.

SEVEN

MONSOON DIARY

I KEPT A DIARY WHILE I WAS IN BHUTAN. In retro-spect, it is a bit of a disappointment—not in the least because, in its pages, I discover that I am not nearly as interesting or as insightful as I remember myself being—but I thought it would be a shame if I did not include at least one chapter of diary extracts, even if just to capture some of the immediate day-to-day frustrations of learning to cope in a new culture. The following chapter is composed of selections taken from the diary I kept that first summer in Khaling, during my first monsoon season.

Monsoon Diary

Everyone goes a little crazy during the monsoon. Father Cherion's solution, I quickly discovered, was to keep everybody busy. He asked me to plan regular Saturday evening features—dancing, singing, skits—that would be run as competitions between the four colour houses. At today's staff meeting, he also enquired after the progress of the school yearbook (something else that he'd assigned to my direction) and complimented me on the bulletin board newspaper I had done with my Class Nine English students: "A wonderful idea!" he enthused, "Great for school spirit." Then he announced that Mr. Ken would extend this exercise, creating a new newspaper every week. At the end of the staff meeting, almost as an afterthought, he asked me to organize monthly staff dinners too.

∞∞∞∞

The school's water supply stopped. I tracked down Ramgi and he said it was just sedi-ment in the storage tanks. He sent some small boys into the tanks with scrub brushes.

We opened all of the taps and let them run. Pure mud ran out of the taps for about an hour. After that it was still murky, but at least we have water. I boil my drinking water thoroughly now and run it through the filter even before I make my tea. The porous stone in the filter needs daily scrubbing.

On Sunday, some Indians arrived in a jeep and commenced shooting stray dogs with a single-barrelled shotgun that fired poison darts. The students watched with disapproval. Now there are dead dogs strewn about campus stiffening in the rain, growing cold and pale and bloated.

There is a Brokpa shepherd down in the bazaar standing on the peak of the roof of one of the shops. He has a striking red wool jacket worn under a yak skin vest and a yak felt beret on his head dripping rain. I'm not sure what he is doing. He is just standing there with his hands stiffly at his sides staring across the valley, looking perfectly forlorn.

My ankles are covered in tiny bites that swell into tiny pustules. They are not flea bites, as I first feared, but sandfly bites. Like the leeches, they will apparently plague us as long as the monsoon lasts. The Indians call them "dum-dums"—a term the locals have also adopted. Some of the primary school students' legs are horribly scarred.

∞∞∞

I ran the first of the Saturday evening entertainments tonight. I have decided on giving each evening a different theme, trying to balance the different languages and cultures at the school. It's like summer camp. Tonight's theme was: Songs in English. Father C and several of the teachers agreed to be the judges and each Colour House presented three items. Lots of pop songs, but not always recognizable because the tempo has been slowed down and they are sung to South Asian rhythms. Weird, but interesting. I was number thirteen on the program and sang "When the Iceworms Nest Again" to banjo accompaniment. The humour was lost on my audience. (Of course! What was I thinking?) Afterwards, Ray invited me back to his place for a beer. At least he got the joke.

∞∞∞

Took class pictures for the yearbook today just before morning assembly. Complete disaster. I had chosen the stone bleachers on the football field as the location, since the students could stand in rows and I had the morning sun over my shoulder. Father Cherion wanted the photos on the front steps of the school, but I pointed out that the steps were in shadow and the morning sun would be shining right into my camera.

Mr. Reghu said I should have the students line up against the side of the gymnasium. I pointed out that the sun would be shining into the students' eyes, causing them to squint, and that the glare off the whitewashed wall would probably overpower the picture and leave the students' faces too dark to see anyway. Nobody was happy with my arrangements and immediately everyone took it upon himself to be in charge. All of the teachers were shouting at once, countermanding each others' orders. Also, every time my back was turned, someone would fiddle with my camera or move the tripod. In the end, everyone was grouchy and the whole exercise took far longer than it should have. As he stalked away at the end of the photo shoot, I heard Father Cherion mutter under his breath that the pictures would be terrible, and that it had all been a complete waste of time. I was ready to tell him just where he could stick his yearbook, but in the end I bit my tongue.

∞∞∞∞

Michael invited me to accompany him on a walk to the Hydel complex today. [Hydel was the name of the Indian construction firm that was building a small hydro-electric plant on the upper reaches of the Jeri River.] He had heard that there was a small shop there that stocked Indian goods that were unavailable in our local shops. The Hydel shop proved to be a disappointment, and coming back I nearly lost my head, literally. Here is how it happened.

Passing through the bazaar on our way to the Hydel, I stopped briefly at the Dantek Canteen and bought a package of *jalebi*, a sweet consisting of sugar, ghee, and flour trickled into a pan and then baked in an oven like a pretzel. On the way home, I was reading the sheet of newspaper that the sweets had been wrapped in. I was engrossed in a quiz, shouting out the questions to Michael who was walking a little ahead of me, when the crossbeam of the road barrier at the entrance to the Hydel compound caught me right across the bridge of my nose. It was one of those barriers with a heavy counterweight at one end, so that when it was unhooked the arm swung up of its own accord, like one of those novelty storks that drink out of martini glasses. I hit the barrier so hard, crunching the newsprint into my face, that I unlatched the arm. It bobbed down, then snapped up, catching me just under the chin, lifting me right off my feet and laying me out cold on the road.

When I came to, a concerned, but grinning Michael was bending over me, saying, "How many fingers am I holding up?" I've got a big scab on the bridge of my nose, but otherwise, okay. No headache, but it sure cleared the sinuses.

After the Saturday evening entertainment, Karin stopped at my place for a cup of instant coffee. It was a dark night with a heavy fog, so I decided to walk her home. The beams of our flashlights—mine, weak and yellow, and hers, strong and white—were clearly defined cones in which water droplets hung suspended and which terminated in haloes on the road's surface (mine looked appropriately tarnished). We heard a guttural coughing bark, which Karin identified as the tiny deer called *gasha*. The fog was so thick that we actually walked right past her house and did not realize it until we reached the basic health unit and had to backtrack. I walked home alone, my flashlight slowly failing until it finally went out completely. Not knowing where you are going makes the route seem longer. I felt my way home by sticking to the hard surface of the road. Since there were no streetlights and no electric lights in the houses nearby, I sensed rather than saw the huts I passed in the dark. A child coughed in a bamboo hut and I was startled; it sounded so close. I felt that if I had reached out in the dark, I could have touched his tousled sleeping head. Walking the last leg up the drive to the school something jumped out of the dark and brushed past my leg—a cat, I think. I jumped—*yallah!*—and could smell my own fear heavy in the damp air.

∞∞∞∞

All of the kids at the primary school have had their heads shaved. Lice problems. They are running around on the football field below my window in their blue ghos, flapping their arms and legs as they chase the ball. They look like a clutch of newly hatched chicks, with the shell still on their heads, following the mother hen.

∞∞∞∞

Classes went well today. I had the students parse a page-long sentence of Ronald Reagan's that he spoke in his own defence at the Iran-Contra hearings. Even they could see that it was a piece of evasion and had no verb to boot.

Met an old woman on the road today. She was [I was told] on a penitential pilgrimage, measuring the distance with her body. She had a thatch of unruly grey hair and damp travel-stained clothing. She had made an apron of burlap sacking to protect her *kira* and had wooden pattens on both hands, worn smooth and shiny from use. The clogs were held in place with leather straps across the backs of her hands. She moved in slow stages. First, she raised the clogs together to her chest and clapped them together. Then she raised her pressed palms to her forehead, praying continuously, and extended her arms above her head. She went down on her knees and stretched out full-length on the road in the rain. She crawled forward, inchworm style, placing her feet at the point occupied by her hands. She then rose to her feet and began all over again. In this way, she slowly crawled through the bazaar, oblivious to the curious spectators, the mud, and the rain. I did not know where she was coming from or where she was going or why she was taking this journey. Curiouser and curiouser.

∞∞∞

Heavy driving rain today. Storm wind blew mercilessly at my windows and water sprayed across the desk, finding its way in through ill-fitting casements and cracked windowpanes. When the wind slowed down and the rain became a steady drizzle, a strange thing happened. Along the tops of the windows, where they fit poorly, a fog started to creep in, whirling convulsively. It was like theatre fog pumped onto the stage, clinging to the walls and ceiling.

Fog does weird things in general. The other day I was waiting for the mail at the post office, standing on the porch, and I turned to look down the valley. The whole valley was socked in with fog except for a window exactly in the centre of the picture through which a view of the spur of Deiwoong and the rocky pillared cliffs beyond was framed. The sun was in my eyes and so the whole valley was tinged with silver. The fog was in constant motion. It was like watching clothes tumble in a dryer at the laundromat—a very pedestrian simile, but one that perfectly describes the very odd behaviour of the clouds as they swirled around this vortex, rolling up one side of the valley, arcing over, falling upon themselves, and unfurling again in a perpetual loop.

Sunset from the girls' study hall mysteriously otherworldly tonight. A cold mist swept up the ridge and soon the temple and the holy tree were only grey silhouettes, but very sharp and distinct. A line of cows, followed by a man bent under a stack of firewood, trudged slowly, head to tail, up the sharp line of the spur under the vast tree. It was like something cut out of grey paper. Behind the tree, in the swirling cloud, the sun shone like burnished steel.

The lights never went on in girls' study, so I fetched my banjo and we sang songs by candlelight instead. They really liked the old Band number "The Night They Drove Old Dixie Down." They called it "Oldixiedown" or "Nana, nana." We must have sung it twenty times.

∞∞∞

I thought it was wet here before, but now everything is turned to mud and jungle. We have torrential downpours every day. In fact, it is raining as I write this. Blue fuzzy mould is growing on every damp surface of my room: on my window casement, on my food, on my broom, on my baskets, on my books, even on my clothes. It's really depressing. You just can't escape the dampness. Many of my cassettes have stretched because of the high humidity. Neil Young now sings "Heart of Gold" under water. The rain also brings out the leeches that lurk in the tall grass and on overhanging tree branches, or along stone walls. They wait for you to brush pass, so that they can adhere to your pant leg or running shoe and inch their way to some spot where they can insinuate themselves between layers of clothing onto bare flesh.

The valley has changed. I rarely see the sky anymore, which I fondly remember as a lovely Dutch-tile blue. Now, a grey lid of cloud covers us, as if someone had dropped the seat cover on a toilet bowl. I don't go hiking much anymore; the paths are too overgrown, the leeches too numerous. The dominant colour in the landscape is green. It is layered onto the mountains as with broad strokes from a palette knife. Underlying this, like a foundation colour, is an ochre of mud. It is more something whose presence you sense than actually see, like a skin tone. Where you notice the ochre colour most strongly is on the occasional dead tree. The dead limbs and their browning foliage are, surprisingly, the same colour as their gummy foundation, as if the tree's vascular system were sucking up this gumbo and transforming the corpse, chameleon-like, into the liquid dust from which all things come and to which all must return.

∞∞∞

The Bhutanese are delightfully unconscious of any shame associated with bodily functions. Even the shyest, most delicate girl in my class will stand and pick her nose while talking to me and think nothing of it. I also love their scolding voice—a special deep gruff commanding tone, like that of a Japanese male actor—that is assumed for certain occasions and then dropped. It sounds to an outsider as if one person is dreadfully and seriously angry with another person, but it is really a formalized way of establishing authority. Once the issue is resolved, the pose is dropped and, two seconds later, the same two people will be laughing and hugging each other.

Holiday today: First Sermon of Lord Buddha. But did I have a holiday? Ooh, no, not me. Spent the morning directing play rehearsal, the afternoon marking notebooks and supervising a makeup exam. Not that I could have gone anywhere or done anything anyway. Nothing but rain, rain, rain, rain.

∞∞∞

The only vegetable I've had for weeks now is potatoes. I've made just about every potato dish you could think of, but it wears a little thin. Still, it beats eggplant. I ate eggplant for three weeks straight and I don't even like eggplant. I think of food, dream of food constantly—pizza, hamburgers, cheddar cheese, bread and butter, cold water, cold beer, fried chicken, steak, spaghetti, ice cream, real coffee...it's a kind of self-inflicted torture. I try to stop, but I can't. It's like getting a song stuck in my head that I can't stop humming.

∞∞∞

Finished exams finally after marathon marking session on Sunday that ended at 1 A.M. Completed them by candlelight. Rain has got everyone down. Play rehearsal went poorly. Students are just reciting their lines. The initial excitement seems to have worn off.

∞∞∞

Play rehearsal went considerably better tonight. We had to practise in the prayer hall, since the actors from the Dzongkha drama were using the stage tonight. Walking home afterwards was wonderful. There was a three-quarter moon shining brightly in a mostly clear sky. The stars seemed farther away and yet brighter somehow. There was a rose and blue halo about the moon where a stratum of cloud intersected it. We saw a falling star, a thread of gold spun across the sky above our mountain. A man left the *gompa* with a bamboo torch, running along the ridge, throwing huge yellow shadows on the underpinnings of the trees.

∞∞∞

Rained all day yesterday, all last night, and all day today. The school building is awash, like an island in a lake. Rain pouring off the gymnasium roof sounds like water over a dam.

∞∞∞∞

The Jeri Chhu is swollen from so much rain. You hear it so continuously that it becomes unheard. It strikes you as surprising when you notice the sound because you realize that you have been hearing it all along, but have simply blocked it out.

Not enough time in a day. I simply can't keep up with the marking.

∞∞∞∞

We have been experiencing a series of late afternoon thundershowers in recent days. Today, I was almost caught. Took 9A outside to enjoy the break in the weather and it started to drip rain, then great grey clouds came rolling in off the Holy Lake and engulfed the valley. In a matter of minutes, we were in the middle of a fierce downpour. So much water was flowing down the road that it lifted up great slabs of tarmacadam and carried them away. Play rehearsal went much better tonight.

∞∞∞∞

Last of the Saturday evening features for a while. Thank goodness. Now I can concentrate on the play. Had dinner with Ray and Mr. Mukherjee and inevitably the conversation turned to West Bengal and its relationship to the rest of India and whether or not Subash Chandra Bose was a patriot or a villain. Same old arguments. I have discovered one of the drawbacks of living in an expatriate community—all conversational gambits are quickly used up and endlessly recycled.

Many of the thorny fence posts around the school have burst into bloom. Huge orange pagoda-shaped flowers called kharshing in the local dialect—"coral tree" in English, I think. The flowers are used in the fermentation of grain.

∞∞∞∞

I have seen ferocious thunderstorms before, but this beats all. It lasted four days! The road became a river, the football field, a lake, and water started dripping through my ceiling. I stopped wearing shoes to school and went barefoot, carrying my shoes until I reached the classrooms. Even my umbrella proved rather useless as the rain struck the fabric with such force that my head and shoulders were bathed in a fine mist.

∞∞∞∞

Finished the yearbook. Everything is finally typed, pasted up, and camera ready. I hope Father is happy with the result, as I would like to wash my hands of this matter and get back to teaching.

∞∞∞∞

Took my Home Form class on a picnic today. When I suggested the idea a few days ago, they were wildly enthusiastic. I had visions of packing a few sandwiches in our jolas and going for a hike, but I was quickly disabused. That is not the way these things are done in Bhutan. A picnic in this country is a feast and the logistics of planning our meal and of choosing our picnic site made the planning of the D-Day offensive seem, in comparison, to be, well, a picnic. First, I had to get permission and file all of the paperwork. Then I had to start stockpiling supplies. A visit to the school store required the requisite chits. Great quantities of food in jute sacks were carted to my room and stacked in readiness. Next, a great leaning tower of battered and blackened cauldrons and kettles was assembled from the school kitchen and set beside this mountain of food.

Dawn rose on the day of the picnic and, for once, the weather seemed willing to cooperate. It was sunny and humid. The class collected on the stage outside my door and we parcelled out loads of picnic supplies. Only the poorest students were still wearing their school uniforms. Most girls were wearing their best summer-weight *kiras*. The boys were dressed in shirts and trousers. We filed down the drive and out along the road toward Dowzor, bundles slung over shoulders or balanced on heads, looking like a line of porters accompanying Henry Morton Stanley through darkest Africa. The site for our picnic, chosen by a couple of boys who had volunteered to scout it out a few days before, was just below the road near Dowzor, in a small clearing above a brook. When we arrived, everyone immediately set to work, gathering firewood, drawing water from the brook, washing rice, re-hydrating vegetables and fish. Everyone was busy and happy. I could hear conversations in at least four languages and reflected that, while this really wasn't my idea of a fun outing, they were clearly having a great time. Though I volunteered to help, they wouldn't hear of it. Instead, they insisted that I sit comfortably to one side and provided me with a cup of milky tea. Only when all of the pots were on the fire and bubbling away, did people start to relax. I walked down to the river with a few of the boys and we went for a swim. They taught me to play a game with flat stones, similar to quoits, called *dekor*. Miraculously, my team won, but that may have been by good-hearted design. By now our guests had started to arrive, for my students had also instructed me that you could not have a class picnic without inviting all of the teachers and staff. The students and I were kept busy seeing that everyone had plenty to eat. Later, some of the Nepali boys got me on my feet and we danced a complicated folk dance to everyone's amusement. (Durga

Class 10 picnic.

called it "The Pundit's Dance," but I'm sure he was pulling my leg.) The day had been a great success, and coming home, while I was walking along the road and chatting to little groups of laughing and singing children, Father sidled up to me, gripped my hand companionably and said, "Mr. Ken, that was a very successful event. I commend you. Well done, young man, well done." He squeezed my hand and patted it, refusing to let go. "The children had fun and the staff is growing closer together. I think events like this are important for the school, so much so, that I would like you to consider the following." Oh, no, I thought. Here it comes. "I would like you to consider organizing more picnics, perhaps on a weekly basis—one for each class. It would make the students happy in their studies and do wonders for staff morale."

@#%&*#%*@ !!!

EIGHT

CULTURE SHOCK

WORKING AS A VOLUNTEER in the developing world is not for everyone. Most people recognize this. And I sometimes wondered if we did more harm than good. Some certainly did no good at all—to themselves or to anyone else for that matter. Volunteer agencies try their best to screen out the worst characters. For example, WUSC volunteers all had to get a note from our physicians declaring that we were not only in great physical shape but that we were mentally fit, as well. In particular, they were trying to screen out those people who had just been through a traumatic experience, like the death of a child or a messy divorce, and who felt that working in the developing world would be just the thing to bring them out of their depression.

I know of one case where it was the volunteer's doctor who hid her patient's mental history, thinking that two years in Bhutan might be just the thing her patient needed to regain his sanity. The patient also happened to be her brother. Things went well at first, but gradually his old illness reasserted itself. His increasingly irrational behaviour and frequent binges alarmed his friends and colleagues. Then, one day, he disappeared. He ran off into the jungle and tried to live as a wild hermit, retreating deeper and deeper into the forest as the authorities pursued him. Eventually, he was coaxed out of the woods by a Canadian volunteer he trusted, clapped in handcuffs, and flown home.

I tell this sad story for two reasons. The first is simply to illustrate the point made above, that working as a volunteer is not for everyone. Lots of people crack. The second point is that you can't remake yourself. Going into an unfamiliar environment simply strips you down to the person you are. It forces you to face your demons.

And maybe this is a good thing. It was fortunate for us all that the Bhutanese were so accepting of our strange and often erratic behaviour.

When we had our orientation in Ottawa, we were given the classic profile for culture shock. The lecturer drew a diagram, shaped like a large letter **V**, on a flipchart using a black marker.

"Culture shock is a disease," she told us, "and you will all experience it to a greater or lesser degree. There are four stages of the disease."

She began to label the diagram. She wrote "Honeymoon Stage" at the top left, then "Conflict Stage" on the descending slope, "Critical Period" at the bottom of the **V**, "Recovery Stage" on the ascending slope, and "Cultural Adaptation" on the top right.

"The first stage is called the 'Honeymoon Stage' and for good reason. When you first arrive in Bhutan everything will be new and exciting and appealing. You will be treated as honoured guests. New experiences, like eating unusual dishes or haggling in the bazaar, are still fun and have not yet become tiresome. But soon the novelty will wear thin and small annoyances will begin to assume outsize importance. You will grow increasingly irritable and be angered or depressed by inconsequential things. You will long for the familiar. These symptoms will indicate that you have entered the second stage of the disease: the 'Conflict Stage.' Now you will begin a slow slide into the depths of despair until a point is reached when you hit rock bottom and you will say to yourself, 'To hell with this! I can't take this anymore! I wanna go home!'" The lecturer circled the sharp end of her diagram with broad strokes. "This is the 'Critical Period.'"

She paused and looked at us. "The thing to do at this point is to remind yourself that what you are feeling is perfectly normal. Everyone feels this way. It's just part of the disease. So don't throw in the towel just yet. If you persevere, you may climb back out of this valley of the shadow and achieve a kind of working equilibrium. This is 'Cultural Adaptation.' But let me warn you: however hard you try, Bhutan will never feel like home. You may learn to be content, but you will never entirely escape feelings of nostalgia for home. Cultural adaptation does not mean that the traveller has come 'home,' only that she has 'adapted.'"

We were warned that that not everyone would experience culture shock in the same manner or to the same degree. For some people the pattern would be cyclical and there would be several depths to plumb before they achieved a degree of cultural adaptation. Many people gave up when they hit rock bottom. Not too surprisingly though, Bhutan had a higher success rate than most postings. Most people fell in love with the place and stuck it out, sensing the reward at the end of the dark tunnel. Many renewed their contracts. Some few never left.

My Slough of Despond came at about the middle of August in the first year. Knowing it was bound to happen helped a little bit. We had been told to expect to hit the critical period about a quarter of the way through our contract, and so it was in my case. I guess it began with the giant centipede in my bed.

It had been raining for three months, not a steady rain, not even a heavy rain for the most part, but a reliable dousing of rain each day nonetheless. And even though it was summer, the rain kept things cool. At no time in Khaling did I ever feel like wearing shorts and a T-shirt—clothing that would have been considered immodest in any case. With the rain came a change of mood in the valley. The rusts and ochres of winter were replaced by the vibrant green of the monsoon season. There was so much green it became suffocating. We were choked with green. Bare sparse hillsides disappeared under jungle. Even the fence posts sprang to life. I had never been to a place before where you could shove a stick in the ground and grow a tree. So it was in Khaling. The crabbed and hunchbacked willows around the campus sprouted new and luxuriant growth (like the flyaway hair of carnival trolls), which the local farmers harvested with billhooks and machetes as fodder for their cattle. There was a leak in one corner of the library ceiling. When I enquired, I was told that nothing could be done until after the rainy season. All I could do was shift the books out of the path of this delicate waterfall and watch the mould grow. And mould grew on everything that would support it. My leather shoes, my belt, my hiking boots, all sprouted a blue fur. There was no point in buying bread. By the time it arrived from the bakeries in Samdrup Jongkhar, it was already spotted with green furry warts. Laundry took days to dry.

That evening, after dinner, I waited on the stage outside my room for my actors to arrive to rehearse our drama, Moliere's *A Doctor in Spite of Himself*. Raju, one of my Class 9 students, arrived alone. He made a stiff bow.

"Good evening, Sir."

"Good evening, Raju. Where are the others?"

"They are not coming, Sir."

"Not coming? May I ask why?"

"We need to rehearse the Nepali dance item for Saturday entertainment, Sir."

I did my best Ed Sullivan stoop, scratched my chin ponderously and paused to digest this. "So let me get this straight. You cancelled my play rehearsal, so that you could practise your dance number for Saturday's program?"

He smiled. "Yes, Sir."

I could have gotten angry, I suppose, but I was too depressed. I went back into my room and closed the door. I looked at the stacks and stacks and stacks of marking neatly piled on the bench along the wall. I looked at the layouts for the school yearbook spread across my desk, half-finished. I decided to do my laundry.

I filled a metal pail in the washroom and carried it to the sole electrical outlet near the door. I could hear footsteps pounding across the stage as other damp boys arrived for dance practice. There was lots of yelling in Nepali. Teenagers don't talk to each other, I had discovered, they yell. I plugged in my immersion heater and dropped it in the bucket. The lights in the building dimmed for a moment and then came back on. At least the immersion heater was working. When I had first moved into the gymnasium, I kept blowing fuses, but I found that when I replaced the old fuse wire with 0.010-gauge banjo wire I had solved that problem. Outside the door there was a shuffling and banging as the dancers took their places and the musicians adjusted their instruments. Someone shouted directions. A pause, and then the clap of the tabla, the wheezy inhalation of the school's ancient harmonium sucking air, the nasal delirium of the singers' voices, and the dancers began: shuffle, shuffle, swish, glide, twirl, twirl, shuffle, stop.

I was beginning to feel nauseous. I hadn't really been feeling right all day. I tried marking an essay while I was waiting for the water to heat up, but I couldn't concentrate. I decided to work some more on the yearbook. I hadn't been typing for more than five minutes on the old Remington portable when there was a delicate tapping on the door. I realized with a start that the music had stopped. It was Raju. Could Sir please stop typing? It was putting the dancers off the beat.

I sighed. "Very well," I said. "I was going to do my laundry anyway." I closed the door, unplugged the heater, and carried the bucket to the washroom. The music started up again. I poured some soap flakes into the bucket and then stuffed all my dirty laundry in on top and began swishing it up and down, raising a froth that spilled over my elbows and onto the floor. For the really dirty items, like shirt cuffs and collars, I slapped them on the concrete floor and scrubbed them with a bar of lye soap. Then I rinsed everything well under the tap beside the squat toilet and dumped the water. The grey water swept across the floor and disappeared down the throat of the cracked porcelain bowl like Poe's maelstrom. I wrung out the clothes as best I could and draped them over a line I had strung between the light fixture above the stage door and the curtain rod. Now it was a race between dryness and mould. If mould won out, I would have to start all over again.

My cheap travel alarm read 8:55, so I lit the kerosene storm lantern on my desk. True to form, the power went off at 9:05. There was a collective gasp on the stage outside, some crashing about and cursing, then silence. I waited for it.

Knock, knock, knock. It was Raju again. Could he borrow Sir's lantern, so the boys could finish their rehearsal?

"Sure," I said. Why the hell not. There was no point in sitting in my room in total darkness, so I followed him out on stage and plunked myself against the wall and watched the rehearsal. Raju set the lantern down at the front of the stage. "Good evening, Sir..., Good evening, Sir..., Good even—" The greeting rippled across the stage like a wave as each boy sprang to his feet and bowed. Several of the boys grinned and nodded. Ruefully, I smiled back. Raju crossed the stage and took his place behind the small orchestra seated on the floor: tabla, harmonium, and beat-up guitar. He evidently had been one of the singers. There were five boys standing on the stage in a horseshoe surrounding the glowing lantern. They were all dressed more or less the same: lopsided topi, jodhpurs, loose white shirt worn over their trousers and a red sash at the waist. Some boys wore canvas running shoes; some were barefoot. None wore socks. With a warning clap of the tabla, they started. The boys were good, several were very good, and I reflected that a comparable high-school class in Canada could not throw together a comparable entertainment. We had no living folk culture any more, though it was not so very long ago that a rural community could have had a country dance hosted by a local band and everybody would have known the steps. Today if we wanted to learn country dancing, we would have to take lessons from an expert and the music would probably be recorded. Of course, if I was not depressed enough already, this train of thought made me feel worse, for, I foresaw the day when the students at Jigme Sherubling would have forgotten how to dance to the beat of the tabla.

When the boys said goodnight, I reclaimed my lantern and prepared to turn in. I set the lantern on my nightstand, stripped down to my boxers, and slid into bed. Suddenly, the big toe on my right foot was clamped in a paroxysm of pain. It was like a bee sting only worse. I yelped and threw back the bedcovers. The world's biggest centipede slithered into the shadow of a fold of linen. I reached under the bed for a *chappal* and scooped the centipede to the floor. Then I whacked it as hard as I could with the plastic sandal. Once. Twice. Three times. Four. Whack, whack, whack, whack, whack. I struck it again and again, but it would not die. Ten times I had to hit it before it stopped moving. Five more before I was sure it was dead. I examined it with awe. It was at least twelve inches long and amber in colour, with turquoise stripes on each of its long segmented legs. The two legs on the one end were as long as my fingers and arced together like pincers. The exoskeleton on this beast was easily as thick as a crab's. No wonder it had been so hard to kill.

I left it where it lay, determined to dispose of it in the morning, blew out the light, and went to sleep.

I was awoken at 5 A.M. by the sound of drumming against my skull. Ah, I thought, basketball practice. One of the great drawbacks of living in the change room of the gymnasium, I had quickly discovered, was 5 A.M. basketball practice. One of the nets was attached to the wall of the gym immediately opposite the head of my bed. Every shot that struck the backboard or the wall beside the backboard rattled the headboard of the bed. Since it was impossible to sleep through basketball practice, I put on my bathrobe and tried to mark a few essays before breakfast. I was not feeling very well. I was a little feverish and my stomach was unsettled. I could not face solid food, so I made myself some orange squash and sat and daydreamed at my desk until it was time for morning assembly. My stomach was now doing back flips and the thought of wearing my gho with its tight sash made me blanch.

I heard the door open on the far side of the stage. In the past two weeks I had gained a temporary new roommate. Dorje Tshering was a recent college graduate who had just been appointed to teach science at our school. It was no secret that he was courting a teacher at the primary school and that they were only waiting for a teacher's cottage to become available before they made their intentions public and moved in together. I opened my door and yelled across the stage, "Hey, Dorje. Come and look at this." He entered my room shyly, looked around hesitantly, and wondered what it was I wanted to show him. I pointed at the prehistoric insect on the floor beside my bed. His face turned white and he took a step backward in obvious alarm.

"It's okay," I said, "it's quite dead. I found it in my bed last night."

"You are very lucky, Mr. Ken. Those centipedes are very poisonous. If it had bitten you, you would have died a most painful death."

There was an awkward moment while I digested this bit of information.

"But...it did bite me," I ventured meekly.

"My goodness, we must get you to the health unit at once—"

"No, Dorje, you don't understand. It bit me last night, before I went to sleep."

He looked at me dumbstruck. "Yallah, but you are very fortunate then." He took his leave, shaking his head in concern and disbelief. I said I would join him in a moment, wondering at my own good fortune and perhaps the thickness of my hide.

When I could put it off no longer, I packed my notes and marking in my *jola*, tugged on my cleanest shirt and trousers, knotted a tie about my neck, grabbed my umbrella, and walked to the assembly ground in front of the school. A huge pool of muddy water had formed between the gymnasium and the classrooms. A dismal drizzle struck the pond, stuccoing its surface. Bhola and Wangpo were wearing old feed bags on their heads like tents in an effort to keep dry and were standing knee-deep in the water wielding short-handled hoes. Their arms and shoulders were glistening with sweat as they swung their tools and grunted with each stroke, trying to clear a weed-choked channel and allow the water to escape. "Hi," I said as I nimbly skipped past, outside the growing circle of water. Normally, they would have greeted me cheerfully, leaned on their tools, and chatted, but today they just grunted and did not even look up. The weather had defeated even these two stalwart souls.

The students stood in straight lines by the flagstaff, their collars turned up against the falling drizzle. Many of the boys' sleeves hung empty as they hugged themselves under their uniforms to keep warm. The country's distinctive dragon pennant hung limp from the mast. The air had grown very still—so still, in fact, as to be quite unnerving. Everybody sensed it. The students shifted uneasily. The ever-present pye-dogs whimpered to themselves as they shifted on the cold asphalt, circling and circling, trying to find a dry berth. There was a stillness like unheard thunder, a phantom stillness, a lurking, preying thing. The hairs on my neck rose. A clammy hand insinuated itself through the weave of my shirt and began to tickle the ladder of my ribs. I shuddered and turned. A cloud bank was rolling up the valley. The insidious fog curls slithered forward, unfurling, embracing, and covering everything like a misty succubus. The bald curs whimpering on the pavement suddenly leapt to their feet and twisted to face the oncoming fog. Hackles raised, fangs bared, tails tucked under their bellies, they snarled uncertainly into the mist. The fog bank rolled over us, obliterating the landscape, swallowing us up in a damp grey suffocating womb, like stillborn children. On a dead tree near the assembly ground, a black crow cackled and gargled insanely, knowingly. And then it passed, leaving us all feeling foolish.

Father Cherion walked to the front of the assembly and stood at the top of the steps facing the students, a dapper scowling little cherub in a charcoal grey suit. He stood erect with his hands folded in the small of his back and rocked up and down on the balls of his feet while he waited for the completion of the national anthem. When the dirge was completed, he rocked forward and addressed the assembled throng.

"The *Gapu* has informed me that there is a headhunter in the area and he asks that students and teachers be on their guards. Until the police catch this man, students must be in their dormitories immediately after final study. Students should travel in groups for safety. Any strangers on campus should be reported to me immediately. Dormitories will be locked at night. Is this understood? Hmm, yes? Then that will be all. Dismissed."

There was a buzz of excitement following assembly. I turned to one of my students. "He can't be serious?"

"Oh, yes, Sir! There was a headhunter in my valley last year. He killed two girls."

"Indeed. But why would anyone do such a thing?"

"They needed heads for the new bridge."

"Heads?"

"Yes, so it would not fall down."

Headhunters, I was told, were called *khag-pa*, though I have never been able to confirm this. This particular headhunter had borrowed money from the local Hydel on behalf of his brother, pledging the life of one of his children. When his brother defaulted on the loan he desperately sought to find a substitute for his child. At least that was the gossip, and obviously it was taken seriously enough for the *Gapu* to issue his warning. The belief that human sacrifice was required to ensure the structural integrity of a large public work, it seemed, was not unusual, nor, if you think about it, is it restricted to Bhutan.

In my first English class of the day I presented the students with exercises in paragraph writing that I had felt would actually be too simple but which most of them found too difficult. Were they stupid, I wondered, or just being deliberately thick? At one point in the lesson, a sparrow flew into the class through a broken pane of glass. It fluttered about in a panic, seeking an escape, beating its wings frantically against the windows. Then it turned and ricocheted off the walls of the classroom. The students ducked below their desks and shrieked. The bird flew around and around the room, seeking an exit, returning after each sortie to punish itself against the glass. Several of the more enterprising boys were standing on their benches trying to slice it with their rulers as it darted past. They began to roughly herd the poor frightened creature with shouts and open textbooks, and they managed to corner it in an ever-tightening circle of bodies. Just as one foul little beast was about to deliver the *coup de grâce*, a stentorian voice screamed:

"GODAMMIT, SIT DOWN, LEAVE THAT BLOODY BIRD ALONE THIS INSTANT! IF ONE OF YOU TOUCHES EVEN ONE FEATHER ON THAT POOR CREATURE'S HEAD, THEN BY GOD, I'LL BLOODY WELL SKIN YOUR HIDES!"

The shrieking and laughing ceased immediately. The students quietly returned to their seats. The only sound was the frantic beating of the little bird's wings.

I sighed.

"Will someone please open the windows?" No one moved a muscle. They were all staring at me open-mouthed. "Karma Dorje, Sangye, Thuckten, please open the windows." The students so named quietly did as requested, keeping their eyes fixed on me. The sparrow lit on one of the windowsills, looked around the classroom, bobbed twice, and was gone. As I followed its departure, I caught my reflection in the open windows. They formed a series of ghostly images repeated in the cracked glass, the reflection of a madman with wild sunken eyes above a Rasputin beard.

"Please get your notebooks out again and finish the writing exercise I assigned. I will collect them tomorrow. Right now," I paused and looked around the room, looking, I guess, for sympathy or understanding, but seeing only shock and fear and my own disturbing reflection, "right now, I am going to see Father Cherion. I'm sorry. I am really not feeling very well today." I quickly gathered up my books and left the room. The students did not rise or thank me for the lesson.

As I walked down the stairs to Father Cherion's office I felt awful. Of course, I had been feeling out of sorts for a couple of days now, but this was a different kind of awful. I had never raised my voice to the students before. I had never needed to. Once when I was ten or eleven years old I had thrown a snowball at a girl I liked—I suppose, when you are that age, pelting someone with a snowball was one way of showing affection. The girl had squealed, turned her back to me, and the snowball had hit her in the back of the head, cracking her scalp. There was a lot of blood, of course. When the principal gave me the strap, I didn't even protest. It didn't seem enough pain to punish me for the enormity of my crime. I had that same feeling when I knocked on Father Cherion's door and asked him for the afternoon off. I had hoped he would cross-examine me, expose me as a whiner or a slacker, but instead he showed immediate concern and asked me about my symptoms, clucked his tongue, and sent me home to bed. "Take as much time as you need," he said. "We can manage. I will send Sister Leonard over to see you when she is free."

I returned to my quarters, stripped off my good clothes, and went into the washroom-cum-kitchen. I stood in front of the mirror and peered at my reflection.

I turned sideways and hiked up my T-shirt. My god, I looked like I was pregnant. I gently tapped my ballooning stomach and it answered with a resounding *ping*, like an over-inflated basketball. I made myself some more squash—mixing the sickly sweet bottled extract with some water from my filter—carried the tumbler over to my nightstand and crawled into bed. I stared around at the three undecorated walls, with their bleeding whitewash, and the bank of ill-fitting windows through which wisps of theatre fog penetrated like unseen stagecraft in a production of *Macbeth*. The room was damp. I felt chilled. I snuggled down under my sleeping bag, so that only my nose was protruding. I felt miserable. I wanted to go home.

Mostly what I wanted was, for a couple of hours, to forget I was in Bhutan. I wanted to cocoon. I got up from my bed, drew the curtains, lit a couple of candles, and opened up my trunk. I rooted around for a couple of minutes and then sat back with sigh of satisfaction. Before I had left for Bhutan my sister had given me a boxed set of Tolkien. I grabbed the first volume, folded down the first page and disappeared into the Shire.

By the time Bilbo Baggins had crossed the boundary into the unknown, I had completely forgotten where I was. The illusion would have been complete if my bowels would have cooperated. As it was, I had to leap out of bed every ten or fifteen minutes for what my students had aptly named "shooting diarrhea." Bilbo was in the grips of the cave trolls when a knock came at the door.

It was Sister Leonard, who, in the midst of all of her other duties, operated the school dispensary. We both agreed that I probably had giardia, a result of drinking water that had been contaminated with fecal matter. She had some medicine, but I expressed some concern since I have a great number of allergies.

"Tut, tut," she said and told me not to worry. She bade me lie down on my bed and hold the pill above my stomach, pinched between my thumb and forefinger. Then she reached into the front of her habit and withdrew a chain that was hanging around her neck upon which were suspended the medals of two saints. Alas, I was so ill I never thought to ask her which two. She held the chain above the pill and it began to spin and then settle into a gentle rocking back and forth. She followed the movement of the chain closely and then nodded with a little grunt of satisfaction. "It is as I thought," she said. "You will be fine."

"I will?"

"Yes, yes. Of course. Take the medicine. You will see."

So I did and she was right. Within a few hours my diarrhea had ceased and the subterranean rumblings in my bowels had begun to subside. I withdrew to my cave and returned to my reading. By the time I had finished *The Hobbit*, I was feeling much better. I started the next volume in my Tolkien series. It was still raining outside. I could hear the constant gurgle of rainwater in the drainpipe outside the bathroom window. I read right through the afternoon and into the evening. By dinnertime I was actually feeling a little hungry. I crawled back out of bed and rooted through my trunk once more. With a cry of triumph I discovered a crumpled bag of sour cream and onion potato chips, which a friend had sent me in a care package from home, and a large bottle of apple cider, which I had picked up in Bumthang on the way to my posting. I had been saving them both for a special occasion and had all but forgotten them until now. I crawled back under the covers and plunged back into my book, munching chips and licking the noxious chemical flavouring off my fingers with relish.

Outside, the world was shrouded in mist, moisture dripped from the leech-ridden jungle, the pond in the schoolyard continued to grow, the headhunter prowled the valley looking for unguarded children, but I did not care. I was far away.

Suddenly, the hair rose on the back of my neck and I had the feeling I was not alone. I lowered the book slowly and observed that a large grey rat was sitting insolently in the middle of the bathroom floor watching me. I scooped up a sandal and pitched it at him. The rat disappeared down the toilet.

Oh my god! So that was how they were getting in! For months I had been plagued by rats and had plugged up every possible opening with scraps of wood and flattened tins and still they managed to find a way into my abode and chew holes in my clothes and knock over my dishes on a nightly basis until I swore in frustration. Now all was clear. They were swimming up the toilet. When the implications of this discovery sunk in, I thought, yuck. I will never be able to squat comfortably on that toilet again. I did not want to think about it. I returned to my reading.

As it grew darker, I lit my hurricane lamp. Moths punished themselves against the glow of the whitewashed wall and against the hot glass of the chimney, occasionally settling fretfully on an open page or becoming tangled in my hair. I ignored them. I read on. I finished the second book and moved on to the third.

But the world would not let me alone. I became aware of the moon peering in at me through a gap in the curtain, throwing a shaft of pale blue light across the warped and curling floorboards, straight toward me on the bed. My undershorts hung above the foot of my bed, pinned on the clothesline, white and luminous, like seven picnic hams in a butcher's window. I responded to the moon's call and moved to the window, pushing aside the curtain. It was a white moon in a sapphire sky, a man-in-the-moon

moon painted by Chagal. It was intoxicating. A dog beneath my window responded to the moon's call, as well. He started up a banshee wail that was soon answered by dogs up and down the valley, blending but not quite blending together, each voice united but distinct. There was a deep "ruck, ruck," from a dog in an orchard across the valley, a "wruff, wruff, wruff," from a stray in the bazaar, a bass *aria di portamento* from a mastiff by the school kitchen, and a castrati yipping from a scavenging mutt in the school's garbage pit. A lone star rested on a pinnacle of rock, on its highest point, like the beacon on a lighthouse. The world began to revolve about this point and its beacon flame stabbed me with pale blue fire. I was drawn out, into the night, apotheosized. I closed the curtains, extinguished the lights, and went to sleep.

In the morning, I was woken once more by the canine chorus. Morning and night—same old story. But there was a difference. Evening was clamorous; morning was regular, sonorous, and mechanical. Evening was frenzied; morning, a quiet measured invocation to the dawn. I opened the curtains. The sun was just rising, but you could already feel that it was going to be a hot day. Flies were buzzing against the windowpanes and, outside, I could hear crickets under the windows. There was also a dull roaring in my ears and it took me a minute to realize it was the river racing by in full flood. A hoopoo was spearing worms on the grassy knoll above my septic bed. I opened the window and leaned out. I could hear children's laughing voices, and the sound of cowbells descended to me from the pastures above the *gompa*. I could see Bhola and Wangpo leaning on their hoes, watching a rivulet of water spill down the hill to the drain by the football field. They smiled and greeted me and asked me how I was feeling.

"Fine," I said. "Much better, thanks. I feel much better today." And I did. I really did.

NINE

KHALING GOMPA

IN SEPTEMBER I FELT A SEA CHANGE in my opinion about Khaling. We felt the sun more. Mornings had a lazy warmth, with sunlight reflecting white off the dew-laden blades of grass and the willow leaves sparkling in the slight hot breeze. Students and villagers would sit on the hot asphalt, soaking up the sun's heat and gossiping in quiet voices. The air, so long oppressive and chill, was still but for the lazy calls of a few birds. Sounds travelled incredible distances. A truck shifting gears by the weaving project sounded as if it were right outside my window. A bird's warble under the vaulted metal ceiling of the gymnasium reverberated in a high-arched echo.

In the evenings, I would sit at my desk looking out the window and watch the light fail. A smoky mist not so much hung over the jungle as emanated from it. The mountains turned grey except here and there where a ridge would poke to the surface and the trees emerged blue-green and wraithlike. The whole scene felt primeval. The mountain itself seemed to be alive with a glowering intelligence, its brow turned broodingly upon us. No wonder people assigned personalities to mountains, turned them into gods.

One night in early September, I was returning home after a visit to Karin's home near Dowzor. There was a full moon. The road, still wet from the rain, was a silver ribbon in the moonlight. The valley was so peaceful. I turned off my flashlight. Patches of fog in the trees caught the silver light and absorbed it. There was a thin wisp of cloud across the moon, enough to make it seem brighter, as a shade does a lamp. But you could still see the stars. It was painfully beautiful. I wanted to show it to someone, but there was no one with whom to share this scene—the white light on the cliff face, the trees hanging in heroic silhouettes against the night sky—so I settled for the night itself, and in a ghastly and maudlin moment of weakness I shouted, "It's so beautiful; it's so beautiful."

Somewhere down the slope, a door creaked open abruptly, and a voice called out, "Oi! *Ibi-rang cha-mo?*"

I ducked down and held my breath. After some time, the door creaked shut on its wooden axle. I slunk home.

I don't remember exactly how I got to Khaling Gompa the first time. Whether it was the boys' idea or my own, whether they asked me where I was going and tagged along, as often happened; or whether in some abstracted moment I expressed a desire to visit the *gompa* and they had organized the trip, I can't say. All I know was that night after night as I supervised study hall I would look up the mountain to the small plateau of Khaling Gompa and watch longingly as the copper rays of the setting sun reflected off the square white temple. The ridge and the giant cypress by the *gompa* would grow dark, silhouetted like a black Chinese papercut against an azure sky. As each night drew quickly on I would see a line of cattle strung out along the ridge, bells clanking, heading down from alpine pastures to their byres within the village, accompanied by a diminutive cowherd who skipped along after them singing. It was a shadow play enacted each night for my enjoyment, and each night I would tell myself that one of these days I would find the time to visit the *gompa*.

Well, days stretched into weeks, and weeks into months, and life at the school became all-consuming. Less and less did I raise my eyes unto the hills, and I found myself burdened with marking and with extracurricular duties and with my own insecurities as a first-time teacher. Then one day in September I found myself heading up the mountain in the company of three of my students. We were, they had announced excitedly, going to visit Abi Gompa (literally the "grandmother of the monastery"). Was that okay, I asked. Arriving unannounced? Oh sure, they replied. She was always happy to have visitors.

There were two ways to reach the small plateau upon which the village and the temple presided. One way was to approach from the bazaar and follow a steep zigzag course up the face of the rocky ridge. The second and easier route (and the one we chose that day) was to walk to the top of the school property, past the student dorms and the Sisters' house, and up through an overgrown pasture to the fence that bounded the school grounds. Here a crude wooden stile crossed the wire fence and if you turned left, a gently rising path took you along the face of a steep grassy slope and

Khaling Gompa in winter.

up to the plateau. This was the easier route but the more problematic, as I found out later. For in the monsoon, the wet chest-high grass became the lair for thousands of leeches.

Each year the *gompa* became the home of a three-day religious festival called a *tsetchu*, and the first thing you saw as you crested the plateau, coming via the school path, was a crude wooden two-hole privy. It was a bad first impression and a bit of a letdown after months of imagining the appearance of what had become, in my mind, an ideal community. The students told me that the privy had been constructed by one of the graduating classes of Jigme Sherubling as a work of community service. It was a bit of an eyesore most of the year, but for three days in October, when hundreds of people ascended to the plateau for the annual three-day festival, it proved invaluable.

However, my spirits were immediately revived by the next thing I saw. The feature that dominated the village, indeed dominated the entire valley, was a giant cypress. There were actually three cypresses standing in a line on the ridge at the back of the village, but one towered above the others and was so large it could be seen from miles away. It was ancient, and its enormous roots gripped the earth like giant's fingers. I am not sure exactly how tall it was, but it was easily three times as high as the temple that had been erected beside it and this temple was four storeys tall. The legend of the cypress was this: In the sixteenth century a Buddhist missionary travelling south from Tibet reached this spot, liked what he saw, stuck his staff in the ground, and said, "Here I will build my monastery." From his staff grew the giant cypress and the present temple at Khaling Gompa is a later version of the monastery he first established.

I have used the words *gompa* (a small monastery without novices, as opposed to a larger teaching establishment—*dratshang* in Sharchopkha, *shedra* in Dzongkha) and "temple" (*lha-kang* in Sharchopkha) interchangeably here, but they are really two separate things. There are no longer any resident monks in Khaling, the last lama having passed away some years earlier. So, in practice, Khaling Gompa is no longer a *gompa*, though the name persists. However, it remains the most important religious structure in the valley, and all of the important religious festivals are celebrated here. Sometimes a monk or lama from outside of the community officiates; more often though, it is a local *gomchen*, or lay priest, who leads these *pujahs*.

The boys led me to the *gompa*, but first we circumambulated the cypress, and I noticed that its roots were festooned with slabs of carved slate, each bearing sacred characters in Sanskrit, most often forming the phrase: OM MANI PADME HUM. Then we passed through an open space, a sort of village green, though bereft of grass, which contained a derelict standpipe. Next, we ducked through a grand gated arch of undressed whitewashed stone and into a large flagged courtyard that fronted the temple. The temple was imposing but fairly simple in design, a giant white cube topped with a red-peaked corrugated metal roof. A broad red horizontal stripe circled the wall of the building just below the line of the roof. This stripe is called a *kemar* and indicates the building's religious function. *Kemars* are found on temples, monasteries, and *dzongs* all across Bhutan. Only the front of the temple, that is the side facing the stone courtyard, had any real windows and these were thin gothic slits covered with sliding wooden shutters. The first floor had an undercut porch, which I later observed served as a waiting area—or the stage wings—for masked dancers at *tsetchu*. Several wooden doors at the back of this porch led into a gloomy storage area and to a rickety interior staircase that wound its way up to the remaining floors of the temple.

We did not enter the temple that day, but rather passed by, crossing the courtyard and passing through another lych-gate and into a smaller courtyard, where there was a comfortable whitewashed stone cottage. The cottage was built into the slope of the mountain and rested on a stonewalled platform. This flagged platform formed a kind of **L**-shaped apron or uncovered terrace around three sides of the cottage. On the short side of the **L**, which jutted out from the slope, stood a separate wooden hut that was the kitchen. Within the embrace of this raised platform was a large kitchen garden that was surrounded by a woven bamboo fence. It was a delightful spot, the sort of hermitage I'd always imagined for poets like Basho or Wang Wei. In fact, it had been constructed as the residence for Khaling's lama. From the kitchen window, the home's single occupant could look down upon the school where I worked.

The boys shouted greetings as we passed through the gateway, "Wai, Abi. Kuzu zangpo-la," and a voice answered from inside the kitchen. The person who emerged from the smoky kitchen door was a jolly old soul, with a remarkably fleshy, almost rubbery face that was covered in wrinkles and good cheer. Her thatch of grey hair was short and stood out at all angles. The striped kira that enclosed her rotund form was soiled with sweat and kitchen grease. This was Ugyen Lhamo, the widow of the late lama of Khaling. She was pleased to see us, particularly me. She had heard that there was a new teacher at the school, and she had been hoping that I might visit. Students, I learned, were regular visitors and frequently came to chat. Many a homesick boy and girl found a listening ear in Abi's kitchen.

We removed our shoes at the threshold, and Abi hustled us into the stone cottage, which proved to be one small room. She bade us take a seat on embroidered cushions on the polished honey-coloured floorboards and returned to the kitchen to rustle up a pot of tea. The boys slid open the window shutters and revealed the exquisitely painted murals that adorned the four walls. The murals seemed to be all of a piece. The same grey-bearded figure appeared again and again on the plaster, each time in a different setting, interacting with different characters, both human and divine. The painting was beautiful, within the limited freedom allowed the artist in such an iconographic tradition, and I admired the skill with which it was executed. I wondered if it was by the same artist who had decorated the temple at Dungray, with its similar narrative style.

When Abi returned we settled into a circle on the floor and she served tea and roast corn. We began to chat. It was a little awkward because my command of Sharchopkha was such that most conversation had to be filtered through my students. My eyes kept straying to the paintings on the wall, until finally I asked if Abi would explain the meaning of the paintings to me. Who was the old man, I wondered? What was he doing?

To my surprise, she considered my request for a moment and then said, "No."

The students were a little embarrassed, but I persisted.

"Why not?"

"Because you are not ready," she replied.

I was perplexed, but it was impossible to be offended because she had been so nice about the whole thing. She had recognized an idle question and had answered it accordingly. Someone less wise would have attempted an answer, but she could see that any explanation she might give me would be useless. She had politely but firmly put me in my place. I was not ready.

Looking back on that day, I am embarrassed. I had behaved thoughtlessly, like a tourist. She was not about to tell me a story for my own amusement. Even if I knew the story, I would not understand it. That would take years of study. I would have to earn the right to waste her time.

I quickly apologized for my presumption and my trespass was immediately forgiven. The conversation turned down more congenial pathways and the afternoon passed pleasantly by. Eventually, we sensed that it was time to go. We thanked Abi for her hospitality, and she invited us all, but specifically me, to come back at any time.

As we left Khaling Gompa that day, I paused by the low stone wall that surrounded the flagged courtyard and looked down over the little village that encompassed the temple. Each whitewashed house stood apart in a fenced field. Cats prowled after mice in the cornrows. Pigs squealed and grunted in stone-lined pits. Children's voices echoed down the leafy lanes between the houses. I heard the clack of a shuttle as someone wove on a loom, unseen in some sheltered courtyard. Smoke billowed out of the gable-ends of houses. An emaciated cow strolled nonchalantly down the hard-trodden mud path, followed by a barefoot young girl carrying an enormous bundle of firewood on her back, suspended from a tumpline around her forehead. Two women were pounding corn into flattened tengma in a large pestle constructed from a hollowed stump. It was a world a hundred miles away from the school below and separated from it by as many years. I vowed to return, and often.

It was mid-December and school was winding down. Students were preparing for exams. We were all thinking of holidays and the freedom to come—a delicious feeling that we had all earned. Only one thing bothered me and that was the thought of returning to my quarters in the gymnasium. They were comfortable enough for a bachelor like me, but far too public and noisy for my liking. I resolved to seek accommodations off campus. Michael was leaving us to teach in New Guinea, and his quarters would be empty, but I thought that, with a little persistence, I might do better than two unfurnished rooms over a shop in the bazaar with no source of water other than a sink in my landlady's kitchen. I knew myself well enough by then to realize that

I would find it awkward barging in each day and asking permission to fill my bucket with water from her tap.

One day I was taking tea with Mr. Mukherjee in the administration office and I happened to mention my quest for accommodations. Tandin Zangmo overheard my musing and piped up: "If you are interested, the house behind mine is vacant."

I was immediately interested. Tandin lived with her parents in Khaling Gompa. She had invited me to tea several times over the past few weeks, and I liked her family. The possibility of having them as neighbours was very appealing.

"Do you think it is possible?" I asked eagerly.

"Sure. I will speak with the owner. Mind you, it is pretty dirty. No one has ever lived in it, and he has been using it as potato storage for many years."

Tandin borrowed a key and we had a look around. It was very dirty. The kitchen was piled high with potatoes. I never learned the full story, but it appeared that the house was being constructed for a family member who, in the end, did not need it, and so the structure was hastily completed and never lived in. The house was constructed in the middle of a small field owned by a man who actually lived in a much larger house located between the school and the bazaar. Tandin and I arranged to meet with the owner in his home over tea, terms were discussed, and the house was rented to me for a year. The owner would rent me the living quarters on the second floor and agreed to clean out all of the potatoes, but he wanted to retain access to the ground floor. For my part, my only condition was that he construct a latrine—a condition he found bizarre, but he agreed to it nevertheless. So it was settled, and, just before I left for the winter break, I was able to move my things out of the gymnasium and up the mountain to Khaling Gompa.

I became very fond of that little house. Not that it was exceptional. It was not. It was a typical house for Eastern Bhutan and, as I mentioned above, had been finished off in rather a hurry, as it had whitewashed wooden planks along the front in some places where it should have had the more traditional and more functional wattle-and-daub. No, I grew fond of the house because of its lovely location. The tiny village that clustered about the temple and its courtyard had seventeen houses, each sitting in a small fenced field of one acre or less. There was one other house farther up the mountain, isolated and empty, and reputed to be haunted. The lanes between the dwellings ran between high bamboo fences and were shaded with willow branches that sprouted from reincarnated fence posts. Each house was painted white and had a flagged courtyard or a porch. There were enormous kitchen gardens with climbing

My house in Khaling Gompa, winter of 1988
(you can see the new power line in the background).

flowering plants, free-range chickens, tabby cats, and cows in wooden sheds. It was very medieval in flavour, very pastoral. I loved it, and I was happy there. Living among such wonderful people and being invited to become a small part of their lives was a rare privilege—one that I was wise enough to appreciate at the time.

The ground floor of my home was built of stone, mortised with mud, and had a large plank door that could be bolted. Two tiny barred openings flanked this door and served as windows. Had the house been occupied by a Bhutanese family, this dungeon would have served as a stable and as storage for farm implements. As it was, my land-lord continued to use it to store potatoes, which perhaps accounted for the many rats that shared my domicile.

The front wall of the second storey was pierced with arched window slits, and while the back and side walls continued as rough stone right up to the eaves, the front wall was vaguely Tudor in appearance, having been framed in heavy timbers and filled in with wattle-and-daub and the aforementioned whitewashed planks. The second floor was reached by a set of exterior stone steps at one end of the building that led to the living quarters. The landlord had constructed a flimsy bamboo porch at this end that stood on posts and was screened in and roofed with bamboo matting. This porch had a hole in the centre of the floor, which normally would have functioned as a toilet, but since I had a proper outhouse, the porch became my shower. The first room one entered from here was the kitchen, which occupied half of the interior space. At the north end, against the stone wall, was a clay stove, or *chula*, which I did not use. Beside it was a barrel of water, which I kept filled with buckets drawn from a spring near the temple. On the far side of the stove was a set of floor-to-ceiling shelves that held biscuit tins full of staples: rice, oatmeal, cornmeal, and *atta*, the coarse-ground local flour. There were also tins of cooking spices and a large cardboard box full of potatoes. On the outside wall to your left as you entered was a crude workspace, a counter I had created by balancing a large plank across some empty wooden crates. On this counter were the two kerosene burners upon which I cooked my meals, as well as a water filter. The crates contained my cheap enamelled dishes, my aluminum wok, my pressure cooker, several smaller pots, and a wash basin. Suspended from the rafters were a number of hand-woven baskets that kept my vegetables—garlic, onions, chilies, eggplant, and radishes—from the rats.

There was no furniture to speak of. I had covered a fish crate with plastic to serve as a low table, and I had purchased a number of foam cushions for my guests to sit on. The interior walls were eventually covered with children's artwork. I kept a large tin of pencil crayons and felt-tipped markers and a stock of scrap paper ready for when the village children visited—also, a stack of old magazines, whose illustrations they delighted in tracing. It kept them busy while I was trying to get my marking done. I remember once a child bringing me a science magazine and showing me a coloured picture of human DNA. "What is this thing?" he asked me. What, indeed? When a child had finished a drawing, she or he received a gold star and we tacked it to the wall. In this way, the empty rooms began to feel like home.

The other two rooms were smaller. One, the larger and airier of the two, had originally been the altar room. It became my bedroom. I moved in a small table and chair upon which to do my work and a wooden bed frame that I borrowed from the boys' dormitory. When I first entered the house, there had been an altar set up in the room. There had been a gilded clay statue of the Guru Rinpoche, surrounded by tiny figures of minor deities and incarnations. All were arranged in a brightly painted wooden proscenium arch, like a miniature model of a vaudeville stage, and a row of brass butter lamps acted as footlights. I had been pleased to discover this and had planned to leave it intact, but when I found there was no way in which to place the bed where my feet were not facing the altar, I decided it would be disrespectful and so carefully packed everything away in a wooden trunk. The altar though had rested on a cunningly crafted and brightly painted bureau, and so I made this my dresser.

The bureau did not have drawers, but it had many hidden doors that swung open to reveal shelf space behind, much like the cardboard windows on a child's Advent calendar.

The final room in the house was the smallest and occupied a dark back corner. Its only light source was a tiny square window set high in the stone wall. This was the storeroom, and it was lined with shelves and full of dusty wooden boxes and trunks, old shattered baskets, butter churns, and broken wooden bowls. I stored the altar here. It was also in this room that I found a large empty trunk that I washed out, lined with moth balls, and used to store my winter clothes.

There was one more floor above, or rather a large attic, which could be reached by climbing a notched log to a square opening in one corner of my kitchen ceiling. The attic was open at both gables, only closed in by a loose screen of plaited bamboo. On a working farm, this would have been the granary and hayloft, and sometimes the extra bedroom for visiting guests. I have slept in such attics in my travels, nesting in the sweet-smelling hay. It can be most pleasant. My attic, however, was empty but for some lumber and an enormous collection of empty liquor bottles. It made a cozy aviary for a variety of birds and was a haven for bats.

Village life began each morning, before the rising of the sun, with the lowing of cattle crying to be milked and the clanking of pails as their sleepy owners tottered to the cowsheds. Then, as the babies started crying for food and people began stirring from their pallets on the floor, the fires in the chulas were revived by blowing through a bamboo straw, and a few sticks of firewood were shoved into the clay firebox, while a kettle of water was put to the boil. Bedding was rolled up and piled neatly against the walls or on top of trunks. And then the sound of churns would begin to be heard in each kitchen. These were not butter churns, though each house had one of those, too, but tea churns. Each was a long narrow cylinder of bamboo into which was poured hot water, leaves broken from a brick of Tibetan black tea, a pinch of baking soda, salt, and, implausibly to a newcomer like myself, butter. The top of the churn would be fastened, and the woman of the house or perhaps an older daughter would stand beside the churn, which came up to her waist, and would drive the plunger up and down until everything had blended together. A wooden bowl of sujah, the hot buttered tea of the Himalayas, along with a handful of tengma, a flattened cornmeal, was a common breakfast in Khaling. The hot tea was especially inviting on a cold winter morning when the greasy butter seemed to pour liquid fire into all the muscles of the body. A foreign tea drinker trying sujah for the first time usually found it revolting because the taste was so unexpected—it was a betrayal of tea. Why, they would sputter, would anyone do this to tea? Why ruin it in this way? But I found that, if I stopped thinking of it as tea and imagined it as broth, it was quite delicious.

After breakfast was cleared away, it was time to fetch water. As I mentioned at the beginning of this chapter, there had once been a standpipe in the little muddy square that stood roughly in the centre of the village, just outside the gate to the temple compound. The water for the standpipe had come from a spring high on the mountain. The spring had been dammed to form a reservoir, and an underground pipe ran down the mountain to the standpipe. The standpipe itself was a concrete platform out of which rose a concrete pillar from which sprouted an iron spigot. The demise of the standpipe was due to one thing and one thing only: cattle. First of all, the cows found the standpipe the ideal thing to scrape against to rid themselves of shedding hair and insects, and in no time the iron spigot was snapped off, the concrete apron was cracked, and the square pillar was rounded off. Secondly, the engineers of the standpipe had decided to bury the feeder pipe directly below the path that the cowherds used to lead their cattle up the mountain to pasture. This was fine in good weather, but in the monsoon, when the ground was soft and the path a river of mud, the cows' sharp hooves eventually cut the water pipe in several places.

My neighbours, however, solved the problem with some ingenuity. They continued to use the reservoir, but they purchased about half a kilometre of black, flexible PVC piping and ran the water line above ground. The new pipe ran overhead, fed by gravity, usually lashed to the top of a convenient fence, and where it had to jump across a path, a bamboo bridge was constructed. The waterline ran right through the village, down the main lane, and spilled down the mountain on the far side. Where the waterline passed each gate, the pipe was neatly cut and then spliced back together with a short piece of bamboo. The idea, and it was good in theory, was that, if you needed water, you could break open the waterline, fill your bucket, and then re-attach the two ends of the pipe when you were done. In practice, however, this only worked for those houses at the top of the slope. Those of us who lived at the lower end of the village—and this included myself—usually found the waterline empty when we went to fill our buckets. I found it easier to rise with the sun and carry my two plastic buckets up to the temple. There, at a flat place beside the ancient cypress, was a communal filling station, and I would add mine to the line of buckets. As one pail filled, you would shift it aside and move the black plastic hose into the next in line. I would sit with the village women and endure their good-natured ribbing about my bachelor status, while we waited for the pails to fill. Some of my best memories are early morning ones, sitting in the embrace of the giant tree roots, with the smell of wood smoke and damp earth in my nostrils, watching the thin rays of the rising sun smoke the dew off the bamboo thatching of the village homes.

When I first moved in I was overwhelmed with visitors. My neighbours would drop in, household by household, always with a couple of bottles of *ara*. I would pass around biscuits and *ara*, and the family would poke through my belongings and quiz me. Conversation was pretty rudimentary, but I had a lot of photos of my family and my home in Canada, and this helped bridge the gap. I did not have sufficient facility in Sharchopkha to have any meaningful discussions, but I could explain family relationships, occupations, gardens, household appliances—things like that, things that fascinated my visitors. I slowly began to sort out my new neighbours and figure out who lived where and with whom. I was touched by the welcome I was given, but I still did not feel comfortable just dropping in at their homes unannounced.

Strangely enough, the thing that concerned them the most was that I lived alone. The other houses in the village were the same size as mine but contained between four and ten people. Living alone was regarded as a trifle eccentric. "Where is your wife?" they each asked in turn, and then, when they discovered I was unmarried, "Are you not lonely?"

Directly behind my house lived Tandin's parents. The space between our homes was filled with a large vegetable garden the size of a tennis court. When I came home from school I would often see Tandin's father hoeing his radishes, and he would bob his head in greeting. He was a tiny man with a shock of white hair, an elfin beard, and a face lined with wrinkles that spoke of a lifetime of toil.

My other nearest neighbour, and one of my more frequent visitors, was Sonam Lhamo. She lived in a tiny house across the lane with her husband and son. Sonam was a skinny elderly woman, with a thatch of untidy grey hair. She was missing all of her lower incisors, and when she smiled, particularly when she was chewing *pan*, she had the appearance of an amiable vampire. Sonam's husband and son, both named Lungten, were alchoholics. There is no point in beating around the bush here; alcoholism was a serious problem in Eastern Bhutan. Heavy drinking was part of the culture and far too much of the local corn crop was turned into *ara* each year. Lungten Senior spent most days sitting meditating in the sun, like a dried-up mummy with a Fu Manchu moustache. Lungten Junior spent most days being depressed and making new resolutions. It was Sonam who held the household together and made sure that no one went hungry. She was cunning. She had a small career as a moonshiner—I purchased most of my *ara* from her.

One day in early May, my door was pushed open (no one ever knocked, or if they did, never waited to be admitted) and Sonam Lhamo entered. She reached her bony hand inside the fold of her very threadbare kira and produced two eggs. I thanked her and beckoned her to sit on the floor while I poured her a cup of tea. She cast covetous eyes about my kitchen. As we sipped our tea, she made little observations between sips. She played on what good friends we were. Oh, I am so old, she began. Sip, sip. You have so many things for just one person, sip, while the three of us have so little. Sip, sip. We have become such close neighbours, have we not? Sip, sip. Oh, there are so many things I would like to give you, if I only could. Sip, sip. I am always so cold, sip, and my teeth are so bad. Sip, sip. I am like your mother, am I not? Sip. And you are like my son. We have had so many good times, yes. Sip. Remember, it was I who taught you the parts of the body in Sharchop; ah, yes, that was such fun. Sip. Hmm, your rain barrel is really much too large for one person. Sip, sip. And that kira (pointing to a kira I had hung on the wall as decoration), ugh, it is not good enough to give to your wife. Sip, sip. Aeiyah, I am so cold. Sip. How cold I am all the time in this old thing. Sip, sip. How many shirts do you have? (She pointed to the four that were drying on the clothesline). Surely, one man doesn't need so many, and my husband is such an old man. Do you have any rice? Chilies?

It was shameless, but very effective. When she left that day, her arms were full of empty bottles, one of my shirts, an old pair of shoes, all of my chilies, and half of my rice. At this rate, I reflected wryly in my diary, I would soon have nothing left to give away.

Another neighbour and my best friend in the village was a kind and gentle man named Tashi Dorje. I met him quite by accident. One day, shortly after I had moved to Khaling Gompa, I went to the bazaar to do some shopping. A stranger approached me and asked if it was true that I lived in the Gompa, as people said. Yes, I replied. Then would I take a message to his sister, Mokhu? Tell her that her brother had to go to Rashung and would not be able to come for dinner. I agreed, and he thanked me warmly. Only after he had left did I realize that I didn't know who Mokhu was.

A few questions, however, soon led me to the proper house. It was just down the hill from mine. It was the house I saw each day when I looked out my kitchen window while sipping my morning mug of tea. I knocked on the door. A pretty teenaged girl answered, still laughing from something someone inside the house had said. She stopped when she saw my face.

"Yallama."

What is it? Someone asked.

"*Ama*," she said, "It's the *lopen*."

I slipped off my shoes and ducked inside to the smoky kitchen. They ushered me to a spot by the fire, where dinner preparations were underway. I relayed my message in Sharchopkha, carefully rehearsed on my way up the mountain. "Ahh," they sighed with disappointment and then perked up, "Well, then you must stay for dinner." I demurred, but they insisted, and soon we were seated in a big circle on the kitchen floor. Mokhu was a large handsome woman. You could see where her daughter got her good looks. The girl I met at the door, whose name was Sonam, was the eldest of five children, the youngest still an infant. The head of the household was a tall well-knit man with a very sad face. This was Tashi Dorje. Seven people in all, living in a home little larger than a one-car garage. That evening, Mokhu's parents were also present. Her father, Tschewang, was a tiny leprechaun with a perfect Amish, half-moon beard. For dinner, we had wooden bowls of rice topped with cold boiled lima beans and rashers of bacon. I had far too much *ara*. They seemed really pleased that I had stopped by, were convinced I had a wife in Tashigang and wouldn't be dissuaded on this point. I had a wonderful time and sensed that I had found friends amongst this affectionate close-knit family. The family insisted that I learn more Sharchopkha, so that we could communicate better in future. At the end of the evening, Tashi Dorje took me by the hand, led me home and put me to bed.

Coming home from school a few days later, humping an enormous load of notebooks up the mountain and breathing heavily, I passed the temple and realized something was going on. The windows were open; music was coming from inside. Tashi Dorje leaped from the lych-gate, as if he were expecting me, and grabbed my elbow.

"*Odo, lopen. Odo.*"

He led me through the gate, across the courtyard, and into the undercut porch of the temple. A side door was ajar, and we passed through, into the gloom beyond, and began to climb a spiralling wooden stairway, lit only by narrow arrow slits in the stone wall. We ascended to the second floor. The chanting was louder now, and there were bursts of cacophonous music, which punctuated the droning like blasts of circus music played on an old Victrola at the wrong speed. He bade me leave my shoes outside the threshold and ushered me through the door. The room was darkened, the only light coming from the narrow windows to my right and the flickering butter lamps on the altar to my left. My first impression was one of confusion. There were people everywhere. And noise, not just the noise of the chanting and the music, but of laughter and gossip and babies crying. There was a constant sense of movement. The floor was covered with people sitting in family groups. Children were dashing about, and red-robed figures solemnly moved here and there on mysterious errands. I was guided to an open space on the floor and pushed to a sitting position. Unseen hands set a plate before me, heaped with food. A cup of *sujah* was forced into my hand. Faces in the crowd bobbed and smiled in friendly recognition.

Later, I realized that what I was attending was a monthly *pujah*, following the lunar calendar. (I found it strange that the *Khaling-pa*, or people of Khaling, seemed to prefer the Hindi word, *pujah*, over their own word, *rimdo-phile*, to describe these regular religious observances). As I sat quietly, watching what was going on around me, I was able to make sense of what I was seeing. Sitting with their backs to the windows on a low dais were a few men in red robes. Some were playing musical instruments—small double-sided drums hit with a curved striker, a pair of *dungchen*, and an oboe-like instrument, called a *galing*—others were chanting from long rectangular prayer books held lengthwise across their knees or placed on small wooden desks. Opposite the officiants was the highly decorated altar, draped with silk, peacock feathers, and accoutred in brass vessels, butter lamps, and flasks for holy water. Upon the altar, was a collection of gilt statues, and behind them hung several *thankas*, religious icons painted on linen and framed with silk. All four walls were decorated with frescoes, covered, floor to ceiling, in religious iconography. It was a small room, foggy with incense, and somewhat overwhelming. There was so much to take in at once. It was nothing like the spare Protestant churches I had been raised in, and (I had to smile) my parents would have had a fit if I had wandered about, as some of these children were doing, in the middle of a church service. Religious services were supposed to be solemn, right? Apparently not...in Khaling, that is.

I looked around at the faces in the crowd. I was surprised to note that many of the red-robed officiants were faces I recognized: Tandin's father, for one, and Old Lungten. It seemed that Khaling Gompa was a village of *gomchens*. The man scurrying about the most was a deaf mute with a long face and monk's tonsure. He was called Yongba and he was the caretaker for the temple. *Yongba* in Sharchopkha means "dumb" and carries the same unfortunate connotation as it does in English. Everyone in the room was eating, and I watched as Yongba scurried about, removing food offerings from the altar and scraping them onto peoples' plates. Ugyen Lhamo was there, smiling contentedly, chatting with a neighbour whose daughter appeared to have

Down's syndrome. Ugyen Lhamo, though unacknowledged, was the presiding spirit of this feast. Tandin was there with her family, as was Sonam Lhamo. I felt a warm glow. I realized that I had unexpectedly found what I was looking for, without even knowing I was looking for it: a community. Here they were: the priests, the matriarch, the rich, the poor, the afflicted, the weak and the strong, linked together through a sense of shared history and culture. And they had welcomed me.

TEN

DOUBLE MIRACLE AT DOCHU-LA

AT THE END OF MY FIRST YEAR, once the school had closed down, I started to head west under my own steam, walking and catching lifts where I could, backpack in tow. I intended to meet my brother in Calcutta and then spend the winter break travelling in India. I broke my journey briefly in Bumthang, in central Bhutan, to celebrate Christmas with some other foreign volunteers at the Swiss guest house and to make a short three-day detour, trekking through the Tang Valley in the footsteps of the famous Buddhist saint and treasure-discoverer, Pema Lingpa, before continuing my journey to India.

And so it was that in late December, I found myself on the public bus en route to Thimphu with two other volunteers, Mary and Lily. It was getting late in the day, darker than usual because we were driving into a blizzard as we climbed to the pass at Dochu-La. The tires on the bus were bald and our tired driver, nervous. He was clearly not used to driving on snow-covered roads. He kept riding the brake, causing the bus to slide all over the road. The bus was overcrowded. Seats designed for two were holding three or four persons, and the aisle was crowded with passengers standing or sitting on their luggage. I was sitting behind the driver, sharing the hard seat with a mother and her three children. Her broad backside occupied most of the bench seat and she held two children in her lap. I was sitting slightly sideways with the third child standing on the floor between my legs, resting his bum on my knee. Every time the driver braked, passengers gasped in fright, as we slid toward a precipice or into the mountain wall. Passengers were throwing up, some out the window and some into their capacious sleeves in order to spare the rest of us, but the smell of vomit lingered. As night fell, we met a car full of monks coming down from the pass. There was a quick confab between our driver and theirs. It was clear that our driver was being told it was impossible to get through and that he should turn around. But he decided to press on. Snow fell like needles in the headlights. Three inches of slick wet snow covered the road. Then it happened. We had pushed our luck too far. The bus started to slide. The driver panicked. The wheels locked. Everyone was screaming as the bus careened toward the edge of a precipice and into a white void.

And then the first miracle happened. The bus was actually sliding out of control while travelling uphill and, as it lost momentum, it began to spin. Instead of hurtling over the cliff, it now slowly began to charge into the rock cutting on the other side of the road. The bus slammed into the exposed rock face, hurling luggage and passengers to the floor. In the silence after the crash there was a brief pause as it registered on the passengers that they were not dead after all—bruised perhaps, but not dead. Smiles were exchanged all around, and we all clambered out of the bus to inspect the damage.

The nose of the bus on the passengers' side was rubbed up against the face of the mountain and both tires on that side of the bus spun uselessly in a snow-filled ditch, but the damage appeared to be minor. There was some discussion of pushing the bus out and continuing, but the driver had had enough. His nerves were shot. We were staying put until morning, he announced, then we would see how things stood. We boarded the bus and tried to make ourselves comfortable for the night.

I nestled down with my new family of five on a bench seat made for two. It was cold, damned cold. Many of the windows, of course, were missing, and passengers did their best to stuff the openings shut with saris and boxboard to cut the icy wind. Still, we were kept reasonably warm just by body heat. The bus was designed to carry forty people. It contained perhaps one hundred. This did lead to cramping. I slept with the profile of an Egyptian pharoah, hips square in the seat, child in my lap, shoulders pinned against the side of the bus, and cheek pressed against the cold glass of the window, which, given the general state of disrepair, was mercifully intact.

With so many people packed into this glass and steel carton there was bound to be some condensation. It began as the windows fogged up and then beads of water began to trickle down the glass into my collar. But it was a long night and soon the condensation spread from the windows to the walls and gradually to the ceiling. I was too uncomfortable to sleep, or so I thought, and I tried to imagine I was somewhere else to keep my mind off the screaming agony of my cramped muscles. I dozed. I was under water. It was cold and I could not get warm. I was in a submarine. I begged the captain to take me up, out of the cold depths to the ocean's surface. I implored him. There was sun up there, I pleaded, and I wanted to feel the sun again on my skin, strip off my damp clothing and bask in its warmth.

Then a drop of water landed on the end of my nose and I woke up. I was still in the bus and my arm had gone numb under the weight of Ama's broad back. All around me water dripped constantly. Clothes steamed. The bus had become an ocean grotto. I tried to extricate my painfully dead arm, but it was no good. Ama was built with very ample proportions and there were two kids in her lap whom I did not wish to wake. I resigned myself to the agony and waited for the illumination of dawn, many hours away.

In the morning, we awoke to stretch our muscles and regroup. The khalasi, or driver's assistant, built a fire under the engine block and several women used the embers to roast potatoes. One man had just purchased a new head for his pick-axe at market, and he quickly whittled a serviceable handle with his chhowang. He and another man attacked a frozen gravel bank, and we quickly relayed hatfuls of gravel to spread under the wheels. There was one shovel on the bus, but the rest of us improvised with scraps of wood torn from packing crates, crooked tree branches, and the soles of our feet to clear away the snow around the bus. When the engine oil was flowing, the driver started the bus. Women with children boarded and resumed their seats. The rest of us found a place to apply our shoulders and began to heave. The bus lurched out of the ditch, onto the road and once more began its slow ascent to the pass. We collected our makeshift tools and loped along behind. In no time, the bus was stuck again, and we attacked the snow and pushed her forward. This became the pattern of our slow progress. Still, the sun was shining and everyone was in a holiday mood. When I tired of walking behind the bus, I taught the young khalasi the fine art of "bumper-hitching," something I had not done since I was a kid. We gripped the bus's rear bumper, feet sliding in the tire-wipes, laughing like idiots.

Things progressed in this fashion until, rounding a great corner in the road, we were confronted with our first real obstacle: a large drift across the road and, protruding through this barrier of snow, the windshield and roof of an automobile. The driver brought the bus to a halt and put on the parking brake. We all gathered around the car and discussed the situation. Someone waded through the drift and wiped the snow from the windshield. The car was empty, probably abandoned the night before. We decided that, if we cleared the snow away, we could probably just squeeze by on the outside, between the stalled automobile and the precipice. We set to with our makeshift tools. Those who were not shovelling, including my friends Lily and Mary, retired to the bus to keep warm.

As we were working, we saw a vehicle approaching from the pass, a small luxury coach, nothing like the old school bus we were travelling in. The coach was moving cautiously through hubcap-deep snow and when it reached our drift it came to a stop. A military man emerged from the heated coach. He was wearing the red beret of the Royal Bodyguard (RBG). We noticed that there were four other men in the vehicle, all officers in the RBG and all wearing dangerous scowls. They appeared to be accompanied by their wives and a considerable amount of luggage. The first man looked like a thug. He began to abuse us. Get out of the way you stupid peasants, he screamed, veins standing out like rope on his neck. Move that great ugly bus out of the road. And where is the owner of this car? If he values his life, he had better move it immediately. He scowled around at us. Which of you owns this piece of shit? He walked up to the nearest man and screamed in his face. Well, is it yours, son of a dog? The man so addressed, a sizable farmer who probably could have broken the arrogant soldier in half, looked at the ground and whispered submissively into his cupped hand. What? Speak up, you moron.

When the situation was finally made clear to the officer, he stomped around some more, cursed futilely, and then yelled at the bus driver. Well, at least move that bus out of our way and the rest of you, hurry up and clear away this snow, so we can pass. And with that he retreated to the warmth of his vehicle, encouraging our efforts periodically with impatient blasts of his horn. Our driver backed our bus down the road, parking as close to the precipice as he dared, so that the other coach would be able to pass him on the inside. He set the parking brake once more and rejoined us in our efforts to move the snow. However, the officers did not have the patience to wait until we were finished. The luxury coach attempted to blast through, honking its horn, scattering workmen like a football tackle; but after a few yards it was sucked into the soft snow, trapped. The passengers slid open their windows and harangued us from the comfort of their padded coach seats until we had pushed them through the remains of the drift. Watching the vehicle retreat around the corner out of sight, I noticed something that set my heart racing. Our bus was moving. I shouted, dropped my makeshift shovel, and sprinted toward the bus as fast my legs would carry me.

It moved slowly at first, almost imperceptibly, but gradually it gained momentum. As long as the bus stayed on the road everything would be okay, but what I saw, and what immediately became apparent to the passengers on the bus, was that if it reached the bend in the road, it would topple backwards over a high cliff and there was little likelihood that anyone in the bus would survive that fall. There were only a dozen or so people clearing snow, so the bulk of the passengers, the women, the children, and the elderly, were all on the bus. The passengers were all trying to exit at once, but there was only one door, at the back. The general panic insured that it was firmly bottle-necked with screaming passengers. I caught up with the bus and ran alongside, watching helplessly. A woman tossed her baby to me through an open window and I caught it, but I could not keep up. The bus was now travelling far faster than I could run. Two men were clinging to the front bumper, desperately digging in their heels, trying to slow the bus down, but it shrugged them off and they fell face-first in the snow. A knot of women pressed against the window beside the driver's seat. The window was hinged and opened outward like a door, but the handle was on the outside and they were trapped by the latch and their own weight. I saw a long pale arm reach forward from an open window and turn the latch. A tangle of bodies exploded through the window, as if shot from a cannon, and landed heavily on the road. Parents were now flinging their children from the bus through the windows. My running steps slowed to a jog, and I watched helplessly as the inevitable catastrophe unfolded before my eyes.

Then I witnessed my second miracle in twenty-four hours.

The wheels must have found some purchase, for the bus began to slow down. Slowly, excruciatingly slowly, the bus began to glide to halt. It finally came to rest with a sigh of crunching snow, its tail end protruding out into the void. We quickly got everyone off of the bus, for it was by no means certain that the bus would not carry on in its final suicidal slide, so close was it to the tipping point. Then what a scene of family reunions did I witness. What tears! What embracing! I returned the child to its mother and then I found Lily and Mary and we collapsed onto the snow, emotionally exhausted but enormously pleased to be alive. It was Lily who had released the door catch. If the bus had gone over the cliff, six women would have owed their lives to her, but she certainly would not have survived the fall.

When everyone had gathered their wits, the bus driver clambered back into his seat and started the engine. Slowly, he eased the bus back onto the road. We pushed the bus the last half mile or so to the top of the pass. No one wanted to ride inside anymore, so we all plodded through the snow in the bus's wake and it was then I noticed that many of our number did not own shoes. It seemed funny that I had not noticed this before.

Throughout our ordeal everyone has demonstrated the greatest good humour. No one had whined. No one had demanded their money back or threatened to sue the bus company. But now everyone was dead tired. By the time we had trudged to the top of the pass the snow was spotted with blood from cracked and bleeding feet. Once over the saddle the snow disappeared—one of those strange climatic phenomenon one experiences in mountains. Two hours later we reached Thimphu in the dark, and we took our leave of each other in silence, never to meet again perhaps, but never to be entirely forgotten either; for I am sure that the story of our dangerous journey will be retold many times before the glow of the kitchen fire while the *ara* circulates in wooden bowls and the wind howls outside the door.

ELEVEN

MASTER Of THE DAY

WHEN I RETURNED TO JIGME SHERUBLING after the winter break, I sensed that everything had changed. There were the obvious changes, like staffing changes, but there was something else, as well, something more difficult to define, an undercurrent of unease. Michael had left for a job in New Guinea. Chogyal had been transferred to a junior high school in south-central Bhutan as its new head-master. (He did not really want the job, for reasons I did not fully understand at the time, but he was given no choice.) We had a new history teacher, Mr. Roy, an elderly bachelor who was probably past retirement age but whose zeal for his chosen profession was undiminished. We also had a new science teacher, a young Canadian named Grant, who had been a graduate student in organic chemistry before coming to Bhutan.

The really big change though was a regime change. I returned to find that we had a new principal, a Bhutanese. He was a handsome strongly built man who always sported a brush cut and a freshly pressed *gho*. He was very strict and formal, and he rarely smiled. His appointment was part of a larger plan. The government was concerned with the erosion of their traditional culture, and so they were replacing foreign administrators with their Bhutanese counterparts as quickly as they could. It was for this reason that Chogyal left us, as well. We were told that the Jesuits would soon be leaving the country. Their presence was no longer required. By the end of the year, all of the Scandinavian missionaries would either have left or would learn that their work visas would not be renewed. The Teaching Sisters would also be asked to leave. This was particularly hard on Sister Leonard, who had worked most of her adult life in Bhutan—indeed, who was now teaching children whose parents had once been her pupils.

I should have sensed the change coming the previous fall, just before winter break, when the school had received an unexpected visit from a senior government minister. Unscheduled visits from important *dashos* were not that unusual in themselves. Remember, we had no telephone service in Khaling, so we had become quite adept at receiving unexpected guests and at throwing together a proper reception at a moment's notice. No, the fact of the visit itself was not unusual, and to be honest, it was not until after the reception line, and not until after the minister had examined the students in some of their traditional cultural practices—the way they bowed, the manner in which they presented their ceremonial scarves of rank, the manner of their address—and it was not until we were all seated in the prayer hall and the minister had been speaking for some time, that I started to detect that there was something different about this visit, something troubling.

On the surface, the speech was about the practice of Buddhism, but it quickly became clear that the real message of the speech was about something else entirely.

"What is Buddhism?" the minister began. "I will tell you. It does not exist. There is no such thing!"

What? What was he saying?

"It does not exist because it is a made-up word. It is a nonsense word invented by ignorant foreigners obsessed with 'isms'—communism, capitalism, feminism, sexism, ageism. The list goes on and on. Everything is an 'ism.' And yet, do the foreigners say, 'Christianism?' No. Do the foreigners say 'scienceism?' No, of course not. Science is not an 'ism'; it is a thing. So why do they say 'Buddhism' when the Lord Buddha is a person, and not a thing. Why? I will tell you: Because there is no good reason to do so. And that is why I say to you, do not say 'Buddhism'; that is the height of ignorance. Use the proper words, 'Buddha Dharma.'"

He had our undivided attention now. He continued on in this vein for a while, lecturing the students on Buddha Dharma, but after a time a pattern began to emerge. His speech on Buddhism was really a cover for an attack on anything foreign.

"In your schools, they teach you science. Science, you are told, is height of human achievement. Everything else is superstition. But I ask you, what has science brought us? Has it brought us happiness? No. Science has brought us the atom bomb. Science has polluted the environment. Science has given us the Holocaust..."

I wanted to dispute his thesis, point out that "science" wasn't a thing, it was a method, and that the scientific method had resulted in improved medical care, if nothing else. But I bit my tongue. In this culture, you did not argue with someone of the *dasho's* high station. The proper response was to remain submissive, and, if a rhetorical question was addressed to you, to answer, "Yes-*la*" or "No-*la*."

"The dharma teaches us to respect and honour all life, but can democracy say the same? No. And foreigners have no respect for tradition. When their parents grow old, do they care for them and listen to their wisdom? No. They lock them away in old-age homes. They imprison them. Dharma teaches us that the world is *samsara*, or illusion. Do the foreigners understand this? No. They are obsessed with material possessions. Their hunger for new things is never satisfied. The whole world can never satisfy their greed."

Whenever the minister would make one of these barbed asides, he would pause, like a comedian looking for a cheap laugh, glance my way, and smirk. Some students found this amusing and obliged him with a chuckle, but most were uncomfortable with this sort of persecution and shifted uneasily. While I could understand his concern for the erosion of Bhutanese cultural values, I could not help thinking that this was the wrong approach to take to preserve them. Particularly since a third of his audience was not even Buddhist, but Hindu. An attack on non-Buddhists was likely to make them uneasy, too.

We noticed that the new regime paid greater attention to traditional discipline or *Driglam Namzha*. *Driglam Namzha* has been defined as "the way (*lam*) of conscious (*namzha*) harmony (*drig*)." One writer, in a felicitous turn of phrase, has described *Driglam Namzha* as an "elaborate choreography of deference."[5] All extracurricular activities were suspended for a month and classes were frequently cancelled so that students could practise draping their *kabne*, or ceremonial scarf of rank (white in the case of the students and other commoners), in crisp and elegant folds over their arms, practise the proper forms of address for different ranks of society, practise how to correctly serve tea, and practise how to bow in the approved manner. There was something inherently charming about all this old-fashioned court etiquette, but not everyone was pleased by these disruptions. The boys missed soccer and basketball practice, and some of the teachers muttered mutinously about all this "*driglam* nonsense."

I felt a little sorry for our new principal. Clearly, a great deal was expected of him. He was to tighten discipline, purge foreign influences; and yet the bulk of his teaching staff was foreign. His only model for leadership was that of the despot and a despot does not ask for help. He cannot seek advice; he can only pronounce. Rather than creating a collegial atmosphere and inviting input from his staff, he preferred to rule from the top down. A more experienced administrator could have managed his multinational work force with more tact and created a sense of common purpose. Instead, we all felt that we had become subjects to a dictatorship. If he made a bad decision, the principal could not reverse his action; he could only take it a step further or shift the blame to someone else. Backing down from a bad decision was not an option, for it involved a loss of face. Staff meetings became more frequent and there was very little give and take.

The principal used the staff meetings as a platform for his latest ideas. Teachers were lazy, he announced early on, and undisciplined. From now on, teachers would be expected to be in the school until the end of the school day, whether or not they had classes to teach, and they would require passes to leave the campus to go to the bazaar. Since I lived off campus, this was obviously an ill-conceived notion. The reaction of the teachers to these pronouncements was interesting to note and usually broke down along national lines. The Bhutanese simply bowed and accepted the new rules, regardless of how they felt. The Indians were very irate, but never challenged the principal directly. They simply grumbled among themselves like a bunch of sea lawyers. Grant was the only one who openly and repeatedly challenged the principal's authority in these meetings. He once even went so far as to say that he thought the principal's new idea was "dumb" and then proceeded to give a carefully reasoned argument why this new idea would never work. Teachers loved these exchanges and followed the arguments with a mixture of alarm and ill-concealed delight.

One of the principal's most unpopular edicts was the introduction of the practice of Master of the Day (or M-O-D, as it became known). He had picked up this idea at some conference, and it appealed to his Machiavellian sense of authority. Since he was convinced we were all a bunch of slackers, he would get us to police each other. Each of us would take turns being the Master of the Day. In addition to his assigned duties, the MOD would spend the day with a clipboard tucked under his arm, following his colleagues around the school, making sure they were fulfilling their extra-curricular responsibilities, and then reporting on any malefactors to the principal at the end of the day. I hated this job and it eventually died a slow death of neglect as people simply let it slide, handing in phony reports, or ignoring their duty altogether, and later saying that they had forgotten. Eventually people just stopped bothering and the principal gave up, his enthusiasm caught up in some newer, more impractical scheme that would make his administration a model of efficiency throughout the country's school system.

Here is my diary entry for May 9, 1988. If nothing else, it gives you a fair idea of a typical day at Jigme Sherubling under the new regime:

5:00 A.M.

My cheap alarm clock kicks in with the raw gravelly clack of cartwheels over cobble-stones. Roll out of bed and push back the shutters. Light is halftone. Low clouds, leaden and oppressive. I scowl up; the clouds glower down. It's gonna be another grey one. I grab my *jola*, the one the women in the bazaar finger so lovingly, and check its contents: literature notes, *Julius Caesar*, poetry anthology, sock with a stone in the toe, tin plate, enamel mug, and spoon. Slip into my clothes. Have to knot the tie four times before I get it right. I slip quietly from the house like a shadow and filter through the burgeoning willow lanes toward the school, unnoticed but by a few early risers milking their cows. Have an extended and completely unintelligible conversation with Yongba under the temple wall and then descend into the valley of the shadow. Mission: MOD.

5:30 A.M.

I arrive at the boys' dormitory to the macaw screeching of whistles. Kick open doors as I pass down the halls, am greeted with the cloying stench of mouldy footwear and thrice-breathed air. Most students are reluctant to leave their beds and pull the blankets over their heads. Lopen Pema is nowhere to be seen. Debate whether or not to awaken the girls: decide against it. Lopen rises at 5:45 looking rough around the edges, prowls around the dorms with bamboo rod for the tardy and glass of water for the dream-filled, filling their ear with its sudden poison.

6:00 A.M.

Lopen Chuwang arrives ten minutes early for morning study, sits himself cross-legged on a desk in the corner, and begins rocking back and forth, counting his prayer beads and muttering his mantra, oblivious to all presences. Students, oddly enough, do not misbehave, though many put their heads down on their desks and fall asleep.

7:20 A.M.

Hostel clean-up well supervised by Lopen Pema and "Lopen Shing."[6]

8:00 A.M.

Eat breakfast in the dining hall: Scoop of gritty bulgar (gift of the people of Canada) refried in Canola oil (also a gift of the same), washed down with a mug of tepid milky-sweet tea. Boys want to know if I like living at the Gompa. Does Sir live alone? All alone? Does Sir not perhaps have a girlfriend? Is Sir not lonely? Would Sir like some help finding a girlfriend? They seem very concerned. It is not good apparently to live so alone. Their concern is very touching, but their solution is a little alarming: for about five hundred *ngultrum* I could probably rent a girlfriend for the year. They are quite matter-of-fact about the whole thing. If Sir finds a girlfriend (and it would be easy because Sir is a handsome devil and very rich) he would also get a family and so Sir wouldn't be lonely. They smile brightly all around. I think about it for a moment, the idea of coming home to a crowded kitchen each night with my in-laws grinning gap-toothed around the *chula*, pushing cups of warm *ara* into my hand, nephews and nieces colouring on pages torn from my novels and notebooks, loud folk songs playing on my two-in-one, brother-in-law importuning me for a loan, while his infant child in a leaky cloth diaper, suffering from pinkeye and gastroenteritis, lies asleep on my cot...and politely decline.

9:00 A.M.

Morning assembly. Students stand in silent, straight lines, organized by grade and sex, collars turned up against the damp. Principal harangues them for a few minutes on their duties to the school and the Fatherland to which they dutifully listen. We glumly intone the dirge-like national anthem. A serious gloomy crowd until the principal releases them to go to class, and then—our morning miracle—they break into chattering groups and become children.

9:10 A.M.

First Period. Class 7 Geography. Yesterday introduced chapter on the earth and the moon from the textbook. Copied down definition of "centrifugal force," but I could see they didn't get it. So today I reach into my *jola* and take out the old sock with the stone in the toe. I begin to twirl the sock above my head. Everyone ducks. "What would happen if I let go of the sock?" I ask. They grin. "That's 'centrifugal force.'" You could see the comprehension in their eyes. "Now here's a question. If the moon is affected by centrifugal force, like the stone in my sock, why doesn't it go shooting off into space? What holds it in place?" This leads to some speculation and class goes very well from there. Trying to explain tides tomorrow will be more of a challenge, since none of them have ever seen the ocean, let alone a body of water larger than our Holy Lake.

11:30 A.M.

Lunch. I approach the kitchen with trepidation. What gastronomic delight has Mr. Chola co-ordinated for my cringing palate. When I reach the surging and ebbing serving line my worst fears are realized. A fly kicks feebly in the scum on the surface of the dhal. Huge naked vertebrae arch through the film of the curry like the carcass of an old horse at a glue factory. The place smells of wet dog. I can see the dirt under the student server's fingernails as he cheerfully flings a fistful of compressed rice and sand onto my plate.

1:00 P.M.

Class 10 English. Review Act II, Scene I, in *Julius Caesar*. I draw a big rectangle on the blackboard. "Imagine this is the stage and you are the director of the play. I want you to decide where to place the actors. From where do they enter? Where do they go? Why do Decius, Casca, and Cinna have a ridiculous argument about where the sun rises? Where do Brutus and Cassius go during this debate? Why does Shakespeare feel it is unnecessary for us to hear what they say?" I break them into groups to discuss the staging problems, and then each group presents their solutions. We finish the class with volunteers acting out the first meeting of the conspirators. Then I walk down the hall and repeat the lesson all over again for another group of students.

5:00 P.M.

Students slow to arrive at study. Father James coolly unaware of my presence at first, sitting in a corner reading a book. Upon noticing me, immediately becomes hysterical. In a loud voice, he denounces the boys who are present—for being late! "Yes, yes. You should come on time. I tell you, but you are late, always. Why are you being late? Hummh? Why? I tell you, because you should be on time. This is no good, isn't it? You must improve in future, *acha*?" All of this to a group of polite, but confused (and present) schoolboys.

6:00 P.M.

Prayer Hall. A fog of incense. Prayers chanted in haunting ululation, filling the room with shapes of sound. Though I don't understand the words, I enjoy being there. Clearly the music itself serves a function; the pulsing rhythm resonates in the breastbone, inducing a trance-like state. I find it meditative and relaxing (as, of course, I should).

7:00 P.M.

Girls' study. P.C. Roy paces the aisles muttering to himself, the two-sided, highly articulate conversation of a kindly madman. When he sees me, he forces me into a chair and groping in his pocket produces a clasp knife with a handle shaped like a fish wrapped in newspaper. Opening it and with manic jabs in the air, he whispers, "If they speak, cut out their tongues." Then he leaves, handing me the knife. Bewildered, I stay on and complete his study duty.

8:30–9:00 P.M.

I sit in the empty study hall and write my MOD report. Wet, tired, redundant and absurd. Most teachers resented my presence, carefully thanked me for coming, and hoped I would go away, soon.

These new rules, the increased emphasis on *Driglam Namzha*, and the repatriation of any foreigners with religious affiliations created an atmosphere of unease, but, living far from the capital, we did not get the full picture of the dark forces at work. Students returning from the winter break brought back disturbing tales. There was a new Citizenship Act and a census was being conducted in southern Bhutan to implement it. Nepali students spoke of families being broken up, of parents or grandparents being escorted out of the country because they could not produce proof of citizenship. We also learned that a new national dress code was being enforced. This code required that all Bhutanese, regardless of ethnicity, were required to wear the *kira*, *gho*, and *kabne* when entering any public building, even in the tropical south, where such dress was obviously impractical.

While these new political developments were unsettling, in truth they did not affect me very much. My focus was on teaching, and by my second year I had become much more comfortable in my role as teacher. I had more confidence. Classes were actually going quite well. I had also picked up two classes of Class 7 Geography, which I was enjoying. On April 1st, I taught an English class in costume, something I would not have had the audacity to attempt a year earlier.

I borrowed a lab coat, a pair of oversize glasses with the lenses removed, stuck on a rubber nose, and powdered my mussed-up hair with talc. I strode energetically into the classroom a few minutes late and launched immediately into my lesson, not giving the students a chance to gather their wits.

"*Guten morgen*," I announced to the startled class in a thick German accent. "Mein name ist Professor Horst Manhoor of the University of Wurtenburg. Herr Ken has not been able to be with you this morning, but has asked me to teach you about the pronunciation of English consonants." I had prepared diagrams of the human throat and palate to show the correct placement of the tongue for different consonant sounds and I had the students rehearse a series of tongue twisters for sounds like that of the letter "R," which they had difficulty with. There was added humour because, as a German, I could not pronounce the English "w" to save my life. At the end of the class, I was exhilarated. The students had participated enthusiastically in a drill, which, let's face it, under normal circumstances would have been dead boring, and I had never had more fun.

My real coup was that on my winter holiday I had visited the department of education warehouse in Phuntsholing and convinced the guardians to release more textbooks for my Class 10 English students. When I arrived back in Khaling, there was a crate awaiting me with crisp new copies of *Treasure Island* and *Village by the Sea*. Now at least my students would have a fighting chance on their ICSE.

These days there are small things, seemingly inconsequential things, which can trigger memories of Bhutan. Smells can do it. Opening my hockey duffle bag always reminds me of the stuffy Pema bus. Dry grass reminds me of winter pastures, rancid butter of temple lamps. Sounds, too. Rain on the roof always takes me back to Khaling Gompa during the monsoon. The other night, though, it was a children's book that transported me back twenty years.

I always read to my daughter before I put her to bed, and this particular night she surprised me. She handed me an old paperback and said, "Daddy, tonight I want you to read this." It was one of her mother's old books: Rudyard Kipling's *The Jungle Book*. She is only six years old, and I wondered if she was old enough to appreciate these stories, but I said, "Okay. We'll give it a try." She pulled the quilt around her and curled against my chest. "Thumb out," I said. She rolled her eyes but withdrew the offending digit from her mouth. Then I opened the book, turned to the first story, "Mowgli's Brothers," and began to read.

The last time I had read this story was in Khaling, standing in front of a class of tenth form students. I had forgotten how good it was and how well-suited to reading aloud. By the end, when the pack turns on Mowgli and when he feels their betrayal ("I would have been a wolf with you to my life's end"), my daughter and I both had tears in our eyes. What a powerful moment, tying together the themes of friendship and loyalty, honour and self-discovery. Did my daughter understand all this? Most of it, I think, even if she could not articulate it. But did my students in Khaling?

This was my struggle as an English teacher in Bhutan. Teaching grammar and composition was one thing; teaching literature was quite another. How did one teach literature, particularly in a second language? Too often my lessons became nothing more than lengthy vocabulary lists and sets of comprehension questions. Joseph Conrad, in his famous preface to The Nigger of the "Narcissus," wrote that the artist "appeals to our capacity for delight and wonder, to the sense of mystery surrounding our lives; to our sense of pity, and beauty and pain...and to the subtle but invincible conviction of solidarity that knits together the loneliness of innumerable hearts, to the solidarity in dreams, in joy, in sorrow, in aspirations, in illusions, in hope, in fear which binds men to each other, which binds together all humanity—the dead to the living and the living to the unborn." But did my students feel this solidarity when they read stories like "Mowgli's Brothers?" I fear that on most days they did not. But on those rare days, when everything went well, we could be translated; we could weep with Mowgli; we could say, "What is this, Bagheera? Am I dying?" (No, Little Brother, the panther would reply, those are only tears such as men use).

I had no control over the curriculum. It was determined by those who set the exam-inations in India. It was heavily weighted toward safe, dead, and, with one exception, male English and Anglo-Indian writers. All in all, though, it was not a bad curriculum. There were a few inspired choices. The short story anthology we used was excellent, with lots of good narrative tales, many with twist endings, and nothing too literary or introspective—stories like "The Monkey's Paw," "The Gift of the Magi," "An Astrologer's Day," and of course, "Mowgli's Brothers." The sole woman writer on the course was Anita Desai, and we read her novella The Village by the Sea, a story of two determined children who learn to cope and adapt in the face of family tragedy and poverty. This was fairly easy for my students to understand. The world Desai described was not too far removed from their own. But Treasure Island was another kettle of fish. It should have been an enjoyable romp. Instead, I spent hours on vocab-ulary, drawing diagrams of ship's rigging and explaining terms like "keel-hauling" and "manning the capstan-bars." Pirates they understood—they had all had experi-ences with dacoits—but sailing was a mystery to them. What saved me here was my father's initiative (bless his heart!). I had written my father telling him that an aid organization had donated a television and vcr to the school. Could he send me a video of *Julius Caesar*? He did better than that; he found a video of the old black-and-white version of *Treasure Island*, starring Jackie Cooper and Wallace Beery, and mailed it to me in a cavity hollowed out of an old book.[7] Now, at least, my students could see an old sailing ship, even if the scriptwriters had played havoc with the plot of the novel.

The poetry anthology was also often difficult. Some of it was fairly straightforward; narrative poems like "The Highwayman" or "Aurangzeb at his Father's Bier" were relatively easy to teach. Much of it was frankly patriotic, like Henry Louis Vivien Derozio's hyperbolic "To My Native Land" or this one by Sir Walter Scott:

Breathes there a man with soul so dead,

Who never to himself hath said,

'This is my own, my native land!'

Not too much subtlety here. But I struggled with the lyric poems. How does one teach Lord Byron's:

She walks in beauty, like the night

Of cloudless climes and starry skies;

And all that's best of dark and bright

Meet in her aspect and her eyes:

Thus mellow'd to that tender light

Which heaven to gaudy day denies.

I love this poem, but I'm afraid I did not do it justice. My students struggled with it and grew to hate it. I began to wonder if English literature was even a proper discipline in the same way that math or science was. What was the body of knowledge to be imparted in a poem like this? In the end, I just said (to the male students): "Boys, trust me on this: one day, you will meet the right girl and the words will suddenly ring true and no one will have to explain them to you." "The woods are lovely, dark and deep," wrote Robert Frost in another poem on the curriculum, but could I really teach them about those deep dark woods? Most of the time, they could not even see the forest for the trees.

It was ironic that the thing that should have been the most difficult to teach turned out to be the most rewarding. Each year the Class 10 students had to study one play by William Shakespeare. It was my task to teach them *Julius Caesar*, and I was dreading it. But to my surprise, once we got past the difficult vocabulary, most students loved it. They committed huge chunks of the play to memory and would surprise me at opportune moments with apt quotations.

Before an exam: "Well, Sir, 'The Ides of March are come.'"

Before looking at the posted results of that same exam: "'Cowards die many times before their deaths;' Sir, but 'The valiant never taste of death but once.'"

And after seeing the results: "'O mighty Caesar! Dost thou lie so low?'"

Discussions about republican versus imperial government became coded debates about contemporary politics.

> I was born as free as Caesar; so were you:
> We both fed as well, and we can both
> Endure the winter's cold as well as he.

Or:

> Men at some times are masters of their fates:
> The fault, dear Brutus, is not in our stars,
> But in ourselves, that we are underlings.

Shakespeare was also useful for coded criticism of one's masters. When yet one more soccer game had been cancelled so that students could practise *Driglam Namzha*, a student would exclaim: "'This was the most unkindest cut of all.'"

"Yes," another would mutter, "but 'Brutus is an *honourable* man.'"

A third would add: "'So are they all, *honourable* men.'"

And that was the problem, wasn't it? We were all honourable men, or wished to be. We were doing what was best for the students and for their country. We were sincere. We were only forcing them to conform because it was in their own best interest. We were not teaching them *how* to think, but *what* to think. We did what we were told.

TWELVE

THE RODENT CONTROL EXPERT

ONE DAY AFTER SCHOOL, I dropped in to see Tashi Dorje and discovered him in his kitchen surrounded by cuts of meat. He was butchering a calf, cutting the beef into long strips to cure over the fire. The meat looked a bit green and smelled off. The eye sockets in the small skull had been picked clean by scavenging birds. Tashi looked unhappy.

"What happened?" I asked.

"It fell off a cliff," he grunted as he chopped at the carcass with his *chhowang*. "It took me three days to find the calf. Much of the meat is spoiled." He sighed and shook his head. "*Aiyi*. What to do? What to do?"

I had been told that Buddhists revered all life and went out of their way to avoid giving harm to other sentient beings. Yet, not one of my neighbours was a vegetarian. I was surprised and wondered how they managed to resolve this apparent contradiction.

The bottom line, it turned out, was that while the Sharchopa were devout Buddhists, they were also extremely practical. Living as they did at high elevations, herding cattle was often a more viable way of earning a living than vegetable gardening. Maintaining a balanced diet was difficult. Indeed, in some valleys I visited at 2,700 metres (9,000 feet) and above, the only crop that could be grown was buckwheat. The main sources of protein were milk, cheese, butter, and eggs, but meat was eaten when it was available and was considered a treat. Almost everyone I knew was raising a pig to be slaughtered in the fall for winter rations. Walnuts were gathered in season, but other meat substitutes, like lentils or chick peas, had to be imported from India and so were too expensive for most *Khaling-pa*. And while no one objected to butchering an animal, few wanted the bad karma of actually killing it. Bhola sometimes earned a share of meat by slaughtering animals for villagers who were reluctant to do the dirty deed themselves. This reluctance sometimes had surprising consequences.

On one occasion, Father Perry asked Bhola to get some meat for the annual school picnic. Bhola bought a young goat and staked it on a long tether behind the school kitchen until it was needed. The students made a pet of the little goat and petitioned the principal to spare its life. The principal reluctantly agreed. However, tragedy struck. The kid, spoiled through overfeeding, sickened and died and was buried out on a little mound behind the school go-down with a great outpouring of grief. The problem was that meat was still needed for the picnic the next day. Bhola said he knew where he could get some mutton at short notice and was given some more money to procure it. Late that night, he resurrected the kid, washed it off, butchered it, and sold it back to the school as mutton. No one found out about the deception until much later, and strangely enough, rather than be offended by his actions, people rather admired Bhola as a clever fellow.

Like Bhola, I lacked certain scruples about killing, which was fortunate because my new house was full of rats (probably because my basement was full of potatoes). I had been forewarned that this might be a problem and so had brought two rather large and sinister-looking traps with me from Canada. Each night I would set my traps and then lay tensely in the dark as the rats emerged from the depths and rattled about my kitchen. I found that I could never fall asleep until the second trap went off. Once that happened I could then drift into a dreamless sleep. In the morning, while I waited for my breakfast kettle to boil, I would empty the traps out the kitchen window to the waiting cats and pye-dogs in the yard below. I was always careful to look out first to be sure I was unobserved because, while I had no scruples about killing rats, I thought my neighbours might be offended by my casual disregard for rodent life. The rat carcasses were quickly gobbled up, so I knew there would be no evidence of my wanton slaughter.

Once, my traps caught an unexpected guest. It was one of the first mornings in my new house. I had thrown open the wooden shutters and the early morning sun, low on the horizon, was streaming across the kitchen, illuminating in brilliant shafts the swirling dust particles. I was sitting cross-legged on the floor enjoying a cup of tea when I became aware that I was being observed. You may remember that in one corner of the kitchen a notched log served as a ladder to the attic above. My guest was sitting on the top step of this ladder, clothed in glossy black, with his head tilted a little to one side as he watched me closely. "Gronk," he said as he tentatively hopped to the next notch, his glittering eye surveying the scene. I sat very still, hoping he would approach closer. I wondered what had attracted his interest. Was it just curiosity to see the new tenant with whom he shared this domicile, or did he have a more definite object in mind? Ravens are sacred in Bhutan. The raven is one of the forms assumed by the protective deity Mahakala and the king of Bhutan wears a raven crown both as a symbol of his power and as a symbol of his role as protector of the realm and its religion. There is an old saying that it is a greater sin to kill one raven than it is to kill one hundred monks. Ravens also have an incredibly keen sense of smell. They are, after all, carrion eaters. I watched his gleaming eye scan the kitchen, find an object of interest, and then, with a little hop in the air, he glided across the room and landed on my rat trap. He brought his solid beak down on the scrap of cheese and was dead in an instant. I was horrified and I never told a soul. It was a warning. The Powers That Be commanded that I cease my slaughter and so, for a time, I put the traps away.

I was no saint, however, and I could only take the nightly orgies in the dark kitchen for so long. Soon the traps were out again, and I was taking my daily quota of rats. One morning, I was a little slow to get going. It was cold in the stone-walled kitchen, but outside the bright sun was warming the thin air, burning off the early morning haze. As before, I threw open the shutters, let in the light and the heat, and also threw wide the kitchen door. I wrapped my fingers around a steaming mug of tea and sat by the window drinking in the view. I heard a faint mewl behind me and realized that I had another visitor.

"Kuzu zangpo, dani," I said, turning around, and, sure enough, my neighbour's black-faced cat was standing with one paw across the threshold, trying to decide if it was safe to proceed. I looked to the traps and remembered with relief that I hadn't emptied them yet. In a corner by the door a stricken rat lay immobilized in the jaws of the large trap. The cat was safe from the threat of the trap, but all too late I realized I was not safe from the threat of the cat. "NO!" I shrieked. I dropped my mug of scalding tea, and scrambled across the floor on all fours toward the cat. But I was not quick enough. In a flash, the cat had darted in, grasped the rat in its mouth and fled the scene, dragging the trap behind it.

As I ran out of the door and onto the landing—screaming, "Come back here, you little thief!"—a head and shoulders suddenly popped up over the fence. It was Tandin's father. He had been hoeing his kitchen garden and had straightened up at my cry. He looked at me in alarm. "Lopen, what is the matter?"

Me in my kitchen, early morning.

"Dani! Dani!" I shouted, pointing at the cat as it streaked across the cornfield, dragging the rat and the wooden trap. He couldn't see the cat from where he was standing, but he must have sensed the panic in my voice, for he barked a command at the two granddaughters who were helping him. They dropped their hoes, hitched up their skirts, and ran across the garden. In an instant, they were over the garden fence and pursuing the cat through a neighbouring field. Less nimbly, the old man and I followed.

"What is wrong?" he asked me again, looking very concerned.

I managed to communicate to him that the cat has taken something from my kitchen. We chased the cat all around the village, through gardens and courtyards, through cowsheds and over fences. We shouted out as we caught glimpses of our elusive prey. Our voices attracted the attention of others and soon half the village had joined in the hunt, not really sure what they were doing, knowing only that lopen had lost something and they were to catch the cat. Partway through this Keystone Kops routine I realized that I was in big trouble. Up until then I had kept my rat culling a secret. What would happen, I wondered, if we caught the cat? How would I explain my actions?

Then little Tshering Lhamo shouted, "Over here," and we rallied to her. There, in a sunny kitchen courtyard, on a neatly stacked pile of firewood, ignoring us and nonchalantly licking his paws, sat our quarry. Everyone turned to me. They didn't say anything and didn't need to. Their puzzled expressions said enough. We've caught the cat, they were thinking, but why were we chasing it in the first place? I looked around for the trap, but it was nowhere to be seen. How was I going to explain this? I laughed uneasily, ran my fingers through my hair, and took a deep breath.

"Okay, it was like this," I began. And so, in the middle of the courtyard, in a mixture of Sharchopkha and mime, I began to act out the drama in my kitchen. "I am a rat," I announced to a delighted audience, and I began to mimic the rodent's stealthy nocturnal journey around my kitchen, sniffing loudly and squeaking. The children loved this. Then, suddenly, I spied the cheese in the trap. "Ah-hah! The lopen's cheese!" I patted my stomach. "Yum, yum." I began to nibble the cheese and then the trap came down on my head, killing me. This part, they didn't understand. How could the rat be killed by eating cheese? ("Maybe it was bad cheese?" someone suggested.)

Then I became the cat. "Now, I am dani," I explained, pointing to the malefactor who was still grooming himself atop the woodpile and studiously ignoring us. "I am entering the lopen's kitchen." I mimicked the cat's proud walk, perched myself in the doorway and licked my paws. Then I became myself. "Kuzu zangpo, dani," I said, greeting the cat. I became the cat again and grudgingly acknowledged this salute. Then I spied the dead rat. "Yum, yum," I thought, "dead rat. Delicious." I quickly darted into the kitchen and took the rat in my teeth and ran away, followed, in succession, (and I acted out each role in turn) by myself, by Tandin's father, and by his two granddaughters. Then I pointed at each member of my audience and, to everyone's great delight, I briefly became each of them, running after the cat in circles in the courtyard and shouting, "Dani! Dani!" Finally, we all arrived at the woodpile, panting and out of breath. I pointed dramatically at the cat and ended my narrative.

Everyone was greatly amused, but still puzzled. We had found the cat. Now what?

I didn't want the cat, I told them. I wanted the rat.

The rat? They really didn't get this, but it was a tribute to their great good humour and perhaps their affection for me that they shrugged their shoulders in collective bemusement and fanned out to search for the dead rat. Nangsi, Tandin's niece, soon found the rat lying in the middle of a radish patch and gave a shout. We saw her triumphantly holding the rat at arm's length. She offered it to me, but I declined, shaking my head. The trap, I reasoned, must be somewhere close at hand, so I got down on my hands and knees and began to crawl in widening circles, pushing the greenery aside with my hands. I spotted the trap—"Ah-hah!"—and pounced. The crowd gathered as

I held out the trap for their examination. It was passed around the circle. Curiosity had replaced amusement. They had never seen anything like it before.

"What is it?" they asked.

There was no escape. Nothing but the full disclosure of my sins would do; so, using a piece of kindling in place of the rat, I set the trap and demonstrated its operation. I was expecting expressions of disappointment, perhaps even anger, but instead, I received expressions of interest and approbation. My neighbours were impressed. They asked me to show them again. "*Yallah!*" they said, "this is wonderful!"

Tashi Dorje asked if he could borrow my trap. "My storeroom is overrun with rats," he explained. "They are eating all of my maize."

"But Tashi Dorje," I protested, "you're a Buddhist. You aren't supposed to kill other sentient beings. Doesn't this worry you?"

He shook his head. "I won't be killing the rats," he said quite seriously. "No one forces the rat to put his head into the trap. He is killed by his own greed. He is committing suicide."

And so death came to Khaling Gompa, and I found my niche in this community—as *lopen*, neighbour, and rodent control expert.

THIRTEEN

THE DREADFUL FATE

WHILE THE TEACHING ROUTINE HAD GROWN MORE COMFORTABLE in my second year, the extra-curricular crunch had not improved much. There was some relief. The new principal did not want an English drama, though he insisted on one in Dzongkha, and when I approached him about the year-book, he dismissed it as a waste of time and money. On the other hand, Mr. Roy, our new history teacher, was bubbling over with new ideas. For one of our Saturday evening entertainments, he organized a quiz show, with himself acting as the master of ceremonies. His patter reminded me of the late Johnny Carson. He supplied corny jokes between rounds of questions and then waited pointedly for the laughter. You could almost hear the drumbeat—"bud-um-PAH"—between gags. He also convinced the principal that we needed an inter-house debate.

"I have come up with a new idea," the principal announced at the next staff meeting. "I have decided that what the school needs is an inter-house debate." There were to be two debates, he told us, one in Dzongkha and one in English. The debates were to take place in two weeks' time. Organizing the English debate was my responsibility.

To give Mr. Roy some credit, he was not behindhand in offering to help. After the meeting, he announced that he would be my advisor. He sat me down and immediately began to lecture me on how to rig a proper debate. As he warmed to his subject I began to grow alarmed. When he started to explain the proper use of prescheduled "spontaneous irruptions," I irrupted:

"Excuse me, Mr. Roy, but do I understand you to say that we are to supply the students with their arguments?"

"Yes, of course," he laughed. "We cannot expect them to come up with their own ideas. My goodness! That would be a disaster!"

"So this really isn't a debate, it's more of a dramatic presentation?"

"Well, no...I mean, yes...no...don't you see, Mr. Ken? Can you not picture it? The telling argument, the quick riposte, the cunning rejoinder...just like Perry Mason. And we must supply them with some good jokes, too. I can work on that."

He was rubbing his hands together with excitement, picturing the scene in his mind. I held my tongue, figuring that with his long experience, he knew what he was about. We talked to the house captains, asking each to consult with the senior students in their house and to choose a team to represent them in the debate. We called a meeting of the debaters for the following afternoon.

That evening, Mr. Roy dragged me to the inaugural meeting of the Community Development Association, another of his ideas. He asked Grant to come, too, but Grant, with a prescience that, in retrospect, was uncanny, begged off. The meeting was held in the dining room of the primary school. The tables had been pushed into a square and those assembled sat on the outside, looking in. I scanned the square of wary faces. With the exception of Karin, all were male. Most were teachers and missionaries. And except for a few prominent citizens, like the postmaster, most were philing-pa, or foreigners. When everyone had settled himself on a hard bench, Mr. Roy rose to his feet and addressed the assembly. He thanked everyone for coming, flattered them on their sense of community spirit, and began to lecture them on the sorts of services that were urgently needed in Khaling. As Mr. Roy spoke of the need for a homeopathic health clinic, a sanitation drive, a library reading room, and community sports leagues for young people, I looked around at the listeners. A few, like Ray, were paying polite but amused attention, but most I noticed had that glazed poached-cod expression one sees in the pews during a particularly long sermon. A few had nodded off. Before long, I found my own attention wandering. It was a lengthy speech, and it had been a long and tiring day.

Then I snapped awake. I heard my name spoken and people were applauding. As the meeting broke up, several men came over to shake my hand.

"Congratulations, congratulations," they said as they pumped my arm.

Karin approached me, took my hand in mock seriousness and shook it.

"Wha—What happened?"

"Congratulations," she said and burst out laughing.

"For what, Karin?" I said. "Why am I being congratulated?"

"Because you are the new president of the Community Development Association."

"What! How did that happen?"

"Mr. Roy nominated you and it was carried unanimously."

The scoundrels! The room cleared quickly. Everyone was eager to get home to their beds now that they had elected me to the only position of responsibility in the new organization. I need not have worried. Mr. Roy was an idea man, not an organizer. Without him to push us, the CDC died a quick and merciful death of neglect. None of us had enough free time to coach little league baseball or to fundraise for a public library in a valley where the only literate residents were the students (and they already had a library).

The next afternoon, I met with the debaters for the first time. Mr. Roy came, too, and asked permission to address the students. "Certainly," I said, grateful for the help. As Mr. Roy began to speak of his vision for the debate, I could see that the children were growing uneasy. But he seemed oblivious to their unease. Several of the boys interjected meekly with, "Sir? Sir?" but Mr. Roy carried on as if he had not heard them. When he had finished, Mr. Roy looked past the students and their now quite voluble protests and said, "Well, now that you all understand what is expected, I look forward to witnessing the debate on the day itself. And remember, if you need any good jokes or quips, I would be most pleased to supply them." He turned to me. "Mr. Ken, I will turn this meeting over to your capable hands. And remember, any assistance needed," he winked, "...you understand? Don't feel shy. Just ask."

After he had left, the students turned to me in a mutinous mood.

"We will not do it!" they threatened. "It is not a proper debate. It is just pretend, a drama."

Since I had my own reservations about this debate, I asked them, "Well, how would you like to run the debate?" They had several reasonable suggestions, which we adopted. I knew that Mr. Roy would not be happy, and he wasn't. He abandoned us with dire warnings of the consequences of our folly and went to advise the Dzongkha *lopens* instead. They, at any rate, were grateful for his assistance. And the debate in Dzongkha was a great success (at least if one measured success by the amount of laughter it generated). Our debate was not so polished. I coached the teams separately, helped them construct their arguments and counterarguments. On the night of the debate, the proceedings sometimes threatened to stall, but in the end they pulled it off. The principal was not very impressed; in fact, he made no attempt to hide his boredom with the whole affair, but I didn't care. I was proud of the students. They had worked hard, and no one had supplied them with a script. In the end, all of the arguments were their own.

If things weren't bad enough already with the new principal, the *Driglam Namzha*, the debate, and my reluctant presidency of the CDC, the annual visit of the school inspector only served to raise the bar on the level of tension at the school. The inspector stayed for three days, observing each teacher in turn as he or she performed their duties. When my turn came, I was not even aware of it at first. I sailed into the classroom, asked the students to take their seats and launched into my lesson. It took me a few minutes to realize that I had a new pupil in the back of the room, an older gentleman in a brown suit with a clipboard, who was taking careful note of all I said and did. I stuttered for a moment; then carried on, trying to ignore the way the inspector frowned, pursed his lips, clucked his tongue, and shook his head in dismay.

At the end of his visit, a special staff meeting was called, so that the inspector could share his findings with the teaching staff. I entered the staff room with trepidation and tried to slouch in a corner to avoid notice. But to my surprise, the inspector singled me out for praise and several weeks later when the written reports came back to the school, the principal noted sourly that only one teacher had received an "excellent" rating: me. I was dumbfounded. I began to think that maybe, just maybe, there might be a career in teaching for me after all.

Later, at another staff meeting after the school inspector had gone, the principal announced that he would be restoring an old school custom. "It seems that in past years, we have unjustly neglected the school's fate." This seemed dire. "We need to revive our fate and I would like some volunteers to organize this project. Mr. Ken you will chair this committee, and Sister Leonard, Mr. Sarkar, and Lopen Pema will assist you. That will be all. Dismissed."

After the meeting, the four of us, so named, sat around the table and stared at each other. Having been put in charge, I felt it incumbent upon myself to clear my throat and make a beginning.

"So, somebody fill me in. Does the school regularly go through crises of this kind?"

They looked at me blankly.

"Why do we need to save the school?"

No reply. In fact, they were frowning. Sister Leonard looked rather concerned. I thought she might take my temperature.

"The fate," I said, "the school's fate! What are we to do?"

"*Acha*," said Sister Leonard, "You do not understand. The fate is to raise money." She nodded brightly, as if at a particularly dull pupil who finally understood the exercise under discussion.

Ah, so it was a financial crisis. Now we were getting somewhere.

"And how do we do that?" I asked.

"The girls can sell crafts—"

"Tombola—"

"Lucky numbers draw—"

"A fish pond—"

The ideas welled up and I began to relax. Obviously, these three were old hands at dealing with school debt. That fact that the school was in dire financial straits did not surprise me. We hadn't been paid in two months.

"This is excellent," I enthused. "Does anyone have any idea just how much money we have to raise to, well, stop whatever it is that is going to happen?"

"What is going to happen, Mr. Ken?"

"Well, you know, our fate."

Blank uncomprehending stares. "You wish to stop the fate?"

"I thought that's what this was all about."

They looked puzzled. Lopen Pema shrugged, "But this is the fate."

"Ah, I see. Very good. A philosophical point. It is our 'fate' to raise money to avert a worse possible 'fate.'"

A worse fate? Sister Leonard began to look concerned. I believe she thought I was quite mad. Ray was looking down at the table, repressing a grin.

Wait a minute. Wait just a minute. "Would somebody kindly spell 'fate' for me, please."

"Spell, fate," wondered Sister Leonard. "Mr. Ken, what are you—"

"F-E-T-E," said Ray in a soft but clear voice.

I looked at him. "Oh, you mean a fête." I pronounced it in the softer French style; I was, after all, Canadian. We both began to laugh. "You knew all along," I accused him and he nodded, sputtering, "and you just let me..." We howled some more. The others looked perplexed and when we explained the joke to them, they, too, joined in the laughter, relieved, I think, to discover that I was not becoming mentally unhinged. Thereafter, we all referred to the event as "The Dreadful Fate." However, at the next staff meeting everything changed again, for the principal had a new project in mind.

The principal began by placing a stack of school yearbooks on the staff room table. "These," he informed us," have been sent to me by the principals of five other high schools in Bhutan and I have decided that we, too, shall have a yearbook for Jigme Sherubling."

I felt that this was not the time to remind him that, at the beginning of the school year, he had dismissed the idea of a school yearbook as a waste of time and money; or to remind him just how relieved I was to have been let off the hook this year. For it was not just that the yearbook was a lot of work, it was the fact of having to do it in Khaling. The entire layout had to be done by hand with a blue pencil, rubber cement, and an old Remington typewriter. I had the only decent camera and the film had to be mailed to India for developing. When the negatives and prints came back, the former were so scratched that they looked as if they had been washed in the silty Brahmaputra, as perhaps they had. Then everything had to be neatly bundled up and an Indian teacher had to make the two-day journey to Gauhauti in Assam, to the nearest printer, because a foreigner, like myself, would require a travel permit and that was impossible to obtain in Khaling, since the nearest Indian embassy was in Thimphu. Then in three weeks time, another teacher would go to pick up the finished books and return them to the school. There was no chance to examine proofs and so there were always errors that you just had to live with.

"Mr. Ken, as you have the most experience in these matters, I would like you to be the editor of the yearbook again this year."

All eyes turned to me expectantly. "Well, sir. I would be happy to do as you request. [Grant groaned, disappointed in me, as usual, for acquiescing.] However, it is a little late in the year to be starting a big project like this." I paused doing some rapid calculations in my head. "I will have to have everything ready for the printers by the end of the month, if we hope to have it finished before the students graduate."

The principal waved his hand airily. "Yes, very well."

"And so, I was wondering..." Eyebrows around the table rose in expectation of what would come next. "I was wondering if I could be excused from one of my other duties. Perhaps someone else could chair the fête committee." All eyes swivelled back to the principal. It was like a tennis match. Everyone knew what he was thinking. He didn't want to show weakness and lose face. On the other hand, he desperately wanted a yearbook, and a good one. He didn't want it for the students. He wanted it for himself, for he had realized that a glossy yearbook was an excellent propaganda tool, something to send to his superiors and to those he sought to impress, for our principal was nothing if not ambitious. In the end, cupidity won out.

"Yes, very well, Mr. Ken. You are excused."

And so I was off the hook, and I forgot about the fête as I became immersed in a desperate attempt to throw a yearbook together at the last minute. But fate, or The Fête to be precise, had not finished with me yet.

FOURTEEN

THE ROAD CHANGES EVERYTHING

ONE DAY AS I WAS SITTING IN MY KITCHEN, sipping *ara* and entertaining some of the men from the village, talk fell to the old days. The "old days" in Khaling fell within the realm of most men's experience, since the dividing line between old and new was the creation of the vehicle road. And this, you must realize, was the most significant event to happen in the valley since the subjugation of King Dewa in the seventeenth century.

I asked Old Lungten how long it had taken to get to an outside market before the road.

"First," he explained, "we used to do all of our trade with Tibet, but the Chinese closed that border."

"Still," interrupted Tashi Dorje, "there is some smuggling." He pointed to his high-top canvas runners and my bright red thermos.

"Agreed," said Lungten. "The Chinese make better shoes and thermoses. It is worth paying more for these things. Indian shoes are plastic and give you sores." He looked at his own black slip-on shoes with distaste. "Indian thermoses will not keep things warm. But today most trade is with India."

Each man nodded in agreement as I refilled his wooden cup.

"Before the road," continued Lungten, "it used to take a long time to take your goods to India and return. You went in winter, when the fields were fallow, and it was a long journey."

"How long?"

He thought for a moment. "It was like this. We would get our hair cut before we left. When we returned, it would need to be cut again."

What he described to me was an arduous journey, managing a pack train of mountain ponies and mules over a narrow winding path from mountain to vale, from village to village, until after many days one reached the dusty and alien Indian bazaar in Samdrup Jongkhar. The journey home was equally long, if not longer, for there were many visits to be made and much trading to be done along the way. Lungten's description of this journey set my imagination going. Clearly, he remembered his annual journey as a great adventure, as an epic tale of there and back again. He traded his agricultural produce for salt and manufactured goods. Today you could buy these same things in Khaling, or, for the price of a ticket, ride the bus to Samdrup Jongkhar in a single day.

The coming of the road not only meant that these commercial items were suddenly available in the local shops but that the price was lower, as well. Easy access to inexpensive Indian cloth and kitchenware meant that the local trades (weaving, basket making, and wood turning) were virtually disappearing. The weaving project started by the Santal Mission was a heroic attempt to rescue traditional weaving skills, but the products were non-traditional: table-runners and cushion covers for Western European boutiques. There had been a traditional paper mill in Khaling before my arrival—large heavy sheets of paper were manufactured from the inner bark of the *Daphne bholua* tree—but by the time I arrived the workshop was an empty shed. Also, the itinerant blacksmiths who had once supplied the people of Khaling with their ironware no longer put in their annual appearance.

The road changed not only the local economy but also farming practices. Where barter had once been the norm, now people required cash, so crops were sown that could be turned into ready money and cash cropping was slowly replacing mixed subsistence farming. In Khaling the two main crops were corn (maize), which was grown as animal fodder, as a breakfast and snack food, and as the main ingredient in *ara*; and potatoes, which were grown as a cash crop. When the potatoes were harvested, farmers would pile great pyramids of the tubers on the shoulders of the road. Indian buyers would arrive in their brightly painted trucks and dicker with the farmers for their crop. When a price was agreed upon, money changed hands and the crop was loaded into the back of the truck for the journey south. The danger, as I saw it, was the very real possibility of famine, should the potato crop fail.

Everyone kept a few animals, as well: chickens, for eggs and meat; cattle for milk, cheese, and butter; and pigs, which everyone considered the most succulent of meat—not surprising when you saw how scrawny the cows and chickens were (the drumstick

Processing walnuts.

from a Khaling chicken had something sparrow-like in its proportions)—for their flesh. In the higher pastures there were sheep and *dzo* (a yak/cow crossbreed), but we rarely saw these in the valley. They seemed to belong to the Brokpa, a nomadic people from higher valleys farther east, or at least were cared for by the Brokpa for the wealthier *Khaling-pa*.

There were several stone-walled apple orchards in Khaling Valley, guarded by chained half-wild mastiffs, but the apples that came out of these trees were usually not much larger than crab apples and were often dried for cooking or trade, rather than eaten fresh. In the lower reaches of the valley there were other orchards, as well—walnuts, oranges, plums, and a surprising number of peaches—but I rarely saw their fruits for sale in the local shops. I do not want to give the impression that Khaling was a fruit-growing area. In fact, less than 10 per cent of the households had orchards, the fruit produced was small and tough and, for the most part, was consumed by the families who raised it. For example, 85 per cent of the apple orchards in Khaling contained five trees or fewer.[8] Khaling was too elevated to grow other fruit crops, though wild berries, walnuts, fiddleheads, and mushrooms were harvested in season.

I once went on a mushroom hunt with the dance *lopen* from the school. We climbed high up the mountain into the pine forests near the Holy Lake. He showed me where to find large shiitake-style mushrooms in the shade under the trees. "Only take the small ones," he cautioned me, but I could not see his point when the large mushrooms were as big and thick as sirloin steaks. When I got home I fried up my mushrooms in butter and opened a bottle of beer. They were succulent, but as I savoured them I noticed that there were small white granules in the centres of the mushrooms, like grains of rice. I brought my plate closer to the kerosene lamp and realized with alarm that these white grains were actually maggots. Eat the small ones, he had been trying to tell me in his limited English, the big ones are full of maggots. I, of course, had known better. Still, I reasoned, they were not going to kill me, and I was hungry, so I shrugged and ate them anyway. Washed down with Golden Eagle Beer in the dim light of my kerosene lamp, they were delicious.

Almost every one of the Khaling-pa used firewood for fuel. Only the teachers and missionaries could afford kerosene. But the Khaling-pa were not allowed to cut firewood indiscriminately. All forest belonged to the Crown, and one needed permission to cut down trees for lumber or fuel. Having said this, firewood could be gathered from deadfall, or dead limbs could be pulled down "by hook or by crook" as in medieval England. The average householder had to walk one to three hours to reach their source of firewood. This, as you can imagine, took a great deal of time.

In Bhutan, 93.8 per cent of the population was engaged in agriculture and yet only 3.4 per cent of the land area was arable and only 6.4 per cent was suitable for pasture.[9] The rest was forest, rock, and snow. In Khaling, as far as I could see, all of the good land was under cultivation. A few desperate souls were practising slash-and-burn-style agriculture on a steep slope on the far side of the valley near the weaving project. By the summer of 1987 a large bare patch of nearly vertical earth had been exposed, like a large scab in the shape of the continent of Africa. The second summer, after the monsoon had washed away most of the previous year's work, the opening in the forest had grown by half again. At this rate, whole mountainsides, whole watersheds, would vanish. Most farms in Khaling were small, two hectares (five acres) or less, but almost all were owned by the families that farmed them. Only a few of the larger landowners could afford to employ farm labourers.

There were no tractors in Khaling; all ploughing was done with teams of oxen. Given the nature of the terrain and the small landholdings, I doubt that tractors will ever be practical in Khaling Valley in any case. Oxen make more sense. They can be shared by the community and the manure can be used to fertilize the fields. The team that ploughed all of the fields around the Gompa was very mismatched—the Laurel and Hardy of the oxen world (one stood at least a foot higher at the shoulder than the

Rice harvest.

other)—but the fields weren't all that big, so the agony wasn't prolonged. Most of my neighbours used farmyard manure to fertilize their fields, but the use of urea fertilizer was becoming more common. A study published in 2000 showed that 90 per cent of the *Khaling-pa* were using urea fertilizer on their corn. In that same study, farmers reported that the chief problem they faced was animal depredation, which explains why, when crops grew ripe, you would see little watchtowers spring up in fields all over Khaling Valley. Family members would occupy these towers in turns, guarding the crops by throwing stones at unwanted grazers, such as monkeys, wild boar, and deer.

All farms have large kitchen gardens. The most common crops are garlic, onions, chili, sag (a leafy vegetable like chard), and enormous radishes, which look like oversize albino carrots. Small quantities of beans, peas, eggplant, cabbage, tomato, and carrots are also grown, but on the whole the diet is very monotonous: meat, radish, and chili served on a plate of rice—the rice, of course, imported, since there are only 9.7 hectares (24 acres) of paddy in the whole valley, not enough to supply every belly.

That the Bhutanese have supported large families on such small plots of land successfully for hundreds, if not thousands, of years may seem remarkable to us in the West, where larger highly mechanized farms have become the norm. But the Bhutanese model is very successful, and experience has shown that small family-owned plots of land are more productive than larger agribusiness models. Small farmers realize that their health and the health of their land depend upon good farming practices. Subsistence farmers realize that their farms are their survival and that of generations to come. Everything that can be done to conserve soil and keep it healthy is done. A great deal of knowledge about their land is accumulated and passed down from one generation to the next. And when I say that most farms in Khaling contain less than two hectares (five acres) of land, I do not necessarily mean that it is all of one piece. A family farm may consist of several plots of land, each in a different agricultural zone: some high-altitude pasture; some mid-range cropland in small walled semi-terraces suitable for potatoes; and some tropical bottomland, suitable for small orchards or rice paddy. Each zone requires specialized knowledge, and each plot of land exhibits its own peculiarities complicated by the mountain micro-climates. One field may have more frost-free days than another. A plot of land on one side of the valley will receive more rain than a plot of land at the same elevation on the other side. In contrast, slash-and-burn agriculture, called *tseri* or *pangshing*, as practised by the landless rural poor, shows no such concern for the long-term health of the soil. Once the soil is exhausted or washed away, a new section of the forest wall is opened up. Anyone who says that there is no connection between population growth and hunger need only look to Bhutan to see the lie of that statement.

One wonders how things will continue. With the introduction of a cash economy, the encouragement of monoculture over mixed farming, the use of chemical fertilizers and the growth of slash-and-burn-style agriculture, will the 94 per cent of the population who earn their living in agriculture continue to do so? My students would not go back to the farm, in fact we had taught them to devalue the work that goes on there. What will be substituted for a life based on the health of the soil? Tourism, perhaps? A view of the land, not as a way of life, but as a "landscape," a commodity that can be sold to wealthy Westerners with video cameras? It is a short step from this to the corresponding view of culture as commodity, where the annual *tsetchu* becomes a cultural show put on by professional dancers for the benefit of paying tourists.

This may seem like a long digression, but the truth is that it remains to be seen what the future of Bhutanese agriculture will be. Things are only starting to change. It seems to me that the current models are still the best: small family-owned farms under intensive cultivation but with environmentally sensitive farming practices. No one will ever get rich in this manner, so how do you convince people of the value of preserving their own rural culture at the expense of their pocketbook? If you try to legislate tradition, as the Bhutanese are doing in the matter of national dress, you are only admitting defeat.

The other question is this: Is it possible to introduce certain good practices from a foreign culture without introducing all of that other cultural baggage as well? I and other observers have noted that changes in farming practices create subtle changes in community relations, as well. In the past, such large-scale and labour-intensive operations as planting, harvesting, threshing, and the construction of houses, walls, and irrigation channels were communal activities, with the whole village pitching in to help. But with the shift from mixed subsistence farming to cash cropping, the impulse for community cooperation seems to have diminished. Let us hope that such values as family farming, neighbourliness, thrift, craftsmanship, and spirituality are not supplanted by profit. The farms of Khaling are not profitable, but the rich rural culture they support is irreplaceable.

FIFTEEN

THE HOLY LAKE

AS MUCH AS I ENJOYED LIVING IN KHALING, learning the customs of the country, or teaching in the school, my greatest joy was to pack a rucksack and, by myself, set off and explore the hills; for Bhutan is, of all the places I have ever visited, the most wonderful for walking. Hiking in those mountains was a constant delight. Every turn in the trail, every mountain pass crossed, opened onto new vistas; each new valley explored was a new world. It was a place where the works of man and the world of nature seemed to live in delicate balance.[10] There was no noise, but that of bird song, falling water, and the bawl of cattle. There were no billboards, no traffic jams, no parking lots or shopping malls, just the clean pine-scented air, a good trail, and fellow travellers who were welcome because you encountered them so infrequently. The greatest joy, I must admit, was the solitude. I had these mountains, these temples and villages, these forests and their denizens—the barking deer, the bears, the monkeys, the brightly coloured pheasants, the prehistoric-looking hornbills, the chattering mynahs, and the enormous iridescent butterflies—all to myself. The hordes that desecrated Nepal, that littered the Annapurna Circuit with the detritus of their civilization, had not discovered these hills, yet.

The most wonderful thing was that I walked in a country whose citizens understood the joys I felt in the wonders of the trail. When you met a fellow traveller on the trail, he wouldn't ask you about your health or wish you a good day, he would ask you where you were going. "O dele?" he would say—or in my case, because I was a lopen and a foreigner, he might use a more polite form of address and ask, "O jonme?" The wonder of the situation was that it was perfectly respectable to reply, "Korbe dele." Just roaming. People did that here, just went for a walk; maybe they would visit a friend in another village or stop to pick berries or flowers, or perhaps they would just sit on a ridge and watch the shadows of the clouds cross the mountains.

Not that there weren't other forms of recreation. You could drop in at a neighbour's house and sit a spell, sip tea, and gossip. There were archery contests and a game like lawn darts called *korla* that was very popular. Gambling was endemic and so was drinking the homebrewed corn liquor and barley beer. But those were communal activities. If you wanted to get off by yourself, you need only pick a direction. There was a vast network of trails to choose from depending on your mood: perhaps a ramble down the valley through a patchwork of paddies might suit your fancy; or, if you were feeling contemplative, a climb to a mountain pass, there to rest on the base of a stone *chorten* under the crisp snap of prayer flags; or, if you felt you needed to justify your leisure, you might take a stealthy journey through an ancient forest and pick leafy mushrooms for your supper. You could skip over streams that had never drunk the poisons of DDT, or duck under moss-covered branches that had never heard the whine of a chainsaw, or steal upon glades resplendent with orchids that had never known the indignity of a camera.

But how can I share this with you? You would have to see it, smell the wood smoke, taste the air; and even then you might not see it as I do. You might notice the mud and the dirty rags people wore; you might find your gorge rise over the smell of dung and unwashed bodies; and you might choke and cough in the smoke-filled kitchens. You might be put off by the pink eye, the lice, the fleas, and the rats. You might see the evidence of disease and poverty and seek to give my neighbours better lives. And who would say that you were wrong? Who can properly judge these things?

Follow me in your mind's eye, then, and we will take a journey of a half-a-day's hard walking to the most sacrosanct spot in my valley: *Dunglingtso*, the Holy Lake. It is a bright November day, the sky is a brilliant robin's egg blue with only a scattering of clouds; the trails are dry and hard-packed. We begin in my village and put on our best walking shoes, perhaps a pair of Chinese high-top runners purchased in the bazaar, for our boots gave way long ago to monsoon rot and the voracious rats. We've packed a thermos of tea, some Gluco biscuits, an Amul chocolate bar, and some beef jerky to keep us going, snapped all together in a straw *bangchung*, the Tupperware of Bhutan. We have put a sweater and windbreaker in our pack, as well, for it will get cold at the higher elevations when the perspiration begins to cool on our limbs. Let's begin. First, circumambulate the sacred cypress by the *gompa* for good luck; then follow a reasonably level path across grassy pastures up the valley toward the source of the Jeri Chhu.

As we walk along the side of the mountain, the valley floor slowly rises up to meet us. As the two lines converge, the valley narrows and the forests close in on either side. By the time we reach the river, we find ourselves walking beneath enormous ancient oaks whose canopy casts the trail in shadow. High in the mossy branches, we see the stark black-and-white coats of a family of common langurs, which watch our passage with suspicion. There are orchids dangling from the boles of the trees, whose tubers, I am sorry to say, are considered delicacies by the local people. The river is running low, but the reason for that will soon become apparent. It seems we are not quite done with civilization, yet.

We come upon a trench weir, a great pit in the bed of the river covered with steel grating. This weir has been constructed as part of a small hydro-electrical plant to supply electricity to Khaling and neighbouring valleys. When the floodgates are open, this weir redirects the water through a canal that runs along the side of the mountain to a small reservoir the size of a backyard swimming pool. From here the water roars down the slope through twin pipes to two turbines in a brick powerhouse that produces the valley's electricity. The system was introduced the second year of my tenure in Khaling, and it quickly revolutionized life in the valley. That first night the power was turned on, the villagers gasped in awe as their valley sparkled with points of light to rival the night sky for beauty. People who had always barred their doors with the setting of the sun against the demons of the night, found themselves staying up to ten or eleven o'clock at night, and at long last the clock time we had been teaching their children at the school made sense. Suddenly every home had a transistor radio where there had only been a few before. Pop music, Hindi film songs, and Bhutanese folk songs blared out of ornate window slits from cracked speaker cones. One local entrepreneur even opened up a video parlor in an empty room in the bazaar. A nightly showing of old Westerns from the US, kung fu flicks from Hong Kong, and Hindi musicals became very popular. I once paid my ten rupees out of curiosity and watched a Bollywood production where, in the final scene, the hero and heroine dance their way across a gory battlefield, singing a nasal duet, and capping the bad guys with shiny automatics. My neighbours watched in fascination, chewing betel nut absent-mindedly, as trucks exploded and dying soldiers writhed in agony to the frantic beat of the tabla. These gentle people, who hadn't witnessed violent death in more than three hundred years, couldn't seem to get enough of this stuff. Soon there was a new game in the bazaar called "war." Fond parents watched in tolerant amusement as their children waved crooked twigs at each other and mimicked death. The video parlor was short-lived, however. The shopkeeper had hardwired the vcr directly into the power line running past his shop and one day a power surge brought the whole enterprise to a satisfactorily flaming conclusion. However, I digress. Once past the weir, it is easy to put the twenty-first century and its complications behind us.

As the trail slowly rises, following the course of the now-tumbling river, the spirit lifts. Song is called for. My favourite is an old Hank Williams standard. (Yodeling and mountains have a natural affinity, after all.) You are welcome to join in, if you know the tune. Ahem:

I got a feelin' called the blu-ues, oh, lawd,

Since my baby said good-bye

An' I don't know what I'll do-oo-oo,

All I do is sit and sigh-igh, oh, lawd.

Then, inevitably, it happens. It always happens. We will round a corner on the path and there he'll be, a young shepherd with eyes like Little Orphan Annie's and a flock of hysterical sheep trying to fling themselves over a cliff. We feel like idiots but try to bluff it out anyway. We wish him a hearty good day—"Kuzu zangpo-la! O jonme?"—not really expecting a reply. He doesn't disappoint, remaining non-responsive, slack-jawed, and goggle-eyed as he follows our burning necks as we stiffly retreat up the trail, out of sight. You find it hard to stand on your dignity for long, however. For by now you have savoured the unique acoustical properties of these mountains and we experiment with another yodel or two. No wonder the normally dour Swiss have such idiotic folk customs. This is fun.

The valley narrows now until it becomes a gorge, and then we begin to climb a steep incline. The river has become quite shallow again, and we ford it on a series of flat stones. Once across, the trail begins to loop back on itself in an endless series of switchbacks. Gradually, we climb out of the gloom of the forest and into steep pastureland. Then we are above the canopy looking down. We continue to climb until we reach a false summit where a flotilla of prayer flags wave listlessly in the breeze. We are out of breath and our legs are beginning to feel like rubber. As my students would say, "They are paining." It is a good place to take a break. We are now above the few clouds that scatter across the foreground, and from this peak the whole of Khaling Valley unfolds before us. We can see the patchwork of fields, the tiny white villages, the flash of the meandering young river where it catches the sun, the school and its dormitories, and the thin black loop that is the road, where we can trace the ant-like progress of the Pema Transport Bus. The hills are drab in November, but if this were March, this muted palette of brown grass, grey stone, and bare earth would be splashed with patches of vermilion as the rhododendrons burst into bloom. Still, you can't beat this view—at any season of the year. It is time for some of those biscuits and a cup of tea, possibly also time to pull on a sweater. It is also a good time to reflect on our destination.

Dunglingtso, literally translated, means "holy lake." It is the home of Meme Dungling, or the "Holy Old Man." He is the guardian spirit of our valley. In the winter, he travels far afield, and each spring there is a *pujah* at the lake to entice his spirit to return, to insure adequate rainfall and a good harvest. There are many stories associated with this benevolent old man. See those great boulders down there to our right? Those are said to be his shot puts. Shot putting with large stones is a popular test of strength in this country. And see that gouge cut into the mountainside there? That was caused one day when Meme Dungling was putting a shot and slipped down the mountain. That trench, they say, was carved by his heel as he struggled to regain his balance. And there, near the village of Bramang, are three large stones arranged in a perfect equilateral triangle. Those are said to be the fireplace where Meme Dungling cooked his lunch while travelling. Nearby is the crooked tree from which he tethered his horse while he rested.

There are other legends, as well. In the farthest distance, raised from the valley on a small plateau, sits the haunted village of Deiwoong, only recently resettled, where the ploughs turn up mysterious lumps of corroded iron, dropped, legend has it, from the *namdrung*, the ship of the sky. I think it is more likely that Deiwoong is the site of an ancient battle. This would account for the legends of ghosts that haunt the place and the scattered bits of metal found in the soil. We can see my village, Khaling Gompa, looking remarkably small—the giant cypress, a mere smudge of green at this distance. And somewhere down there are the ruins of King Dewa's Palace for which I have hunted in vain on many a memorable afternoon. But where is it? That may remain a mystery and with it any conclusive proof that King Dewa did exist. Enough rest. It is time to move on before we grow too stiff.

The climb is now less steep. We follow a ridgeline and enter a pine forest. Here the trail narrows in places and becomes quite treacherous. Under the shade of the pine boughs, the trail is occasionally covered in ice. In other places, we have to climb giant stone steps, also black with ice, or follow narrow paths along the faces of sheer precipices whose depths are masked in cloud. Eventually we ascend to a rocky saddle where nothing grows. Here, the ground is strewn with thousands of boulders all tumbled together. It is a good place to turn an ankle if we are not careful. Here, too, the trail forks: to the left and up the mountain lie the road to Mera and the valleys of the Brokpa; to the right, down a short slope, and hidden in a vale of pines is our destination: *Dunglingsto*.

The Holy Lake is set in vast bowl of jumbled grey stone. It is one of the favourite pastimes of the idle in Khaling to turn amateur geologist over a peg of rum and to speculate about the lake's formation and the source of its waters. Some maintain it is volcanic in origin and that the water begins deep underground as hot springs. Others say it was formed by an earthquake or by glacial activity. Some contend that the water comes from artesian springs or from a subterranean river. Still others say that the lake has no outlet and it is simply a catch basin for snowmelt and the monsoon rains (my pet theory). To the more devout, of course, such speculations are irrelevant; it is the home of a god. All I know is that each spring, after a long dry winter, the monks file up the mountain to the lake, make *pujah* to entice the god to return, and, shortly thereafter, the monsoon rains come and the lake is full once again.

I have been to the lake several times and each time it seems a different place. I have seen it in the spring when I attended the *pujah*, when it was almost empty. I have also seen it in the summer monsoon, after climbing through the dripping jungle and scraping so many leeches off my legs that they bled bright streams, when it was full to the brim, like a bowl of leek soup ready to overflow. I think it is most memorable as we see it today, in the fall, when the water level has dropped just a little to expose a layer of tumbled grey boulders arranged about the lake like the cracked seats in an ancient Roman amphitheatre. The twisted pines, thickly draped with Spanish moss, close in tight about the lake. The kidney-shaped lake has a great pulpit-like rock standing on the inside bend. The air in the valley is deathly still. The lake is a perfect mirror, so calm in fact, that if you had taken a photo of it at that moment and shown it to me later, I couldn't have told you which end was up.

The lake has an aura. Poets speak of the genius of a place, the *genius loci*, and I think we can feel it here; for some places in the world have a transcendent quality, where the line between what is real and what is Real becomes very thin, and we are allowed a glimpse beyond the tattered veil. Here, for centuries, men and women have felt the power of this place and have been drawn to worship. It is an archetype—the holy lake, the sacred grove—of all early cultures. Druids would have felt at home here. Wordsworth would have had one of his tiresome epiphanies. It is a dark place, surrounded by the musky procreative scent of the jungle, primeval, where an older

The Holy Lake.

earthier god is worshipped, not Lord Buddha. Meme Dungling is no doubt a hold-over, an earlier shamanistic deity, who preceded and was absorbed into the Buddhist pantheon.

There is time for some quiet reflection before we descend once again to the trou-bled life of the valley floor. It is traditional to circumambulate the lake three times for luck, and I will wait here and finish my tea, if you choose to venture forth. It's a tough scramble. Most people give up after one turn. Before we depart, it is customary to leave an offering. In the spring, supplicants bring sprigs of blood-red rhododendron and place them on the surface of the lake. Failing that, we might pin a grubby *ngultrum* note to a broad leaf and set it adrift like a tiny boat. Then, we must go. Take one more look around, fix the place in our memory for when we are too old and too frail to climb mountains, and depart.

SIXTEEN

SNAKES, PARASITES,
AND OTHER NEIGHBOURS

THE DAY STARTED BADLY. The always temperamental kerosene stove refused to light until I had disassembled it and trimmed all of its twenty-five wicks. Then, while it sputtered and smoked, the tea kettle boiled over, filling the kitchen with the aroma of burned sugar. Already late and flustered, I could not get my rebel *gho* to cooperate, and it steadfastly refused to conform to its accustomed shape. I gave up, slung my *jola* over my shoulder, and ran out of the kitchen and down the stone steps in disarray. I turned the corner and put my foot in a bucket of water. *Jettah!*

Ever since the monsoon mud had clogged the village's makeshift water main, I had been forced to collect water by lining up buckets and pots beneath the drip line on my roof. It worked surprisingly well, but now I had a soaker and I was late for school. I removed my suede shoes, wrung out my socks and looked around for something to wear. My eye fell on my leather hiking boots—rat-chewed and rotting, but still miraculously holding together—and I laced them on. A few moments later I was glad that I had.

For the second time I flew out of the house and raced down the mountain path toward the school, *gho* ballooning about my knees. I saw something slither onto the path in front of me and froze, poised on one foot like the principal dancer in a Russian ballet.

There are a lot of snakes in Khaling, and a number of them are poisonous. My neighbours, on the whole, distrusted all snakes. I remember once walking down the valley with two men and casually pointing out a snake that was sunning itself on a low wall beside the path. The first man shrieked and ran away. The second whipped out his *chhowang* and quickly turned the snake into sushi.

"Was it a dangerous snake?" I asked.

"All snakes are dangerous," was his grim reply.

I knew this was not the case; nevertheless, only a few days before, my students and I had come across a dead viper on the road. The boys used a stick to pry open the snake's jaws and, retracting a delicate membrane of skin, showed me the enormous fangs which arched toward the back of the snake's throat. What were the odds? I wondered, as I twisted awkwardly on one foot, trying to see the thrashing serpent that was pinned beneath the instep of my hiking boot. Rusty brown with a large diamond-shaped head: a Himalayan pit viper. Great.

I was in a bind. As long as I remained motionless I was fine. The snake could not raise its head high enough to bite me, but how long could I remain perched on one foot, especially with the heavy satchel of notebooks throwing me off balance? I decided to jump. I slid the *jola* down my arm and wrapped the strap tightly around my wrist. Then I swung my free leg forward with as much force as I could muster and leapt. Fear gave me wings. When I hit the ground I did not look back but ran as fast as my legs would carry me down the hill.

The presence of snakes seemed to be seasonal. In the winter, we never saw them (no doubt they were snug in their hibernacula), but during the monsoon, we saw dozens. Of course, the monsoon also drew the leeches out of hiding. Where they resided the rest of the year was a mystery. By July and August the grass in the pasture behind the school was up to my chest, and picking up a leech on my way to school was not a probability during the monsoon, but a certainty. It was no longer a matter of "if," but of "how many." I kept a coffee can of coarse salt by my back door, and as soon as I returned home each day I would take off my shoes and socks, find the leeches, and apply a pinch of salt to each. They would fall to the floor, twisting in agony.

There were two kinds of leeches in Khaling. The most common were tiny black leeches, no larger than paperclips, which moved inchworm style across your shoes and socks until they could find an opening onto bare flesh. The second kind of leech was much larger, mustard-coloured, with black pinstripes along the length of its body. These leeches could be as large as your thumb and, when engorged, swelled to the size of Havana cigars. I never had the misfortune of being attacked by one of these, but I remember that the village cattle suffered greatly from them. I saw cows with multiple leeches attached to their necks, bellies, and thighs; and I once even saw a poor cross-eyed beast with one of these monster leeches filling up the space between her eyes.

We had other parasites, too, a whole catalogue of unpleasant gastrointestinal critters. Once, in the staffroom, Wangpo was passing the tea tray around, and my hand froze halfway to the cup. A pinworm, as small and as fine as a human hair, writhed on the surface of the tray.

"Sir?"

"Uhh, on second thought, Wangpo, thanks, but I'm not that thirsty today."

"La-so."

It never paid to look too closely at the latrine in the dormitories, either. We had periodic visits from the mission doctors to dose the students for worms. After one such treatment, a group of boys approached me, bursting with news.

"Sir! Sir! You will never believe what we are telling you!" I bit. "Pushpa is having five different kinds of worms! Five!" They slapped their skeletal friend on the back, and he grinned as proudly as if he'd just won the Boston Marathon.

Dogs were also a problem. Pariah dogs were a fixture of life in Khaling and they were dangerous because they were so unpredictable. The same dog that licked your hand one day might bite it the next. Pariah (or pye-) dogs were not wild and they were not pets; they fell somewhere in between, like cockroaches and rats—animals that were comfortable in a human environment but not wanted. I remember that during that second monsoon I not only had to deal with leeches and snakes in the pasture behind the school, but also an elderly mongrel bitch with sagging dugs that looked a bit like that famous Roman bronze of the she-wolf that suckled Romulus and Remus. She had scraped out a den for her litter beneath a large boulder behind the girls' dormitory, and every day on my way to and from school she came roaring out of the tall grass, fangs bared and hackles raised, ready to sink her teeth into my calf muscles as I raced by. No one was happier than I when those puppies were weaned.

I observed that children in Khaling learned to throw stones at stray dogs before they learned to wipe their noses (and their noses ran continuously from the moment of birth until about the age of four). This was a survival tactic. I also noticed that when one threw a stone, one shouted, "Koo!" in a very loud voice. Koo means "dog." Why one should shout, "dog!" when one wants the dog to go away, I don't know. No one could ever explain the logic of this to me.

My most frightening encounter with dogs happened right behind the classrooms. I was supposed to be supervising lunch but was running late, so I decided that, rather than taking the steps, I would take the shortcut up the hill behind the classrooms, across the second soccer pitch, and up the next rise to the dining hall. It may have been the flapping skirts of my *gho* that attracted them or my pale bony legs, but halfway across the soccer field I found myself surrounded by a snarling pack of pariah dogs—the same outfit that skulked around the kitchen looking for scraps. I am not sure why they attacked me—the behaviour of feral dogs is, as I've said, fairly unpredictable—but I am guessing that my helpless condition was fairly irresistible after years of being put upon by fickle students.

A group of students waiting outside the dining hall had seen my predicament and started shouting advice: "Suuur! Suuuur!"

The students were frantically waving and yelling, but they were too far away for me to hear them clearly. The fact that they were all shouting at once did not help either, and there were far too many distractions to really focus on what they were saying—nine distractions, to be precise, which were reducing my knee socks to ribbons. My attention was focussed on the circle of snapping teeth and raised hackles, which I was feebly trying to fend off with my furled umbrella. I kept spinning around, slashing and jabbing, but meeting only empty air.

"Sir! Sick and alone! Sick and alone!"

Sick and alone? Who was sick and alone? And why were they trying to tell this to me now? Wait, no, it wasn't "sick and alone," it was:

"Dig up a bone! Sir! Dig up a bone!"

Dig up a bone? A bone would have been helpful right about now, but how was I to dig up a bone with nine dogs trying to nip my nether parts?

"Sir! Sir! Pick up the phone"

What? Pick up the phone? What phone? There were no phones in Khaling. Ouch! I stabbed with the steel ferrule of my umbrella but met only turf where seconds before a dog had been clamped on my ankle. Damn, they were quick. As fast as I parried, they moved faster. I could only guess that this animosity came from years of serving as targets for hurled stones. Now they had an opportunity for taking revenge on all of humankind in the person of this lone outnumbered clumsy *philing-pa*. If only I had a stone.

A stone.

"Sir! Pick up a stone!"

Of course.

No sooner had the thought entered my head then the dogs turned tail and were gone. Just the act of stooping over was enough to scare them off.

The monsoon brought other, more welcome, visitors, too. There were lots of songbirds and butterflies. Karin once found a remarkable moth attached to her curtains. It was iridescent, with a peacock colouration, and large as a dinner plate. I had never seen a larger or more beautiful moth.

One night while I was marking, I heard a scratching and scrabbling on the shutters. At first I thought that it might be a rat trying to get in, but there was something more metallic about the sound. Curious, I slid open the shutter and in flew an enormous stag beetle, attracted by the light. He circled the bare bulb several times before he came to rest on my kitchen counter. He was as large as my hand, his armour black and glistening, his pincers large and deadly like those of an alien villain in a science fiction film. I kept him in a bucket for several days before my conscience got the better of me, and I reluctantly let him go.

Another day a similar rustling also set me searching, but this time the sound seemed to come from within one of the walls of my bedroom. I listened carefully, moving slowly along the wall, until I located the source of the sound on a spot high above my desk. There was a band of moulding around the room, just below the ceiling. This decoration consisted of a series of flat rectangles, each the size of a paperback novel. These panels were staggered, with one panel flush against the wall and the next slightly protruding in a dentil band. The sound, which had now stopped, was coming from behind one of these small panels. I climbed on the small table that served as my desk and, with my fingernails, carefully prised the panel from the wall. I was surprised to discover a hollow space behind. In this little niche was a nest of grass and twigs cupping three small eggs. Beyond the nest was a small opening to the outside, pecked from rotting wood under the eaves. I carefully replaced the panel and over the next few weeks, checked it frequently when I was certain that the parents were not around. Then one morning I awoke to the sound of chirping voices. For several weeks I was able to check surreptitiously on the young birds' progress. They were swallows. Each day I would race home after school and inspect my growing family. I can't tell you how much I looked forward to this. And then one day the nest was silent, and they were gone.

Of course, the monsoon rains also brought lush growth. The narrow fenced lanes of Khaling Gompa, which in the dry season were open and airy with hard-packed earth underfoot, became muddy gullies in the monsoon, roofed over with willow coppice sprouting from the tops of the fence posts. The path to my house became so close and overgrown with weeds that I felt like a jungle explorer stumbling upon the ruins of Chich'en Itza each time I came home. The corn in the field around my home grew so tall that—well, forget this business about being "as high as an elephant's eye"; you

Boys clearing weeds around my house.

could hide an entire elephant in my cornfield! One Sunday a group of my students came up to the Gompa for a visit. These boys were so appalled at the condition of my yard that they scoured the village for sickles and insisted on chopping down the undergrowth around my house. When they reached the outhouse, they paused.

"Does Sir wish us to cut down this tree?" one of them asked. He was pointing at a massive shrub, at least four metres (13 feet) high, growing beside the outhouse door.

He looked uneasy. "We know that some foreigners are liking this plant. Is Sir perhaps liking this plant?"

"Lord, no!" I said. "By all means, chop it down and burn it!"

A moment later I added, "But stay clear of the smoke, okay?"

They laughed.

I should explain: marijuana grows wild throughout the Himalayas, where it is a common shrub. Surprisingly, while the Bhutanese are aware of the plant's hallucinogenic properties, they do not use it. Instead, they feed it to their pigs. The pigs grow placid and hungry. Fat happy pigs. In Sharchopkha, marijuana is actually called, *phagpa-to*. Pig food.

The coming of the monsoon also brought illness, as water sources became polluted with muddy run-off. Two of the Canadian volunteers became very ill and had to be hospitalized in Tashigang. One had contracted hepatitis and was the colour of a dandelion. The other had typhoid fever complicated with amoebic dysentery. As they had no family to look after them, other volunteers took turns in the role of caregiver. It was during my watch that it was decided that these two needed to be evacuated to Thimphu. Howard wired that the road was out below Thumsing-La again, but that he would drive to one side of the rockslide and that we should meet him on the other side. We would then arrange to have the patients transferred over the rockslide, and he would drive them to Thimphu. The district education officer lent us his car and driver. The car was an Indian Fiat, narrow and boxy, a throwback to European car styles of the 60s. Pietie, a Dutch nurse from Tashigang, accompanied us on the journey. She dubbed the ancient car "The Cookie Box." We spent the first night in the Mongar guesthouse.

That day near the border of Nepal and the Indian state of Bihar an earthquake struck, registering 6.6 on the Richter scale. The earthquake and the subsequent flooding that followed, when a river embankment was breached, took a huge toll of life, close to 1,000 deaths and some 15,000 people injured. Even in Bhutan the earthquake still had enough force to throw me out of my bed in the guesthouse.

The news from Bihar would strike Bhola the hardest. His wife was in Bihar, expecting another child and staying with his family. Bhola had innocently thought that, for her confinement, she would be safer and more comfortable in Bihar than in Khaling. As the news reports came in with the mounting death toll, Bhola became frantic. The disaster had cut off all communication to the region and after several weeks with no word of his family, Bhola asked the principal for leave to return home.

As the months passed and we received no word from Bhola, rumours began to circulate that he, too, had died. Some said he had drowned in the flood trying to reach his family. Others that he had taken his own life when he discovered that his family had perished. In time, these rumours took on the authority of truth. "Perhaps" became "likely" became "probably." Soon, we began speaking of Bhola in the past tense, as in "Alas, poor Bhola, we knew him well." Everyone agreed: It was sad, but undeniable—Bhola was dead. Of course, Bhola was not dead. We should have known better. Bhola was a resurrectionist. But that is another story.[11]

In Mongar, we had no idea of the scale of the disaster. We bashed on regardless, journeying with our charges on a road that slowly deteriorated. Twice we had to stop and drag fallen trees from across the road. Once we had to roll huge boulders off the road and send those bouncing down the mountainside. The streams coming down from the mountains were so swollen with rain that many were flowing over the road rather than through the culverts underneath. In some places the surface of the road was actually washed away. Just before the rockslide, a river had gouged the road so deeply that the car got stuck halfway across the watercourse and water started flowing in under the doors. We rolled up our trousers and waded across the river, ferrying our patients and their baggage to the far side of the washout, slipping on the loose stones that rolled beneath our feet in the swift current. Pietie lost one of her sandals as we were wading through the rushing torrent and we watched, with grim fascination, as it bobbed along, hesitated on the crest and then fell into the abyss. The two sick volunteers were in no shape for a long hike, they looked as gaunt and jaundiced as mummies, but we seemed to have no choice. The car would not travel an inch farther.

We had just transferred the luggage across the washout when the public bus appeared. We flagged it down. The bus was crammed with passengers and the khalasi protested that there was no more room. We finally persuaded him to allow our two patients to stand just inside the doorway, with him on the step outside holding everybody in like a human bungee cord. Pietie and I hefted the luggage and followed on foot. The driver said he would stay with the car, turn it around, and wait for our return. The distance to the rockslide was not more than a kilometre. When we caught up with the bus, it had halted where the road came to an abrupt end. About three hundred metres farther on the road began again, and in between was a sheer slope of loose scree. To reach the other side, passengers had to climb up to a ridge above the rockslide, walk along the ridge, and then descend steeply to where the road began again

months passed and we received no word from Bhola, rumours began to circu-
[...] he, too, had died. Some said he had drowned in the flood trying to reach his
[...] Others that he had taken his own life when he discovered that his family had
[...]. In time, these rumours took on the authority of truth. "Perhaps" became
[...] became "probably." Soon, we began speaking of Bhola in the past tense, as
[...] poor Bhola, we knew him well." Everyone agreed: It was sad, but undeni-
[...]ola was dead. Of course, Bhola was not dead. We should have known better.
[...]s a resurrectionist. But that is another story.[11]

[...]ongar, we had no idea of the scale of the disaster. We bashed on regard-
[...]eying with our charges on a road that slowly deteriorated. Twice we had to
[...]drag fallen trees from across the road. Once we had to roll huge boulders
[...]d and send those bouncing down the mountainside. The streams coming
[...] the mountains were so swollen with rain that many were flowing over
[...]ther than through the culverts underneath. In some places the surface of
[...]s actually washed away. Just before the rockslide, a river had gouged the
[...]ly that the car got stuck halfway across the watercourse and water started
[...]nder the doors. We rolled up our trousers and waded across the river,
[...] patients and their baggage to the far side of the washout, slipping on
[...]nes that rolled beneath our feet in the swift current. Pietie lost one of her
[...]e were wading through the rushing torrent and we watched, with grim
[...]s it bobbed along, hesitated on the crest and then fell into the abyss.
[...]volunteers were in no shape for a long hike, they looked as gaunt and
[...]ummies, but we seemed to have no choice. The car would not travel an

[...]st transferred the luggage across the washout when the public bus
[...]lagged it down. The bus was crammed with passengers and the khalasi
[...]here was no more room. We finally persuaded him to allow our two
[...]d just inside the doorway, with him on the step outside holding every-
[...]uman bungee cord. Pietie and I hefted the luggage and followed on
[...]said he would stay with the car, turn it around, and wait for our return.
[...]he rockslide was not more than a kilometre. When we caught up with
[...]alted where the road came to an abrupt end. About three hundred
[...]n the road began again, and in between was a sheer slope of loose
[...]e other side, passengers had to climb up to a ridge above the rock-
[...]the ridge, and then descend steeply to where the road began again

curtains. It was iridescent, with a peacock colouration, and large as a dinner plate. I had never seen a larger or more beautiful moth.

One night while I was marking, I heard a scratching and scrabbling on the shutters. At first I thought that it might be a rat trying to get in, but there was something more metallic about the sound. Curious, I slid open the shutter and in flew an enormous stag beetle, attracted by the light. He circled the bare bulb several times before he came to rest on my kitchen counter. He was as large as my hand, his armour black and glistening, his pincers large and deadly like those of an alien villain in a science fiction film. I kept him in a bucket for several days before my conscience got the better of me, and I reluctantly let him go.

Another day a similar rustling also set me searching, but this time the sound seemed to come from within one of the walls of my bedroom. I listened carefully, moving slowly along the wall, until I located the source of the sound on a spot high above my desk. There was a band of moulding around the room, just below the ceiling. This decoration consisted of a series of flat rectangles, each the size of a paperback novel. These panels were staggered, with one panel flush against the wall and the next slightly protruding in a dentil band. The sound, which had now stopped, was coming from behind one of these small panels. I climbed on the small table that served as my desk and, with my fingernails, carefully prised the panel from the wall. I was surprised to discover a hollow space behind. In this little niche was a nest of grass and twigs cupping three small eggs. Beyond the nest was a small opening to the outside, pecked from rotting wood under the eaves. I carefully replaced the panel and over the next few weeks, checked it frequently when I was certain that the parents were not around. Then one morning I awoke to the sound of chirping voices. For several weeks I was able to check surreptitiously on the young birds' progress. They were swallows. Each day I would race home after school and inspect my growing family. I can't tell you how much I looked forward to this. And then one day the nest was silent, and they were gone.

Of course, the monsoon rains also brought lush growth. The narrow fenced lanes of Khaling Gompa, which in the dry season were open and airy with hard-packed earth underfoot, became muddy gullies in the monsoon, roofed over with willow coppice sprouting from the tops of the fence posts. The path to my house became so close and overgrown with weeds that I felt like a jungle explorer stumbling upon the ruins of Chich'en Itza each time I came home. The corn in the field around my home grew so tall that—well, forget this business about being "as high as an elephant's eye"; you

Boys clearing weeds around my house.

could hide an entire elephant in my cornfield! One Sunday a group of my students came up to the Gompa for a visit. These boys were so appalled at the condition of my yard that they scoured the village for sickles and insisted on chopping down the undergrowth around my house. When they reached the outhouse, they paused.

"Does Sir wish us to cut down this tree?" one of them asked. He was pointing at a massive shrub, at least four metres (13 feet) high, growing beside the outhouse door.

He looked uneasy. "We know that some foreigners are liki
liking this plant?"

"Lord, no!" I said. "By all means, chop it down and
A moment later I added, "But stay clear of the smol
They laughed.

I should explain: marijuana grows wild througho
a common shrub. Surprisingly, while the Bhutanese
cinogenic properties, they do not use it. Instead, the
grow placid and hungry. Fat happy pigs. In Sharchopl
phagpa-to. Pig food.

The coming of the monsoon also brought il
polluted with muddy run-off. Two of the Canadian
to be hospitalized in Tashigang. One had contracte
dandelion. The other had typhoid fever complicat
had no family to look after them, other volunteer
It was during my watch that it was decided tha
to Thimphu. Howard wired that the road was
that he would drive to one side of the rockslide
other side. We would then arrange to have the p
and he would drive them to Thimphu. The di
and driver. The car was an Indian Fiat, narro
car styles of the 60s. Pietie, a Dutch nurse fr
journey. She dubbed the ancient car "The Co
Mongar guesthouse.

That day near the border of Nepal an
struck, registering 6.6 on the Richter sc
flooding that followed, when a river emba
life, close to 1,000 deaths and some 15,00
quake still had enough force to throw me

The news from Bihar would strike
expecting another child and staying w
that, for her confinement, she would
in Khaling. As the news reports came
frantic. The disaster had cut off all of
weeks with no word of his family, Bh

As the
late tha
family.
perishe
"likely"
in "Alas
able—Bl
Bhola wa

In M
less, journ
stop and
off the roa
down fron
the road ra
the road wa
road so dee
flowing in
ferrying our
the loose sto
sandals as w
fascination,
The two sick
jaundiced as
inch farther.

We had j
appeared. We
protested that
patients to star
body in like a l
foot. The driver
The distance to
the bus, it had
metres farther o
scree. To reach t
slide, walk along

Washout on road below Mongar.

on the far side. After a little rest, we began to climb over and around the slide. As we ascended, we began to meet people coming the other way who had left a bus waiting on the far side of the slide. This practice of exchanging passengers had become so common on this stretch of road that it even acquired a name: trans-shifting. Near the top of the ridge we met Howard and Françoise on their way to assist us. We helped our friends down to Howard's suv and waved goodbye. In a few months they would make a full recovery and would return to their postings. Not everyone was so lucky.

One of the cooks at my school had an infant son who became ill with diarrhea. The cook hired *powahs*, or witch doctors, to do *pujahs* over the sick child, but to no avail. His friends urged him to take the boy to the mission clinic, but it was not until the boy was beyond hope that, in his desperation, he finally appealed to Western medicine. It was too late and we attended a sad little cremation by the riverbank a few days later. The quickness with which dysentery could kill children was alarming. Even those who applied Western medicine were not always successful.

Sven, the nurse at the mission clinic, lost his daughter that summer, as well. She became ill with vomiting and diarrhea, and a few days later, despite his best efforts, she died. I attended the ceremony in Riserboo, the Santal Mission's main hospital located on a misty saddleback some twenty kilometres (twelve and a half miles) south of Khaling. As the child's body was committed to the ground, I felt an utter desolation of spirits. The mission director said some comforting words about the Resurrection. Sven looked bereft. I had not known him well—he had not really encouraged intimacy—but he seemed genuinely pleased that I had come, and he handed me his camera and asked me to take pictures of the ceremony for the grandparents back in Sweden. I agreed—what could I say, after all—but I have never performed a more awkward duty. I walked around the open grave, snapping photographs as unobtrusively as possible. The Sisters, three from my school and three from the college, perched over the open grave in the swirling mist, heads bowed under black veils and shoulders hunched under black cardigans, like a gathering of hungry crows. One of the other missionaries, a simple person with thick glasses and a rather blank expression, used the ceremony as an opportunity to witness to me.

"Isn't it beautiful?" he said, meeting my eyes with his intense, myopic gaze. "She is with God now, singing with the angels."

"Yes," I replied, tripping the flash in his face. "Smile."

Sven's wife was red-eyed and angry—but whether angry at her husband for bringing their family to Bhutan or angry at God I could not say. Only years later, watching my own daughter—her vulnerability and awkward grace, her fragile beauty and loving kindness—can I imagine the punch in the gut Sven's wife must have been feeling on that day.

The mission had had its share of tragedies in more than a decade of service. In one corner of the courtyard at the school for the blind lay another small grave, the child of the school's first headmaster, marked by a small concrete cross. I never passed this poignant marker without feeling melancholy. There were other tragedies, as well, other kinds of failure.

That spring we had seen the retirement of one of the mission's senior nurses, a hardy woman named Greta, who had worked much of her life in a remote clinic in the valley of Thrimshing, which was the centre of the mission's leprosy work. Her replacement, a young attractive woman, passed through Khaling and we wished her well. She seemed a suitable candidate for such a difficult post—tall, strong, self-assured. Thrimshing was a day's journey off the road and the mission provided her with a riding horse and pack mules to bring in supplies. At first, things seemed to go well. Then disturbing stories began to return from the hinterland. One of the doctors journeyed in to check on the new nurse. When he reached Thrimshing, he found a woman besieged within the stockade of her own mind—quite literally besieged, for she had locked herself into the clinic and had refused to come out. She claimed to have heard voices, demonic voices, which taunted her and would not give her rest. Determining that her breakdown was complete and that no amount of psychiatric counselling was likely to help her, the mission sent her home, a broken woman.

I did not know it then, but within a few weeks I, too, would be travelling to Thrimshing Valley.

SEVENTEEN

DIPLOMATIC DINNERS

WHEN I WAS YOUNG, there were two things that absolutely terrified me: rats and lepers. And this was strange, for I had never met either a rat or a leper outside the pages of a book. Nevertheless, my childhood nightmares were populated with darkened rooms where I was pursued by red-eyed rats and lumbering shadowy figures who sought to clutch me with their fingerless hands. At twenty-six, I may no longer have been a child, but I had not outgrown these childish terrors. Bhutan forced me to confront my fears, and for that I am grateful.

With the Thrimshing mission temporarily abandoned, Mark, a Canadian volunteer in nearby Wamrong Middle School, got permission to hike in and spend a weekend exploring, using the empty missionary quarters as a base of operations. Mark invited Grant and me to accompany him. We set out from Wamrong Bazaar on foot.

Wamrong Bazaar was a curious arrangement of huts balanced on stilts on the downward slope of the road embankment. The first stage of our journey was unpleasant, for the shop owners tossed all of their garbage out their back windows, and so the steep slope below the road was a slippery mess of paper, tins, and rotting food scraps, patrolled by mangy pariah dogs. The school was on a level space below the bazaar—hardly a situation to encourage the public health authorities. We continued down the hill to the river and across a picturesque covered bridge to ascend another ridge before descending into Thrimshing Valley. The clinic was on the far hill. The journey took most of the day, but Mark and Grant kept up a constant and amusing commentary on the passing scene. Mark was one of those people whose wit was equal to any situation, whose utterance was always quotable. (He invented the phrase "dysentery donut" to describe the Tibetan dumplings served in the Khaling Bazaar.)

Soon we arrived in Kangpura Village and Mark produced a key and unlocked the door to the two-storey mission house. The clinic was on the ground floor with living quarters above. Curious neighbours looked in, and we were invited to dinner that night in the village's *lha-kang*.

We set off that evening, climbing a gently rising path to the square temple that occupied a point high above the valley floor, facing the setting sun. We were warmly greeted and bade sit on cushions on the floor. We faced the soft golden light on the hills through the open windows. To our backs, on three walls, sat one hundred Buddhas, meditating in carved wooden niches. Wonderful murals glowed in the smoky half light.

A middle-aged woman approached with a crooked grin and offered me a plate of rice, holding out the plate with two hands. I reached for the plate and hesitated. The woman had no fingers. I looked around the room and quickly noted the scabrous brows, the flattened noses, the stumpy digits. Panic fluttered briefly in my chest like a caged bird, but I was determined not to show bad grace. I took a deep breath and forced a smile.

"*Kading-chhe-la.*"

I reached forward to receive my plate and, to my surprise, the little bird had flown. Thank you, I repeated.

The following day we would visit several more households; each contained at least one person afflicted with leprosy. I found that, after my initial panic, my fear of the disease was gone. In its place, I found a growing sense of admiration for those who suffered stoically from the disease, for the families who offered them support, and for the medical missionaries who had made it their life's work to help the lepers. My own volunteer efforts seemed paltry in comparison.

My second story concerns rats, or, more precisely, how I learned to live with rats, if not exactly love them. It all began on the day that a senior Canadian diplomat came for a picnic.

In November I received a letter from Howard informing me that he would be leading a senior Canadian diplomat and his small entourage on a tour of Eastern Bhutan. Could I arrange a tour of the school and could I host a luncheon in my home? I was told not to worry about supplying the food as the delegation would be well-provisioned by the commissary of the Canadian High Commission in New Delhi.

In Bhutan people take this sort of thing seriously. A state visit, even from a relatively unimportant country like Canada, involved a lot of preparation. Classes would be disrupted. There would be receiving lines, perhaps entertainment provided by the students, and certainly a banquet of some kind. The principal would feel slighted if he were not asked to put on some type of show. For, despite the extra work involved, such a visit was an honour, and these things had to be done right. I knew, however, that my principal would be secretly relieved if he were spared all of the fuss and bother. He couldn't let on, though. I think Howard was sensitive to the slight, but he realized that the diplomat needed a break in his itinerary from banquets of this sort, if only for his digestion's sake. I also think that Howard felt it was a wonderful opportunity for the diplomat to visit a traditional Bhutanese village, without having to risk the traditional Bhutanese diet.

The small committee arrived in two shiny new Toyota Land Cruisers. There was the usual reception line of bowing students pressed, dressed, and sashed, and the principal nervously guided the distinguished guests through the school, not quite sure if he should be praising his own progressive administration or drawing attention to the decay. The diplomat was a stocky balding man. What hair he did have was completely white and worn rather long, like Einstein's, if Einstein had used a comb. He didn't seem to be taking much in. He had a grumpy pre-occupied manner. Perhaps he had seen too many such schools. Perhaps it was the elevation, or his stomach. I want to be charitable here. I am sure there were mitigating circumstances, but he wasn't even pretending to be interested and I was a little discomfited by his behaviour.

The rest of the committee was very pleasant. There was a tall slim young man from the Canadian International Development Agency or the World Bank (I cannot remember which) and a young woman who was attached to the high commission in some other official capacity, but the man who saved the day was an older very distinguished Indian man who seemed somehow to be the senior member of the delegation. He asked the most pertinent questions and seemed to be genuinely interested in the answers. I was not sure what his position was with the high commission, but he was obviously important, as the younger members of the entourage tended to defer to him and seek his advice. I was glad he was there because he rescued the situation from becoming downright embarrassing.

And what was the purpose of the visit?

Oh, sorry. It seems that the Canadian government had about $50,000 to dispose of in Bhutan and this commission of inquiry was looking for a suitable project to sponsor. Our school was a very unlikely candidate, however, and everybody knew that. We were just going through the motions.

It was a short visit, a quick walkabout, and the principal queried me again about the luncheon arrangements.

"Should I offer them tea in the staff room?"

"No, I don't think so, sir. I would imagine they would like to get straight to lunch as they have another appointment at the college this afternoon."

There was a struggle of emotions on his face between feeling slighted and his relief at being let off the hook. Relief triumphed.

"Ah well, that is a shame then." He turned to bow once more to his departing guests and wish them a pleasant visit to Bhutan.

We boarded the vehicles and drove down the serpentine drive to the bazaar where the Toyotas were parked, and we drew a great hamper from the back of one of the vehicles.

"So where are we eating lunch?" asked the diplomat looking around the bazaar.

"Up there," I said, pointing up the mountain to Khaling Gompa.

He followed my finger as it traced the zigzag track up the spur of the mountain. The diplomat swore under his breath. "All right, lead on."

The Indian man grabbed one end of the hamper and I grabbed the other, and we commenced the short but steep climb up to the village. The younger members of the party stuck with us and we took turns carrying the heavy basket. Howard trailed behind and encouraged the panting diplomat. When we reached the cluster of prayer flags at the top of the rise, we paused to catch our breath.

"Wow," acknowledged the World Bank Guy resting his hands on his thighs and taking in the view.

"Not much farther now," I encouraged them. We trundled through the shaggy willow-lined lanes of the village, treading warily around the cow plots. Faces peered out of narrow window slits and hailed me. "*Lopen*. What's up?" I tried to explain in broken Sharchopkha that these were big *dashos* from Canada and that they were coming to my house for lunch.

When we reached my gate, I slid aside the peeled willow-coppice rails and my little caravan stumbled across the cultivated ground to my house.

"Voila," I pronounced, indicating my humble abode across the rows of corn stubble. "Chez Ken."

I invited my guests into the kitchen and quickly arranged cushions and folded blankets for them to sit on. The diplomat sat by himself in the corner on my only chair and rubbed his temples in obvious discomfort. The rest of us dived into the food, and a lively conversation ensued in which we shared our impressions of Bhutan and I asked for news of the outside world. The hamper proved to be an Aladdin's cave of culinary delight: Californian red wine, tins of Foster's lager, smoked oysters, Triscuit crackers, goose liver pâté, Danish Camembert, English Stilton, and more wonders too numerous to mention. As the conversation ranged over a number of topics, I noticed that, once again, it was the older Indian man who asked the most pertinent questions and who gave the most closely reasoned observations.

At one point as I was refilling glasses, I took the young man aside and asked him about the Indian. "Who is this guy?" I asked. "He's really sharp. Is he like some senior planner or the deputy commissioner or something?"

The World Bank Guy seemed taken aback. "No," he said, "he's our driver."

As we were talking and as lunch came to a close, the young lady cleaned up. She thoughtfully packed the residuals of this feast into a large green plastic garbage bag she had brought for just this purpose. She turned to me.

"Where do you put your garbage?" she asked brightly.

My garbage?

They assumed, of course, that I would have a means of disposing of so much extra trash, and I did have a system of sorts. I had dug a pit beside my outhouse about a cubic yard in volume into which I pitched my food scraps and in which I periodically burned my garbage. In the entire year I lived there, however, I never managed to fill that pit even a quarter full. It's amazing how little garbage such a society produces. Every tin, jar, or bottle was re-used and what I didn't need was gladly accepted by my neighbours. Every plastic bag was considered a valuable resource. How long, I wondered, before the villagers were sated with such things. There was no organized garbage disposal. Things were just tossed aside when they were broken or worn out, which was fine if they were biodegradable, like wooden bowls or straw baskets; but with the creation of the vehicle road and the intrusion of cheap plastic goods from India, how long before Khaling began to look like an enormous refuse heap?

After I had waved goodbye, I was left with a dilemma. All of this garbage, produced after only one sitting, filled my entire garbage pit; indeed, not only filled it, but rose several inches above ground level. I stood there pondering this pumpkin-shaped green plastic bag filling a square hole in the ground until a wonderful and elegant solution came to me. I hefted the bag over to my outhouse, poured the contents down the hole, and then thought no more about it.

It was some time later, one evening after several days of rain, that I had cause to remember the diplomat's picnic. I had to relieve myself. It was dark and a gentle rain was falling. I grabbed my flashlight and walked through the rows of damp corn stubble to the outhouse. My outhouse was quite simply a rectangular hole cut in a plank floor that was surrounded by a screen of woven bamboo. I was just hunkering down with my flashlight clamped between my teeth when the floor collapsed.

Looking back on it, I can piece together what must have happened. The rats, you see, had smelled the delicious Camembert on the foil wrappers, the pâté adhering to the plastic wrap, and those oily oysters and sardines in the empty tins, and they had tunnelled in from all sides to reach this olfactory feast, thus weakening the floor. The rain had done the rest. Hence the structural collapse.

And so it was that I found myself, with my trousers down around my ankles, falling through the floor like Marlowe's Faust and splash-landing in a slurry of garbage and sewage. The flashlight shot out of my mouth and exploded. It was suddenly very dark and very quiet. I was half-naked, up to my neck in a damp slimy pit, and extremely annoyed. Then I heard the first squeaks of terror and realized I was not alone.

In retrospect, I feel a little sorry for them. I mean, there they were, minding their own business, quietly munching away on whatever exotic scraps were lying around, when suddenly the sky fell in upon them. They panicked, of course. And in their panic chose to flee by the nearest possible exit. (I shudder to think of it even now.) Squeaking furry bodies with rough snake-like tails scrabbled in a terror-stricken rush up my bare legs, across my chest, over my shoulder, and along the bridge of my arm to safety.

It was sometime after they had left before I could bring myself to move. Then, gorge rising, I hauled myself out of the hole and stripped off my fouled clothing. I left the flashlight where it fell. I stumbled to the porch, ripped the lid off my rain barrel, and slopped buckets of water over my head in an attempt to sluice off the slime and the memory of dozens of sharp probing fingers seeking their escape.

From that day, I was never plagued with dreams of rats again. Instead I have awakened to a nightmare of consumer waste, into which I fall only deeper and deeper. The veneer of innocence has been stripped from my world. Only man is vile.

EIGHTEEN

KHALING *TSETCHU*

IT WAS THE DAY BEFORE THE *TSETCHU*, the annual festival in honour of Guru Rinpoche, the last class before the end of a long day, and I was standing at the classroom window, my back to the class, observing the weather with grim interest. A student was standing at his desk, reading a poem aloud. It was a new poem for the class, but none of us felt like making a new start on anything that day.

"Give to me the life I love."

A ribbon of cloud, a cloud snake, was wending its way along the valley wall. A contour line serpent, fitting the green folds of the mountain.

"Let the la...la...

("lave, Pema; it means: something that flows, like a river.")

"...lave. Let the lave go by me,

Give me the jolly heaven above

And the byway—byway?"

("A road.")

"La. And the byway nigh me."

("That was good, Pema. You can sit down. Someone else? Narayan, will you continue?")

"Bed in the bush with stars to see,

Bread I dip in the river—"

It was amazing really. I had never seen a cloud behave in this manner before. A band of mist wrapped itself along the folds of the green hills, undulating like an enormous smoke-snake. A slight breeze kept it moving, slithering over the jungle, enveloping all in its path, swallowing the green in a vacuum of white light. It stretched endlessly along the corrugated ridge, its head stalking closer and closer to the school and its tail neatly wrapped around a corner of the valley out of sight. Constricting, undulating, it slithered over the green—a sinuous purposeful evil. Quite unsettling.

"There's the life for a man like me,

There's the life forever."

A temperature inversion perhaps? The movement could be caused by a mountain breeze, warmer air on the top of the pass drawing the ribbon of cloud up the valley like a serpent. Unusual for the time of year, though. With the tsetchu opening the next day, I knew my eyes were not the only ones watching the sky anxiously. It was grey and ominous.

"Wealth I seek not, hope nor love,

Nor a friend to know me;

All I ask the heaven above,

And the road below me."

"That was fine, Narayan. Thank you," I said, turning from the window and looking at my students. They were as anxious to escape this classroom as I. It was the last period before a three-day holiday, the biggest and most important religious festival of the year. "The poem is called 'The Vagabond' and it is probably the easiest one you will have to learn for the syllabus, once you get past the new vocabulary." A few faces brightened at that. "To begin with, what is a vagabond?"

I knew better by now than to expect a reply. The answers either came all at once in a communal chant or not at all. I continued: "A vagabond is..." and I paused, thinking to draw a parallel with the popular saint, Drukpa Kunley, but then felt that they might draw the wrong conclusions, since Robert Louis Stevenson's character was not a wandering holy man, but more of a gypsy, "...a vagabond is a man with no family, no job, only a few possessions, who moves from place to place making a living as he can. It sounds very adventurous, very appealing and romantic, but the poet is careful to point out the difficulties of this kind of life. What are some of those difficulties?" I looked out at the rows of adolescent faces that were now looking down at their desktops with sudden concentration. I knew that no one would volunteer an answer. They expected me to supply it. That was my role as teacher in this culture, a role I'd been fighting for almost two years. My term of service would be over in a few months, and I would be returning to Canada, but I wasn't about to give up on them yet. I let them think for a moment.

"Dorje Penjore."

"Yes, Sir." The startled youth rose to his feet still regarding the floor.

"What are some of the difficulties of being a vagabond?"

He licked his lips and cleared his throat nervously. "Don't know, Sir," he whispered, ashamed.

"I'll bet we can figure it out together. Read me the first two lines of stanza two."

He began to read, softly, but confidently now that he had a task that he could understand:

"Let the blow fall soon or late,

Let what will be o'er me;"

"That was fine, Dorje. Well done. Let's start with that: 'Let the blow fall soon or late.' I wonder what he means by 'blow?' The wind can blow, of course, we know that, and I can give Ugyen a blow (I tapped the sleeping student lightly on the head with my poetry anthology to the delight of the class. He sat blinking and turning red), but I think here 'blow' is something more sinister. It's the Big Blow. The Final Blow. The Last Blow that you and I, Dorje, will have to face in this world, maybe soon, the poet says, or late, but it will come to each of us in the end—"

"Death!" he shouted, surprised and delighted at his own sagacity.

"Yes, death. Well done, Dorje, you may sit down. Death. But the next line is more of a problem, and to understand it you have to remember that Stevenson is from the West, like I am, and we have different customs for the dead. 'Let what will be o'er me.' 'O'er' is short for 'over.'" I noted this on the blackboard: Blow = Death; O'er = Over. "What do you think will be *over* the vagabond when he is dead?"

"Sir." I turned. It was Ugyen, rising to his feet. I was pleased. Perhaps he was ashamed to have been caught napping and meant to make it up to me. "I am thinking it is dirt, Sir. Foreigners put dead people in holes in the ground." A few students giggled at this, finding the notion ridiculous.

"Sir!" It was Narayan again, rising to his feet. I had always found the Nepali more forthcoming than the Drukpa students. "Why do Western people bury their dead?"

I looked out over the rows of Asiatic faces—most with a round Mongolian cast, but a few sharp-featured Nepali—as they rose from their open texts and regarded me with friendly curiosity. Teenagers, I reminded myself, have more immediate concerns than the musings of dead Scottish poets. I smiled to myself. Oh well, it wouldn't hurt. There were only minutes left of class. I just wasn't sure I could give them an adequate explanation.

"I will try to explain. Unlike Buddhists or Hindus, people in my culture believe we have only one chance at life on this world. So I think we value our bodies more.

We have them buried in the ground and erect grand monuments over them as if this might guarantee our immortality. The custom began, I think, with a belief that, in the beginning, God created the first man and woman from clay and breathed life into them. His breath is that part of us which is immortal. When we die, then it seems only natural that what remains be returned to the soil. When we bury our dead we say, 'Earth to earth, ashes to ashes, dust to dust.' The vagabond, of course, has no guarantee of a proper burial. He may die far from home, away from friends and family, in a foreign country perhaps; with different customs and a language he does not understand, with no covering but the sky..." I stopped, realizing I was being self-indulgent, wondering, too, if what I was telling them was even true. The brass gong sounded, announcing the end of the school day.

"Well, I will see you all again in three days. Enjoy the tsetchu...and, boys (faces looked at me expectantly) don't let me catch you drinking, okay?" A shout of laughter rose up. The students sprang to their feet in unison, and with less gravity than usual intoned: "Thaaank yoou, Ee-Sirrr."

Out on the landing I was pursued by the breathless duosyllabic, "E-Sir! E-Sir!" I turned to find Ugyen running after me, schoolbooks thumping like a beating heart inside the loose folds of his gho. "Sir," he slid to a stop, breathlessly. "Sir. Some of us Class 10 boys are bringing pack lunches to tsetchu. We would like it very much if Sir would eat with us tomorrow."

"Kading-chhe-la, Ugyen. Jang packlunch zale-ga legcha."

His face flushed in approval. "Your Sharchop is much better, Sir."

"I have good teachers, Ugyen."

"Goodbye, Sir. See you tomorrow, Sir."

I leaned on the rail and watched my students run up the hill to their dormitories. Their excitement was palpable, catching. My heart was filled with something like love. Never again, I realized, would I instruct such well-behaved, hard-working, respectful, helpful, not to mention sympathetic, students. I was missing them already.

The dates of the tsetchu were chosen each year with care through astrological consultation. Tsetchu means "tenth day" and the holiday was supposed to fall on the tenth day of the month in the lunar calendar, but in practice it rarely did. We knew, of course, that it would fall sometime toward the end of October; it always did. It was the best time of year for the religious celebration. The crops were harvested and corn stubble stood in the fields like bristles on an unshaven chin. The rainy season was over. The sky was generally a beautiful blue like an invention on the palette of Claude

Lorrain. It was dry and warm during the day, though cold at night. The trails were dry and in good repair, so travelling was good. This was the traditional time of year for trading. Pack ponies were coming and going on the trails to the hinterland. The Brokpa were evident in the taverns of the bazaar or passed out in the dusty street. The luggage on the roof of the daily bus was stacked almost as high again as the bus itself. Life was lived in the sun, under the blue sky. Pillars of smoke rose from the valley floor where farmers were burning the chaff off their fields and the air was filled with its fragrance as the smoke drifted up the valley. Whole families came down out of the mountains like circus elephants walking in graduated scale, from father to youngest daughter, each sweating and grunting under a tumpline, dragging a bridal train of green bamboo; for it was the season for weaving new fences and new roofs from split green bamboo. Rooftops were splashed with the scarlet of drying chilies. Looms were erected on porches in the warm sun, and cloth was hastily woven to complete that new tsetchu outfit begun last winter. A bright new kira perhaps for a girl of marriageable age, with gold or silver thread bartered for in Assam; for tsetchu was also a season of betrothals. Everyone tried to look their best at tsetchu, and if they couldn't afford a new outfit, you could be sure they would bring their Sunday best out of mothballs for this three-day celebration.

In the fall of the year, life renewed itself amid the brown grass. Winter was coming, but it was never very harsh, in our valley anyway. If any snow fell, it quickly melted and its presence was cause for celebration, not consternation, as its white colour was seen as auspicious. Life was good in my corner of the Himalayas in fall and winter—dry and cold and bright. I wonder if I will ever again feel so alive, so vital, as I did then? I thought I had learned to catch each day and hold it, but I've lost that skill. It was linked to a time and a place.

Preparations for the tsetchu began weeks before it began. The courtyard of the temple was scrupulously cleaned, grass and moss pulled out from between the flag-stones. Farmers from up and down the valley met daily to practise the necessary dance steps. The bigger towns had monks to perform, professional dancers, but here in Khaling we relied mostly on local and not always sober talent. Since the death of Ugyen Lhamo's husband, we did not have a resident lama, so this year, once again, we would borrow one from Wamrong to the south. All the children born this year would be presented to the lama for a blessing and a name. The year before, I had asked my friend, Chogyal Tenzin, if he would be taking his son to the lama to be named.

"No," he had replied, shaking his head emphatically.

"No? Why not?"

"The last time this lama was here, he named every child 'Karma.'"

"Every single child?"

"Uh-huh."

"Why in heaven's name would he do that?"

Chogyal shrugged. "No imagination, I guess."

I tried to imagine being the primary teacher assigned to the class of students all named Karma. Ask a student to run an errand and the whole class would be out the door. On the other hand, calling the roll would be dead easy.

There were no family names in Bhutan. The royal family had a dynastic name, Wangchuck, but this was unusual and a fairly recent innovation, only since 1907. In practice then, every Bhutanese child's name was unique to him or herself. On the other hand, there was a fairly small pool of names to choose from, fifty or so. There were a lot of Sonams and Dorjes and Wangmos. On the bright side, spellings were not formalized, so an individual could express his or her individuality through some creative spelling: Sangay, for example, might also be Sangye, Sengye, or Singye. Students frequently changed the spellings of their names, or even decided to change their names altogether, which could be bothersome for teachers. A pupil you had known for two years as Sonam Dendhup could suddenly announce that from hence-forth he would be known as Tshering Tobgye. You needed a lot of white-out for your record books.

The bazaar merchants were busy erecting small bamboo huts around the temple—rustic saloons and restaurants, and booths housing games of chance. It was like a medieval Bartholomew's Fair, mixing religion and dissipation. It was colourful. It was wonderful. It was a time for the entire population of our valley to get together, to wear their finery, to flirt, to gossip, to pray, and to drink heavily. For, while it was a religious celebration, it was also a big drunk, a huge brawling celebration of Life. Everyone in Khaling Gompa had been distilling their own corn liquor for many weeks in anticipation of the many friends and relations who would be dropping in for a visit. I had only managed—and this with a great deal of pleading and persistence—to gather a stock of seven bottles of *ara*. At any other time of the year it would have been easy, but at *tsetchu*, when they might have need of it themselves, people were reluctant to sell me their *ara*. Needless to say, I paid premium prices for the few bottles I could scrounge.

It was not my first *tsetchu* in Khaling, but it would be my last, and I hoped to make it memorable. The previous year's celebration had been cut short by duties at the school and a recurrent bout of giardia, but this year I would be living right in the heart of the village with three whole days to enjoy the festival to the full. I felt that I had earned this break and I meant to enjoy it. I planned to throw my house open to all and sundry and repay some of the many kindnesses I had been shown over the past two years.

Although Khaling's tsetchu was somewhat rough and unpolished, rustic and not nearly the spectacle of larger centres like Tashigang, Thimphu, or Paro, Khaling had the advantage of having one of the few temples in the country that was still open to foreign visitors. For this reason, I had invited a friend, also a Canadian teacher, to visit. Duncan had been teaching in Bhutan for three years, and I felt that he would be comfortable staying with me in the village and could cope with the open-door policy I hoped to introduce.

The first day of the celebration was rainy and dreary. The dancing was postponed, though the temple was crowded with the faithful, the monks, the local gomchens, and the lama. Chanting and incense issued forth under dripping eaves. Children's faces peered out of the temple windows, regarding the grey sky. I went down to the bazaar early, to meet the morning bus and to purchase two bottles of Apsoo rum, to supplement my meagre cellar. The bus groaned and swayed into the bazaar and coughed itself to death, settling into the muddy ruts before the canteen. I saw Duncan's grey and drawn face in a window aperture where the glass was missing. "Rough trip?" I yelled.

Duncan grimaced and laughed sardonically. "Nice weather you have here."

I bowed ironically. "I ordered it especially for your arrival. Here, pass me your bags." He handed down his jola through the open window.

"My backpack is on the roof, I'm afraid," he shouted over the chatter of new arrivals.

I stuck the jola under the eaves of the canteen, out of the rain, and stepped out into the street behind the bus to view the situation.

The bus was a hive of activity. Lilliputian figures clambered over the luggage on the roof, pulling and tugging at sacks and boxes, crates and drums. Loads were lowered to willing hands. It was like the dissection of Gulliver. The miracle of the Pema buses, I had decided long ago—besides the fact that they always began their journey every morning a lovely battered blue and reached their destination a vomit-streaked, greeny-grey—was their amazing capacity to swallow humanity. Just when you thought that not another person could possibly emerge from the narrow door, ten more would unbend and slip out, followed by ten more.

Duncan was among the first to emerge. As always, he was clean-shaven and hulking. He had already lit a cigarette. He was usually reticent and had that Mr. Spock trick of raising one eyebrow at will.

"How are things in Yurung?" I asked.

He shrugged. I took this to mean that things were okay. We trailed out of the crowded bazaar and I led Duncan up the mountain, up the many switchbacks and past lines of damp prayer flags to the plateau where my home and the little village sat. The mountain pastures curved up and away before us into the clouds, and below us, through patches of grey cloud, we could see Khaling Valley snaking away into the distance. The river shone dully like a wire and the little white villages, like pearls, hung on its length.

Khaling Gompa was crowded with the faithful from up and down the valley and from across the district, and many faces registered surprise at the spectacle of a couple of philing-pa wending their way through the narrow lanes that led between the small stone houses. The rain and the heavy pedestrian traffic had churned the paths into a deep chestnut gumbo, but there were a series of flat stones, like stepping stones in a stream, down the middle of the path, and we hopped from one to the next as in a game of hopscotch. The only problem came when two people met going in opposite directions and then one would have to leap to one side and cling to the latticework of the bamboo fences that lined these lanes until the other had passed by. There was much hilarity when someone slipped and fell in the mud. My house, like others in the village, sat in the middle of a small fenced-in field, long since harvested. I slid aside the rails that served as a gate to keep out the cattle, and we stumbled across the corn stubble to my house.

There was an unwritten rule among foreign volunteers in Bhutan: one's house was open to all travellers. It was (and is) a country with few hotels or inns. This offers no obstruction to the Bhutanese who seem to have relatives everywhere with whom to stay. It is an Asian thing, I think—the Big Family, Han Suyin called it, the extended family that looks out for its own—and, in a way, we foreign teachers had adapted to this tradition. Any foreigner travelling through Khaling was welcome at my house. If they were decent human beings, they didn't arrive empty-handed but brought a bottle of whisky or some fresh vegetables, something that was often in short supply in the long winter months when I had to make do with dried chilies, radishes, and shrivelled midget potatoes.

Each volunteer was allowed to sponsor two visitors a year. As I didn't have any visitors my second year, I was often pressured to sponsor somebody else's friends or family members. The responsible volunteers would let you know if someone was expected by dropping a card in the mail stating, "My brother will be travelling through Khaling at such-and-such a time, would you mind..." or it might be, "My cousin," "My roommate from university," "My sister's friend," and once even, "My grandmother." More often than not, though, I would arrive home from school after a long day and some grubby backpacker would spring from my doorstep with an outstretched hand and say, "You must be Ken. Hi, I'm X's friend from Montreal. X said you wouldn't mind putting me up for a few days and showing me around." I shouldn't complain, really. My village was a bit off the beaten track, so I wasn't overwhelmed the way some volunteers were. One teaching couple in Tashigang had visitors every weekend for an entire year.[12]

As we kicked off our shoes and entered my kitchen, Duncan reached into his *jola* and brought out a bottle of Bhutan Mist. "Here you go," he said. "I don't imagine you get too much of the good stuff around here." I thanked him and set down the bags. "Have a seat. I'll put on the kettle."

"Do you have any *ara*?" Duncan asked and when I pointed to the bottles on the counter, he helped himself to a glass. "Ah," he winced with the first sip, "that's pretty harsh stuff." Still, I noticed that he helped himself to a second glass. There was a knock on the door.

"Hello. *Kuzu zangpo*," called a cheerful voice with a rising lilt at the end of each word.

It was Karin, dressed in the Christian Dior of all *kiras*, a drop-dead sleeve of bright colour and gold thread, worn under a lovely jacket of Chinese silk. Karin was accompanied by Phuntsho Lhamo, one of the other teachers at the school for the blind. Phuntsho was slender, very pretty, and wore her hair quite long, unlike most Bhutanese women who wore their hair cut short in the pageboy style. Phuntsho was the only Bhutanese Christian I had met in my two-year stay and, while she was doing well at the school (indeed her talent was recognized and greatly valued), I knew that her apostasy made her superiors in the department of education nervous. They were not comfortable with her attending prayer meetings with the missionaries and had strongly suggested that she stop. I asked her what she would do. She shrugged and said she would probably stop attending. It would be career suicide to continue.

"What to do?" she sighed.

This may be why she socialized with Karin and me. We were also misfits of a sort. No sooner did I have Karin and Phuntsho settled with a glass of tea, than there was another knock at the door.

The door creaked slowly open and two wrinkled old faces peered shyly around the heavy doorframe.

"Ah, *Kuzu zangpo-la!*" I cried. "*Odo, odo. Zhugcho-la.*"

I ushered in my neighbours, two old women curious to see the *philing-pa*, bade them sit on the mats, and filled the *gorbus*, which appeared miraculously from somewhere inside their *kiras*. The older of the two, with a dirty thatch of grey hair, was Sonam Lhamo. The other woman was Nima, a widow who owned a great deal of property. Her eldest son was a monk in Tashigang Dzong and was expected to return home for the *tsetchu*. Her only daughter, who must have been about eighteen, was mentally handicapped and was cared for, in a way I found quite touching, by the entire village.

I had hoped that my house would be a place where Bhutanese and non-Bhutanese might mix in agreeable companionship, but I could see this was not to be. Oh, Karin was trying hard enough. She'd engaged Nima in conversation in Sharchopkha and they were exchanging gossip, which was a good beginning, but Duncan was already beginning to drink heavily, and he was becoming morose. I worried about him. Each time we got together, he seemed to be hitting the bottle a little harder. I suspected that he was developing a drinking problem, which I suppose is an occupational hazard in a country of heavy drinkers. Sonam Lhamo asked in a pleading and ingratiating tone that we take her picture. I had hoped to avoid this. I wanted to hide my camera away during *tsetchu*, as it seemed too intrusive, a barrier between my neighbours and myself, but I could see that this was going to be impossible. And I realized then that my last *tsetchu* in Khaling was not to be as I had planned. My house had become a place where two cultures met to regard each other, not as fellow human beings who might have something to share but as curiosities. There would be no real communication, only snapshots, both figurative and verbal, that would be discussed later in the privacy of one's own cultural milieu.

I arose early the next morning. Through dinner preparations, washing dishes, and ablutions of various kinds, we had used up a great deal of the water in my barrel. I stepped carefully over my sleeping guest, slipped on my plastic *chappals*, and grabbed two buckets from the porch. The rain had stopped, but I still had to pick my way carefully through the mud. There were cattle bawling in a shed as I passed, their udders painfully distended. No doubt their master, his head thick with wine, had slept late after last night's carousals. I made my way through the maze of booths around the temple and past the sleeping figures who were reclining under awnings, or on benches, or under tables, and up to a point near the great cypress where spring water flowed from a bamboo spigot, and I set my first bucket down underneath. The water dribbled in fitful bursts, and as I took a seat on one of the tree's massive roots I picked up one of the incised slates that ringed the base of the ancient tree and ran my fingers over the letters. I couldn't read the Tibetan script, but I knew what it said: OM MANI PADME HUM (All hail the Jewel in the Lotus!), which was the mantra of the Bodhisattva Avalokiteshvara and was chanted incessantly by practising Buddhists throughout the country. I rested the palm of my hand on the cool black stone and looked out over the valley, soaking up the warmth like a cat, as the first rays of sunlight spilled over the mountains. The morning was silvery and far below in the throat of the valley, I could see clouds turning like a millwheel, rising up one ridge, rolling over, and sliding down the opposite side of the valley. It was a very Buddhist image, like the Wheel of Life. There were crows wheeling, too, and darting above the temple roof in the bright air, cawing and cackling, their primary feathers snapping like torn sails in a gale as they dived. Several came to rest on the prayer masts around the courtyard and I counted them: eight. How did the rhyme go?

"One for sorrow, two for mirth, three for a wedding, four for a birth, five for silver, six for gold, seven for a secret not to be told, eight for heaven, nine for hell, and ten for the devil's own self."

Eight, eight for heaven. Well, that was a good sign. But then the eight were joined by two more and then one flew away, and so I supposed it was meaningless after all.

When the second bucket was full, I reluctantly left my warm perch and started down the path, past the temple, through the tent city, toward my home. But first, I decided, I would have to pay a visit. I stopped at one of the hastily erected huts, one with a canvas tarp for a roof and bamboo screens for walls. I pushed aside the corner of a dirty curtain that screened the doorway and peered into the smoky interior. A young girl looked up with a toss of her hair from where she was rolling out a loaf of flat Tibetan bread on a rock. I looked to the smoky corner where her father sat cross-legged on the floor, whirling a tiny copper prayer wheel in his right hand and chanting his morning mantra.

I greeted them, "*Kuzu zangpo.*"

"*Kuzu zangpo-la, Lopen,*" she smiled simply and waved a flour-covered hand to a bench along the wall. "*Zhugcho-la.*"

I left the buckets outside the door and ducked through the curtain. "*Khading-chhe-la,*" I said. I took my seat and turned to the old man. He smiled in my direction and bobbed his head. We talked first of the bad weather, then of his health and that of his stock, and eventually got to the business at hand: I needed more booze and could he oblige me? He nodded and rose to his feet, still swinging the counterbalance on his prayer wheel with a rhythmic snap of his wrist. He poked around in a crate at the back of the hut and produced two bottles of Changta whisky, horrible rotgut, but we had consumed most of my *ara* last night and I wouldn't have been a good host if I had run out of liquor. I paid for my bottles and thanked them. I withdrew, dropped a bottle in each bucket and headed for home with short quick steps, shoulder muscles protesting under the weight of the water.

When I returned home and set my pails just inside the kitchen door, Duncan was already stirring and smoking his morning cigarette. I began to work on break-fast, brewing up a pot of tea in the Indian way—tea leaves, milk powder, and copious amounts of sugar brought to a boil in the kettle—and frying up some chopped vege-tables with the remnants of last night's cold rice.

I had lunch that day with my students. Duncan said he would fend for himself, since there was plenty of food for sale in the stalls around the temple, and he wanted to try his hand at one of the games of chance. Ugyen and the other Class 10 boys found me in the crowded temple courtyard, watching the masked dancing, and reminded me of my promise. We sprawled among the roots of the giant cypress and ate fried rice and chili paste with our fingers out of shallow straw *bangchungs*.

A drunken shepherd staggered toward us and then collapsed at our feet, quite suddenly, as if felled by an axe. I watched his immobile form with alarm, thinking he had suffered a stroke. He didn't move, and when I started to rise to his assistance, Ugyen grabbed my sleeve.

"Leave him, Sir. He is Brokpa. Very dangerous fellow."

I thanked him for his concern, but I thought that the man might be hurt. When I examined him though, I found that he had simply had too much *tsetchu* cheer. I rolled him on his side—what the St. John's people call "the recovery position" (couldn't have him choking on his own vomit now, could we)—and watched him sleep like the dead. Lord, but he was heavy. He was so deeply under, I doubted he would even dream. I sat with the boys and watched his breathing closely.

I'd seen the Brokpa before around the bazaar. They were a tribal people from far back in the hills. They lived at high elevations and earned their livings as pasto-ralists, raising sheep, yaks, and *dzo*. In the winter, they brought their herds to lower pastures, sold the Sharchopa of my valley butter, cheese, meat, and hides, and worked as labourers for the wealthier landholders. They were unlike the Sharchopa—taller, leaner, with thinner faces and higher cheekbones. More than one writer has remarked on their resemblance to the Plains Indians of North America. They spoke a different language, as well; though most spoke Sharchopkha adequately.

It was their costumes though that first caught your attention. Handwoven and handspun from wool they had shorn from their own sheep, their clothes were limited to four colours—black, white, walnut, and a brownish red like dried blood, colours that came naturally to the wool or could be manufactured with plant dyes. The women wore plain red sleeveless shifts and short jackets, which were woven with complex geometrical patterns, often of stylized animals. They also sometimes wore capes of black yak felt that were both warm and water repellent. The men wore black, brown, or red hip-length tunics of heavy wool, bound at the waist with a sash, leather leggings, and a loincloth of white wool. And as footwear, both men and women wore either black rubber boots or green-tanned leather mukluks. But the most distinctive feature of Brokpa dress was their curious hats. These were made of pressed yak felt and looked like Basque berets with five or six legs. The legs, I was told, acted as rainspouts, wicking moisture away from the neck and face. My reaction upon first seeing a Brokpa hat was an intense desire to knock it to the ground and step on it, so closely did it resemble a large black spider. It is fortunate for me that I never acted on that impulse.

Ugyen was still talking: "...they are a very primitive people, Sir. Last year at tsetchu, one Brokpa stabbed another with his knife. I am thinking they were both drinking very much."

I suspected that the Brokpa weren't quite as dangerous as they were made out to be, and that, like most fear, my students' worries stemmed from a lack of understanding. The Brokpa intrigued me. I knew that they lived in two large valleys called Mera and Sakteng in the northwest corner of the country. It was a politically sensitive area, for, not far away, the Chinese and Indian armies faced each other over an ill-defined border between Chinese-occupied Xixang (formerly Tibet) and the Indian-occupied territory of Arunachal Pradesh. As a result, Mera-Sakteng, as this region of Bhutan was known, though itself peaceful, was too close to a disputed territory to allow tourist access. I had been trying unsuccessfully for two years to get a travel permit to see the place for myself.

"Look, Sir," said Ugyen and pointed up the hill. There was a small fenced pasture and a large crowd had gathered there. "Let us go and see, Sir." The other boys shouted

Thankas at Khaling *Tsetchu*.

their enthusiastic agreement, so we left the poor shepherd to his slumbers and struggled up the hill.

Being tall has its advantages. Even though I stood at the back of the crowd, I had a good view of what was going on. The boys abandoned me, worming their way to the front of the press for a better vantage point. It was a Brokpa dance. It reminded me of that old vaudeville routine where two comedians form the front and back of an ass, only in this case the ass was a yak and on the yak's back there sat a white wooden statue of a goddess. A darkly tanned man with chunks of turquoise dangling from his earlobes was clapping out a slow rhythm on a set of brass cymbals and the yak danced a comical jig. Another shepherd walked amongst the crowd soliciting funds with his spider-like hat. The significance of the dance was completely lost on me. I asked one of my neighbours what it was about, but he just shrugged. "They need money to buy *ara*," he suggested.

On the third and final day of *tsetchu*, the *thankas* were brought out. They only showed their faces to the world on this auspicious day. For the remainder of the year, they were carefully stored in the temple attics. They slept, rolled around long poles like furled sails against the mast of a ship in port, until this day each year when they were raised to fill with the reverent gaze of the devout. There was not enough room to manoeuvre the awkward poles down the cramped stairwells, so the monks had to lower them carefully from the roof on long ropes. The masts were met on the ground by more monks and a few prominent citizens, who had been honoured by the task, and were then borne three times around the temple, shoulder high, in a clockwise circumambulation to the accompaniment of chanted prayers. The tide of the faithful swept over the beleaguered monks, a tide of pilgrims eager to touch the sacred images and so gain a blessing. The Brokpa doffed their spider caps and tapped them on the *thankas* as they were carried past. On the final pass of the building the monks paused in the stone courtyard in front of the temple. Ropes were lowered from upper storey windows and attached to either end of the long booms that supported the scrolls. The bearers held firmly to the bottom of the cloth as the booms were raised and the scrolls unrolled, covering the face of the temple. When fully unfurled, the booms were lashed to the window frames and the *thankas* caught the breeze and flapped. But even then, the mysterious and seldom-seen figures were shielded from our eyes by enormous veils of colourful silk. The temple had taken on the appearance of an enormous Christmas present. Finally, the prayers were finished and the veils were raised to reveal the faces of three serene figures: on the right, the powerful seated figure of Padmasambhava (also known as Guru Rinpoche or "Precious Master" in Tibet and Bhutan), the missionary from Swat in present day Pakistan who introduced Tantric Buddhism to Bhutan in the eighth century AD; on the left, sensuous and pale as the moon, the Bodhisattva of Compassion, the eleven-headed Avalokiteshvara ("the keen-seeing Lord, the great pitier and Lord of mercy"); and in the centre, seated in meditation, Lord Buddha himself. The crowd rushed forward to touch the bottoms of the thankas, the hems of their garments, and everyone was lost in private prayer, overcome by the moment.

A voice at my elbow said, "I am told the thanka in the centre is over three hundred years old."

"Really?" I turned to see the speaker. It was my friend Nawang Dorje, the principal of the school for the blind. "It doesn't look that old."

"Well, it has been repaired."

I must have looked confused, for he continued.

"You see, when any part of it has rotted or faded, that section of cloth is cut out and a new piece stitched in its place. The art lopen at your school did the repairs this year, just prior to tsetchu. I think he did a very fine job."

"Yes, it's beautiful." I regarded it closely as it rippled in the breeze. "But I can't tell what is original and what has been replaced."

"Oh, I imagine it has all been replaced. After all, it is over three hundred years old."

"Of course," I said.

"The new missionary has arrived," said Nawang.

"Oh, that's good news," I said. "I look forward to meeting him. What's he like?"

Nawang paused, and by that pause, I knew something was wrong. A Bhutanese is always very circumspect in his criticism. "He seems very interested in the school. I'm sure you will meet him. Karin said that she would bring him to the tsetchu today. In fact, I see them now." He looked uneasy. "If you will excuse me, Mr. Ken," he said and fled, red-faced, through the crowd.

I felt sorry for him. I knew his position was very difficult, for he was caught between two contradictory and often opposing forces. There were those in Thimphu, especially in the monk body, who disapproved of all foreign intervention in Bhutan, especially foreign missionaries, and he had to placate these men. It was the missionaries, however, who supplied the money for the school, provided him with some of his staff and gave him funds to train the others, and who had very strict ideas on how a mission school should be run. That he spoke to me at all and seemed to take an interest in my welfare showed incredible kindness and charity.

"Ken, Ken." It was Karin, working her way through the crowd toward me. "Hei," she gasped as we met and gave me a hug. "Ken, there is someone I want you to meet. Ken, this is Knut. He is the new teacher at our school that I was telling you about."

Knut was about forty years old, rather unremarkable except that he sported enormous mutton-chop whiskers and that the eyes behind his spectacles were perfectly lifeless. He smiled and shook my hand, but his eyes never changed expression. His grip was firm enough, but I found him unnerving. I couldn't decide whether his expression was one of innocence or malevolence.

A staccato thunderclap of cymbals announced the beginning of another dance. The courtyard cleared and four dancers entered in a square with slow prancing steps. They were wearing wooden skull masks and were dressed in white with long talons attached to fingers and toes. They had rich brocade sashes that crossed on their chests and, around their waists, long skirts of multicoloured silk, very bright and somehow incongruous with the rest of their appearance. They carried between them the flayed skin of a condemned sinner. As the cymbals picked up the beat, they began to sway, gyrate, toss their heads, leap, and jerk their arms in a quick staccato rhythm, dancing in perfect unison.

It was *Durdag*, the Dance of the Masters of the Cremation Grounds. I said, "You're in for a treat, Knut. This is my favourite dance."

The dancers dropped the skin to the ground, spread out and began to spin and leap with incredible energy and agility. It was a terrible sight. There was a kind of fierce hard-edged masculine vigour that hypnotized the spectators.

"Devils, ...Devils," whispered Knut. "Such evilness. These people live in darkness."

"Oh, no, Knut," said Karin. "The dances are like stories."

"That's right," I interjected, eager to explain. "They are like the morality plays of medieval Europe. The dances act out the battle between good and evil. They teach a lesson. I guess you could say they're like sermons." That wasn't strictly true in this case; the *Durdag* was a consecrative dance, but how could I explain that?

"Devils and demon worship," spat Knut. "I have seen enough." He pushed his way roughly to the front of the crowd and, for a moment, I thought in alarm that he was going to try and stop the dance, but he was only seeking the quickest escape route, skirting the edge of the dancing floor to avoid the crowds. And that was how the *atsaras* got him.

Atsara. Yongba, the temple caretaker, stands to the left.

The *atsaras* are the court jesters of masked dancing. They wear outlandish clothes and masks that are uncomfortably like caricatures of European features: red face and prominent nose. They wander freely amidst the dancers and the spectators, mimicking, amusing, deflating the pompous. Their presence is anarchic. They parody. They challenge. They hold a mirror up to us. They alone hold the dispensation to mock religion in a society that is deeply religious. No, that's not quite right, for they never mock religion, they only mock the images of religion, reminding us that the images themselves are not the reality, but that the true reality lies somewhere beyond them. The *atsaras'* symbol is a sceptre that is unmistakably phallic. As Knut strode indignantly along the edge of the dancing floor, one clown crept up behind him and goosed him with his staff. Knut jumped and spun around. The other *atsara* ran up from the other side and rested his staff on Knut's shoulder. Knut turned his head and leaped in alarm as if he'd seen a snake. The crowd loved this. One old woman in the front row collapsed in hysterical laughter. Knut roared in anger and roughly shoved the great wooden penis away. The first clown stood at Knut's shoulder and mimicked him, aping his anger, the way he pointed with his finger, the way he stomped his foot. Knut fled *sans* dignity, torrid with humiliation.

"Oh dear," sighed Karin. "I think it is best I should go after him."

As I watched her go, I did not envy her position. Knut's reaction had spoiled my own enjoyment of the dance. I pushed my way into the crowd. I found myself in front

Dancer waiting his cue. Tandin's father is on the left, sporting the goatee.

of the temple entrance. There was a sort of porch with a curtain in front of it. Inside, the dancers were putting on their costumes and their helpers were lacing up the heavy wooden masks: there were animal *rakshas*—stags, monkeys, boars with razor tusks, fierce dogs, alligators, elephants, and a mystical bird called the garuda, all with red-rimmed eyes sockets and protruding tongues; there was a black-faced demon with bulging eyes, bloody fangs, and a necklace of human skulls; there was a tall white-faced saint-advocate in a flowing white robe; and there were two assistants supporting the enormous and scarlet mask of the Lord of Death as a stout monk struggled into his costume. It was a netherworld behind the screen, a fantastic mythical animalia.

I pushed passed the curtain and deeper into the temple. A stone-flagged corridor led to a dark space that was like a mineshaft. Here, a rickety staircase corkscrewed up into unknown regions of the ether. The stairwell was lit by a single shaft of light that speared the darkness from somewhere high above, illuminating spinning dust motes. There were ragged children sitting on the steps, eating rice with their fingers. I stepped between them, unseen as a ghost, and climbed higher in the half-light, ascending to the first floor.

The low portal to the main temple room was crowded with people. I left my shoes outside and stepped over the high sill. It was darker that afternoon than it had been in days, for the *thankas* now covered most of the windows. The greatest part of the light came from the hundreds of butter lamps on the altar. They illuminated the closely decorated walls, the gilt statues on the silk-covered altar, and the fantastic pagodas of rice and butter paste—ritual cakes called *tormas*—made as offerings to the gods. The lama sat opposite the high altar on a raised dais. A small golden bell sat by his hand, which he reached for and rang at prescribed intervals in the prayers. He was flanked on either side by two lines of monks, who were facing the altar and chanting in unison from the rectangular leaves of the prayer books that sat before them on small individual desks.

"Lopen, *Lopen.*" Someone grabbed my hand and I was led through the crush of farmers and farmer's wives and their children, who filled the room and who were busy eating the offerings. There were children laughing and crying, and mothers fussing with newborns, nursing them at their breasts. I was led to a cushion beside the lama where I sat cross-legged in my *gho*. Unseen hands brought me refreshment: hot butter tea in a turned wooden bowl and a chipped enamel plate heaped with dry roasted rice, roast corn on the cob, strips of dried yak meat, gobs of gooey sweet rice, and the pastel rice flour paste from a dismantled sculpture. "*Jai, Lopen,*" I was urged. Take this. You do us honour. The lama looked down on me benevolently from his dais and nodded in approval. I sipped the salty tea and let the room roll around me.

The incense swirled in my brain, the icy stares of the incarnate gilt Buddhas, the fearsome guardian divinities, the saints and mystics, looked down at me out of the shadows, rippling in false animation in the smoky light of the butter lamps. And the sounds of the temple, overpowering in that small room, were worse than any high-school band practice or catfight in a back alley. It wasn't really music at all; there was no score or melody; it was simply a prompted explosion of sound. The deep booming of the *dungchen*; the high wheedling notes of the oboe or *galing*; the hypnotic pulse of the large double-sided drum or *nga*, which was beaten with a curved striker shaped like a large question mark; the clanging cymbals or *rolmo*; the tenor piping of the *kangling*, a trumpet fashioned from a human femur; and the deep bass of the conch shell, from whose heart the Buddhist doctrine is spread throughout the world—all of these sounds, discordant and unharmonious, struggled with each other in a powerful and alien cacophony that punctuated the recitation of the texts and overwhelmed me. But it was the chanting that affected me most, the unknown words striking like a hammer at my temples.

The clack of the lama's muffled bell signalled the beginning of a new round of prayers. The chanting began, low, subdued, and slowly welled up in overlapping layers, growing in volume and in eerie supra-rational pervasiveness. I felt inexplicably tired, and as I hung there and my head fell forward to my chest, I suddenly lost all sense of my body. Its awkward weightiness was replaced by nothing, absolutely nothing at all. I seemed to have dropped into an abyss, into a darkness without walls. About me, the waves of sound swelled like breakers on a beach, or like a pebble dropped in a well. They seemed to be filling space, each swelling a bit over the last, the atonal chanting turning in the air, beginning small, but gradually filling the space with shapes of sound, swell upon swell, until it possessed me; this welling wall of mighty sound poured in and filled my emptiness. It seemed to hold and resonate within my chest, as if a plumb line hung there, quivering. Before my fallen eyelids, from somewhere in the deep recesses of my brain, a picture began to emerge, an image of childhood, I think. I've had this dream before; it's a place I want to go to, or return to, but it only comes in dreams. It was a hazy vision at first, but slowly it swam into focus, as if a breath of wind had cleared away the fog. I saw a ring of snow-capped peaks cloaked with fragrant pines and in their centre, all-encompassed by their majesty, a lake of pure sapphire blue, still as a mirror, reflecting the peaks on its surface. It was an icon of stillness, a deathless, lifeless place. And then someone threw a stone into the lake and the picture dissolved. From a long way off, I could hear voices, angry voices, raised in argument. With indescribable weariness, I opened my eyes.

It was Lungten, Sonam Lhamo's husband, who though aged and alcoholic, was still a *gomchen*, or lay priest, and had been given a small part to play in this ceremony, a part he had invested with outsized dignity and importance. He was arguing with Yongba, the mute caretaker of our *gompa*. Longten was gesticulating angrily. Yongba was making supplicating gestures with his hands and uttering soothing whimpers in an attempt to calm the old man down. I wondered what could have upset him so much. Tandin Zangmo was sitting not too far away, surrounded by her children. I caught her eye and made the sign for "what?" by jutting out my chin and making a peculiar twisting motion of the wrist where the cupped fingers pointed upward. She grimaced and tapped her forehead, the universal sign for "he's crazy, don't worry about it." I turned sideways and looked at the lama. He gave me a reassuring smile and held out his hand, palm down, to show I should remain where I was and not worry myself. Now I was worried because I realized that all of this fuss was somehow about me. Tandin's father had now joined the argument trying to shush the old man, but he just became more vociferous. More and more people became aware of the alter- cation and they looked from Longten, who was now gesturing violently at me with one hand and slapping his knee with the other, to myself. It was the slapping of the knees that clued me in. I had forgotten my *kabne*. I looked at the other men in the room and realized that they all had a ceremonial scarf of rank or *kabne* draped across their bare knees to shield them from the altar. My bony knees were sticking out, facing the high altar, and were all the more obvious because I was sitting on a raised dais. It was an awkward moment, and I cursed myself for my stupidity. I had carelessly introduced discord into what should have been a tranquil event. The best policy under the circumstances seemed to be retreat. I rose painfully to my feet. My ankles were dead from sitting cross-legged for—how long had it been? Hours? Or had it only been a few minutes? People gestured to me to sit. It was okay, they were saying. You didn't know. But I did know, and I should have come prepared and I was ashamed.

I left the temple chamber in despair. I left poor Yongba to take the burden of apology onto himself as I knew he would, and I turned into the dark stairwell and climbed the steep wooden staircase. I climbed past the third floor, where the holy books were kept in great pigeon-holed cupboards, carefully wrapped in silk; I climbed past the fourth floor, where the *thankas*, masks, cymbals, and costumes were stored; I climbed until I reached the great open attic, shaded and airy, inhabited only by sparrows and where the wooden floorboards were covered in bat droppings and dust. The eaves of the temple were open and so I crouched and walked to the edge of the wall, leaning onto the roof trusses for support. Far below, I could see the dancers performing the final dance of the *tsetchu*, the *Raksha Marcham*, or "Dance of Judgement of the Dead." In the centre of the court, cowering on the flagstones, lay a sinner in sackcloth, prostrate before the throne of Shinje Choekyi Gyelpo, the God of the Dead. A bamboo bow lay at the sinner's side. Presumably, he died while poaching the king's deer, breaking the Buddhist commandment against taking life. Animal-headed gods took turns dancing before the throne of judgment, alternately pleading for the sinner's soul or condemning it. I watched the spandrel swirl of the dancers' skirts as they circled the procumbent sinner, opening and closing like the delicate tendrils of the sea anemone.

My *tsetchu* had been a disaster from beginning to end, but from up here it was easy to view the whole thing dispassionately. Watching the dance, I asked myself: what role did I play in this comedy, was I judge or sinner? It would be easier to live like this, aloof with god-like detachment. From here, I could concentrate on the beauty of the dancers' movements and ignore the truths of the human soul. My attempt at socializing, at trying to bridge the gap between cultures had been a failure. The distances

Condemned sinner before the throne of judgement at Khaling *Tsetchu*.

were simply too great. Each to the other seemed ultimately unknowable. A century earlier, when Kipling had written, "East is East, and West is West, and never the twain shall meet," he had felt that such a bridging of cultures was possible when two men met on equal terms on the field of battle. Somehow, in my vanity, I had thought I could do better.

From far below, the shriek of the poor sinner rent the air and startled a pair of rock doves that rocketed about the attic in a blind panic. A troll-like demon, wearing a harness of cowbells and human skulls, seized hold of the trembling figure in sackcloth and dragged him into the waiting maw of hell.

NINETEEN

THE DOPPELGÄNGER

MOST DAYS, WHEN CLASSES WERE OVER and before study duty had begun, I would walk down the mountain to the bazaar and order some syrupy tea and a snack in the Dantek canteen. Most visits to the canteen were pleasant but unmemorable. There was one visit, however, that stays with me—one encounter, though inconclusive, which has continued to haunt me to this day.

On that particular day, I approached the front door of the canteen, greeted the loafers who were sitting on a bench in the weak sun, and held my breath as I ducked through the cloud of flies that always seemed to swarm in the entranceway. I entered the grey interior, allowing my eyes to adjust to the gloom, and strode to the back of the canteen, where a doorway, blocked by a greasy countertop, had been cut through the mud wall. Beneath the counter, an impressive and somewhat incongruous glass display case had been fitted into the gap. The case was, as usual, empty but for a few old newspapers, a broken lamp chimney, and an assortment of dusty flies in the various attitudes of death. I leaned over the counter and peered into the greater gloom of the kitchen beyond. I could see the red flashes of fire and charcoal in the baked-clay stove on the floor and several shadowy figures crouched before this glowing portal.

"*Namaste*, Mr. Das. *Mujha minu dikhao.*"

A chuckle of laughter from the cooks.

One of the grey figures rose to his feet and emerged to the little window in the wall. "You are always joking, Mr. Ken. A menu! What can you think of next? My goodness." Mr. Das was an Indian from Orissa State. He had been a sergeant in the regular army but had left it to manage this kitchen. He was dressed in a worn and patched khaki uniform, as was usual for officers of the Dantek company. He was about a head shorter than my six feet, sported an elegant moustache, and but for his hair, which was beginning to thin at the top, looked a lot like Clark Gable. His eyes sparkled as he rubbed his frayed collar and leaned up to the counter.

"*Apka shubh nam?*"

"'Ken Haigh,'" I said, "Mister Sri Dasho P.K. Das."

He nodded, ignoring my poor attempt at humour. "*Han. Kya baja hai?*"

I looked at my watch. "Three Forty-Five."

"In Hindi, Mr. Ken, in Hindi. You will never learn if you don't practise. Now, once again and slowly..." And we began to count, "*ek, do, tin, char...*" This was our daily ritual. Every day Mr. Das tried to teach me a little Hindi and I did my best to learn. Mr. Das and I had been in the valley for about the same length of time. I liked him. He had left a wife and two small children back in Orissa, and yet I never saw him depressed or cross.

After our little lesson was over, I ordered a tumbler of sweet milky tea and two rupees worth of pakora. In Bhutan, pakora is generally made with green chili, which makes it very hot and spicy. The battered chili came wrapped in a cone of paper—everything is recycled in Bhutan—and I carried it over to a rough wooden table near the back of the canteen and took a seat facing the door. I placed a pile of notebooks on the table in front of me, unscrewed the cap on my fountain pen and tried to get through some of my corrections. I did my marking in green ink, since my students had informed me that red ink was often used to write poison pen letters to one's enemies.

I spread out the paper enclosing the pakora on the tabletop and pinned down a corner with my cup of tea. It was a page torn from an exercise book. The kids were always doing that, trading old exercise books with Mr. Das for snacks. I occasionally lost library books in this way, too. I once ate my afternoon snack off pages torn from *Hedda Gabler*. I began to read the composition on the wrapper:

> I was going through the snow laden pines, singing merrily and enjoying the beautiful sceneries around me, but suddenly at a far distance I saw a dark coloured thing which I could not make out what it was, whether bear or man or monkey. It seemed dark and shaggy, more I knew not. I stood still feeling afraid to move. Now it grew darker and darker as time passed by. I looked back and saw a long creeper hanging over a tree like a snake which made my nerves jingling.

I was now cut off upon both sides, behind me the darkness and before me this lurking creature. I hesitated to go towards it, and didn't take even a step forward, but kept still and numb and thought for some method of escape, and as I was so thinking, the recollection of my knife flashed in my mind, courage glowed again in my heart and I set my face resolutely to...

That was all there was. The composition was entitled, "The Battle I Fought in My Dream," and I was impressed by the naïve, yet effective (though perhaps unintentional) use of imagery here: the Edenic setting and the entrance of the shaggy man/beast and the snake. Freud would have had a field day with this. It was actually not bad when you consider that English was, at the very least, a third, and more probably, fourth or fifth language for these kids. It gives you some idea of the calibre of writing I was receiving in my own classroom, as well.

As I had been reading, a large flatbed truck had pulled up outside with a great grinding of brakes. The road workers began filing in, dusty and dishevelled—exiled Tibetans, thin wild-haired Biharis and Bangladeshis, topi-topped Nepalis: the poorest of the poor, the landless, the dispossessed, the nationless. The government could never get the Bhutanese to do the job of building roads. It was backbreaking work. Roads were carved into the mountainsides with sweat and dynamite, the fatality rate was high, and thousands of bonded labourers had died in the sun and dust, in the monsoon downpours, and in the snow of winter. I had seen women in thin cotton saris breaking stone by hand in swirling snow at 3,000 metres (10,000 feet), no shoes on their feet and their babies in baskets by their sides, covered only with patched black umbrellas.

The Bhutanese had to do a certain amount of the road work. A medieval-style corvée was still in effect and each family owed so many days of labour to the dzong each year. The Thimphu Dzong, which housed the national assembly offices, had been rebuilt with this kind of labour (Lopen Yonten had met his wife on this project), but most of the road work still fell to poorly paid foreign labourers who lived a semi-nomadic existence in hastily constructed shanty towns along the road's edge. There, living in flimsy huts made of bamboo mats and flattened forty-six-gallon drums, they sweated away their brief lives in bonded servitude.

These were the people that shuffled into the Dantek Canteen that dreary afternoon and sat speechless on the dirty benches clutching chipped tumblers of Indian-style tea with dumb-animal expressions of exhaustion on their faces. One man sat slightly apart from the rest at the end of the long trestle table in a corner. He was notable only in his air of detachment from the rank-and-file and by the covert interest with which he took in his surroundings. He was tall and thin and wore a maroon cotton shirt and a pair of worn polyester trousers the colour of chocolate. His sleeves were rolled up to his elbows. His pants were typically tight-fitting with flare cuffs. He was dirty, his brown hair long and matted and unkempt. His nails were cracked and blackened. He had blue plastic sandals on his feet. His face was no cleaner than his hands. He had small rodent features and a wispy moustache and at least two weeks growth of beard. He was altogether unremarkable at first glance. I assumed he was a labourer like the rest. Then he raised his head and looked in my direction, and I noticed his green eyes and it struck me all of a sudden, with a kind of shock, that he was European.

The man sat at the end of the table by himself, clearly desiring no company. He kept nervously stroking his moustache or picking at the tabletop with his long broken nails. He was highly strung and obviously desired to be left alone. He avoided my gaze and kept glaring out the window as if he were waiting for something or perhaps someone to arrive. He had a fugitive appearance, and I was dying to ask him a question, to discover who he was and how he had ended up here in these dire circumstances. Don't misunderstand me. It was not that I lacked sympathy for the others, but their stories I was familiar with—victims of drought or soil erosion, younger sons or daughters of poor peasant families with no other options, victims of caste distinction, victims of foreign invasion and civil unrest. But how had a European found his way to this outpost of progress and fallen on such hard times? Was he a down-and-out dharma bum? A drug addict? An army deserter? In Canada, he would have excited no comment (and probably less sympathy), a skid row bum perhaps, a junkie, but here? Who was he? With the borders so jealously guarded, how did he get in? Here was a story, I thought to myself.

He kept so much to himself, like an armadillo curled into a ball, that I could not see an opening into his world. And then it was too late. Mr. Das was gathering empty glasses and the troop rose as one tired animal and filed out of the door wearing their misery like a pall. I followed them out. They climbed into the back of the open truck. The mysterious stranger stood near the cab, with his elbows resting on the roof. It was even a bleak truck. Most trucks in the subcontinent are gaily caparisoned with mirrors and chrome and streamers and pictures of Hindu deities, but this one was just dusty and battered and painted a dull blue. Our eyes met for an instant, the stranger's and mine, there was a spark of recognition perhaps, of fellow feeling, and then he was whirled away in a grinding of gears and a thick cloud of blue diesel exhaust. My last glimpse of the stranger was of him pulling the collar of his shirt across his mouth like a cowboy's bandanna as the truck ground its way slowly toward the south, and he drifted out of my life as quickly as he had entered.

Looking back on the incident, I fear I may have deluded myself. I never heard him speak, and there are many fair-skinned blue-eyed people living in northwest India and Afghanistan. Why should I assume my mysterious stranger was European? Yet, there was something about the fellow that felt familiar. If I was more superstitious, I would have sworn I had met my doppelgänger, for he was my mirror-image.

TWENTY

THE DREADFUL FÊTE

ON OCTOBER 31, 1988, the King of Bhutan was married. This was the most important event to take place in the country in the two years that I was there. The wedding took place in Punakha Dzong, the traditional winter capital of Bhutan, and following the ceremony there were three days of feasting and celebration to which thousands were invited. It was front-page news in the national newspaper, *Kuensel*. I knew that many people across the country would be relieved. In a monarchy, the issue of succession is tantamount and, at thirty-three, King Jigme Singye Wangchuck had left marriage rather late. Sitting in the staff room, sipping tea, I read the newspaper article with interest, but then I set my cup down in amazement and began to read it again. Had I understood correctly? As I stared at the handsome wedding photograph, I was, well, bemused. It seemed that the king had married not one wife, but four, and all were sisters. I knew that polyandry and polygamy were legal in Bhutan, it was a matter of economics in most cases, but surely the king needn't concern himself with this. Why marry four women? It made no sense. I looked around for some help. At one end of the conference table sat our senior Dzongkha instructor. He was a kind and gentle man, well-respected by the staff and students for his learning and integrity. Surely, if anyone could enlighten me, it would be him.

"*Kuzu zangpo-la, Lopen.*"

"Ah, Mr. Ken," he nodded and smiled. "Good morning-la."

"Have you seen the newspaper, *Lopen*?"

He nodded enthusiastically.

"You must be very happy to hear that His Majesty has been married."

"Yes," he said. "For many years now his people have been concerned for His Majesty's happiness. Now we are most pleased to hear that he is married."

"Yes," I muttered, unsure how to proceed, "but, Lopen, it says here that His Majesty has married not one, but four wives..."

"La."

"And that all four wives are sisters..."

"La."

"Well," I struggled for words. "I don't understand. Why marry four sisters? Please do not be offended, but it seems to make no sense to me. Won't the issue of royal succession become unnecessarily complicated?"

He thought for a moment and smiled at my consternation. "Mr. Ken, it is like this in Bhutan. The four queens belong to a very important family, one that has always been a political rival to the Wangchucks. This marriage will solve two problems: it will provide Bhutan with an heir and it will unite the political ambitions of two powerful families, ending a long feud."

I paused to digest this. "I think I understand, but why would he marry all four sisters? Wouldn't one have been enough? I mean, won't each sister want her own child to be the next ruler of Bhutan?"

"Oh, the king has named his heir already, Jigme Gesar Namgyal, the eldest of his sons."

"Eldest son? You mean he already has children?"

"Yes, His Majesty has eight children."

Now I was really confused, but my friend patiently explained. It seems that the king had been encouraged to court one of the daughters of this prominent family by his royal advisors, to bury old animosities and create political stability. He had courted all four and the results were palpable. He named his eldest son heir at the time of the wedding. After the wedding, each queen would live separately in her own home with her own children. There was something fairy-tale-like about the whole predicament—a quincunx of star-crossed lovers who nevertheless manage to live happily ever after. I looked at the wedding photo again. It was a handsome family, but no one was smiling.[13]

The staff meeting that week progressed much as usual. The principal did most of the talking. Then, as he was wrapping up the meeting, he turned to me and said, "And now, Mr. Ken will tell us about tomorrow's plans for the school fête."

The room fell silent. Everyone turned to look at me. I cleared my throat.

"Excuse me, Sir, but, if you remember, you excused me from the fête committee, so that I could work on the yearbook. You were going to appoint another person to chair the committee in my place."

The principal's face turned the colour of old red brick. He fumed inwardly. We could sense it coming and when it did, we were not disappointed, for it descended on our heads like a prairie hailstorm.

"What! WHAT! Has nothing been organized?" No one answered. "Nothing?" he said in a very arch tone, looking around the room. And then the reality seemed to sink in. "Nothing?" His face fell. "But the invitations have gone out. Dasho Dzongdag, Trimpen, Head of Hydel, everyone of importance has been invited." He looked around the table in anger and dismay, but no one dared meet his eye. "Nothing! Nothing is planned! Must I do everything myself? You are all much too lazy. This will cause great shame to the school. You are a disgrace! I will look like a bloody fool!" He pushed his chair violently back from the table and rose to his feet.

"I am leaving," he announced. And he did. He stomped out of the room to the school Jeep, where he barked at the driver to shift himself. The driver sullenly crawled into the back and winced as our beloved leader bucked the transmission down the serpentine drive. We found out later that the principal picked up his wife and proceeded to the college at Kanglung where he sought solace in the bottom of a bottle of whisky in the company of a few friends.

After the principal left, the meeting broke up slowly. Everyone was talking excitedly about the grand scene. When the staff room cleared there were only four of us left sitting at the long table: Sister Leonard, Brother Frederick, Grant, and me. I raised my eyes from the table and looked at the other three.

"What are we going to do?" I asked.

"Do!" said Grant. "We are not going to do anything. This is Hitler's problem, not ours. He's the one who forgot to appoint a new chair."

"But Grant..."

"But nothing. Let him stew. It serves him right after everything he said. Besides, you heard him, nothing's ready."

Sister Leonard piped up. "Well, strictly speaking, that is not true." We turned to her and she continued. "My girls have been doing handicrafts for months. We have plenty of things to sell at the craft table. Though," and she looked at Grant and nodded, "I agree with Mr. Grant. It is time someone taught this insufferable man a lesson. Still, I do not want to disappoint the students. They have all worked so hard."

Brother Frederick, who was one of the most upbeat souls I have ever met, jumped in. "All is not hopeless," he said. "I am sure that if we call the House Captains together we can organize something. It will not be terrific, to be sure, but it will pass."

"Do you think so?" I asked, still unconvinced.

"Certainly," beamed Brother Frederick. "Let me gather the captains and we will meet in a few minutes on the hill behind the school."

Grant rose to his feet, shaking his head. "I can't believe you guys. You're all crazy. You are going to bail him out, after all he said?" He groaned and threw his hands in the air. "Well, count me out," he said. "I refuse to do anything to help that man."

He left the room, still shaking his head.

A little later we met on the hill behind the school, as Brother Frederick had suggested, and once again I was amazed by my students. In no time, they had everything organized. The boys had plenty of ideas for games of chance, and they volunteered to organize work parties to clean the gymnasium and set up tables and chairs. Sister Leonard was in charge of the craft tables. Brother Frederick would take several boys and canvass the merchants in the bazaar for prizes and would purchase enough orange squash and snacks for refreshments. I was in charge of tickets and money. Everything fell into place with surprising ease. It would not be a spectacular fête, but, as Brother Frederick had said, it would pass.

Throughout our meeting on the grassy knoll, I was aware of Grant lurking just out of earshot. He was pacing, hands in pockets, shoulders hunched forward, scuffing his shoes in the dust. Finally, he cleared his throat, came forward, and threw himself on the grass.

"Okay, what do you want me to do?"

One of the boys, looked thoughtful and said, "There should be decorations for the gymnasium." Another ventured, "Mr. Grant Sir, has a good two-in-one. We will need a loudspeaker to make announcements and to make music so everyone is feeling happy."

"Hurumph" grunted Grant. "I guess I could do that. I will get a couple of boys to help me."

"Thanks," I said.

He grinned ruefully. "Well, since you three seemed determined to make fools of yourselves, I couldn't very well let you do it alone, could I?"

And so we worked hard all that afternoon and evening, and by the time evening study was finished, we were ready. Or as ready as we would ever be. But when we awoke in the morning, another drama presented itself.

It seemed that after his evening visit to the college, the principal had insisted on driving home himself, even though it was clear to everyone, his wife included, that he had had far too much to drink. Just above Dowzor he failed to negotiate an inside curve and drove the Jeep right into a rock cutting, demolishing the vehicle and scaring the daylights out of his pregnant wife. They had to walk back to the school in the dark.

I later talked to the driver, and he was disconsolate. A driver without a vehicle is redundant and so he had been assigned to assist Wangpo in cleaning toilets and sweeping up. As the principal phrased it, "If he can't drive I'm not going to pay him to sit around doing nothing, so he will do whatever I tell him." It was a great comedown for Chimi—from driver to sweeper—and there was no avenue of complaint open to him: no union representative, no ombudsman.

The "fateful" day went fairly well. The dignitaries came and were given a tour of the school by our bruised and hung-over fearless leader. They tried their hand at a few games of chance, bought a few crocheted doilies, and then they left. The only sour note was when the principal's wife insisted that the craft table open an hour early for a private viewing, so that the she could grab all the best stuff.

"Well," I ventured, trying to see a bright side, "her money is as good as anyone's, I suppose."

"It was not fair," replied Sister Leonard grimly.

After the event was over I was sitting in the staff lounge with the other event organizers, adding up the receipts. A young boy knocked at the door and was beckoned in. He handed me a note and left.

"What is it?" asked Grant.

"The principal wants a financial report on the fête."

"When?"

"Immediately." I sighed, showing him the note. "I'm almost done. I should be able to give him something in a few minutes."

"No." We all looked up in surprise. It was Sister Leonard. "Make him wait," she said. She pointed to the chit in my hand. "That should have been an apology or a letter thanking you for your work. Make him wait. The longer, the better."

To my surprise, Brother Frederick reluctantly agreed.

Grant laughed. "All right, Sister!"

The next morning, I knocked lightly on the blue office door. There was no response from within. I pushed open the warped and ill-fitting door—warped and ill-fitting because, like everything else in the school, it had been constructed of green wood—and entered. The plastic lace curtains were drawn and the office was filled with a dusty gloom. The principal sat behind his desk at the far end of the long narrow office, his head bowed and his fingers splayed across his close-shaven scalp. I walked forward silently and placed the envelope on the corner of his desk.

"Here's the money," I said. I would normally have added, "Sir," but kept it back. I placed a ruled sheet of foolscap beside the sealed envelope, covered with columns of figures. "I've reimbursed Sister Leonard for her materials and paid the merchants in the bazaar what we owed them." The principal did not look up. He remained immobile. "We made 695 rupees, most of it from the girls' craft table." And we could have done better, I thought angrily, if everything had not been planned at the last minute. But I didn't say anything. There was no point. The awkward silence lengthened.

"That will be fine."

I waited. I wasn't going to be brushed off that easily. The principal looked up. His face looked old and worn. I felt a pang of remorse. At that moment, I think that I actually felt sorry for the man. I hesitated a moment longer, then turned to go.

"Mr. Ken." I paused and looked back. The principal gazed down at his desktop and coughed awkwardly. "Thank you," he whispered. I found it difficult not to grin. I turned again to leave, got halfway to the door, and then thought, what the hell, he owes me.

"Sir. Miss Karin at the school for the blind is going to Samdrup Jongkhar this afternoon and she has invited me to come along." I expected a battle, especially after his rant at the last staff meeting about teachers leaving campus without his authorization, so I hastened to add, "I will need someone to cover for me at study hall, but I'm sure Mr. Dorje Tshering will help." I waited, amazed at my own audacity.

"Yes, no problem."

No argument! It was unprecedented. I was exultant, but as I looked at the shrunken figure seated behind the desk, I was surprised to find a feeling akin to compassion stirring in my soul. I felt a need to comfort the man.

"Thank you, Sir," I said and left him to his thoughts.

TWENTY-ONE

SAMDRUP JONGKHAR

"LISTEN TO THIS," said Knut as he snapped his newspaper, a Swedish daily, and folded it flat. "In Saudi Arabia, they are to, ah, translate, yes, that is the word, to translate the...hmm...I do not know the spelling of this word in English, Ken," and he proceeded to spell it out, "Q-U-R-A-N."

"Yes, 'Quran,'" I replied. "It's the same word in English, Knut."

"Ach, so." He continued, his voice quivering with indignation. "It says here they have plans to translate the Quran into all of the languages. That is to say that...that... aaach!" He stumbled for the words to express his anger and waved his hands frantically in the air, so that the newspaper slid off his lap and fell to his feet on the floor of the moving vehicle.

Karin and I paused in our conversation in the back seat. "That is very interesting, Knut," she said and turned back to me.

"Interesting!" he sputtered. "Interesting! Do you not see what this is?"

We shook our heads.

"They will use their oil money to spread their heathen gospel to all places in the world. They will take over!" He turned in his seat to face Karin and pointed a threatening finger at her. "And you will have to wear a tent!"

"A tent?"

"You know what I mean!" he cried and his jug handle ears grew pink in outrage. We were winding our way south in the blue Toyota Hi-Lux that belonged to the school for the blind. Karin and I were packed together in the back seat with Sangye, a new teacher to her school, a young man of whom I had heard good things. Knut was in the front seat with the driver and the space between them was filled by a large vinyl carryall—the sort that airlines give away—from which Knut had guardedly extracted the newspaper. It was a very heavy bag and the rest of us had difficulty understanding why it was not on the roof rack with the other luggage.

Karin was angry. The teachers at her school took turns going to Samdrup Jongkhar to do the school's shopping. It was a scrupulously shared perk, a chance to get away, to eat in a restaurant, and to do some shopping of your own. Karin was always very generous with her time and I knew her *jola* was full of shopping lists from a dozen people in the valley who had asked her to pick up things for them. Sangye was along because he was new to the school and to the valley and he was setting up house. It was a kindness that he was allowed to come, to stock up his shelves with canned and dried goods, and to purchase some curtain material, a hurricane lamp, a few jerry cans of kerosene, and perhaps a wicker armchair. But Knut had no business being there. He had already been to Samdrup Jongkhar several times since his arrival. His turn would come again. He had bullied his way into the truck. I tried to remain neutral in the conflict, since I really had no right to be there either, but had come as Karin's guest.

Things were not going well at the school for the blind. Knut had arrived ostensibly as a teacher but had immediately begun making changes, exceeding his authority and countermanding Nawang's orders. "He does not understand," Karin had told me earlier. "I have tried to explain to him that he is not in charge, but he goes around telling everyone what to do. The other day, he told all of the cooks to paint the boys' dormitory. He said it was a pig's house."

"Sty," I said, gently correcting her. "A pig sty."

"Sty? Really?" Karin giggled. "What a funny word, sty. Anyway, the cooks protested, but he yelled at them, called them lazy, and they obeyed. You know how they are; they don't like to argue. Well, lunch came and, of course, there was no food. Nawang was furious. He yelled at the cooks. 'Why are you painting? You are cooks. Where is the children's food? Who told you to paint?' Well. They told him and, of course, he came to me. He is in an awkward position, you see. The money comes from the mission and Knut is the mission's representative, so he cannot yell at Knut. So he comes to me, and I tell you, Ken, I am so stressed. You cannot imagine how it is. I am always the go-between. I just get so stressed.

"And do you know what else? He is a hopeless teacher, simply hopeless. Ken, I don't think I have met a man before who is so stupid. The students have complained to me in a quiet way—Nawang has given him the senior science class—"

"Well, that's good. He is an engineer, after all," I said, trying to be encouraging.

"*Ja*, so?"

"Then he must know a lot about science, right?"

She looked confused. "What? I don't understand." I told her that in Canada an engineer would have to study a great deal of science to qualify for his degree. "*Ach*, I see. No, no, for Knut it is not like that in Sweden." Karin explained to me that the term "engineer" had a fairly broad connotation in Swedish. You could become an engineer at a community college. The nearest I could figure, Knut had been some kind of janitor before he joined the mission.

"So he is hopeless at teaching science. The students say they do not understand a thing that he says. Of course, his English is not so good. I have offered to help him plan his lessons, but he just says, 'Why, so?' How can I tell him that the children are complaining of him? And there is more."

"It gets worse?"

"*Ja, ja*. He is not teaching them the text in his senior geography class. He has them reading Braille Bibles that he brought from Sweden. He does not see how this is. How he could hurt the mission. He is so—*och*, what is the word you use?"

"Dense?"

"*Ja*, dense!" she laughed and then turned serious. "I get so stressed, you know. Because of this, I feel like vomiting much of the time. Yes! Don't laugh. I do. You don't know how I feel when I get so stressed like this."

I didn't know, but I could imagine. And this was the man who had taken up the whole front seat with his airline bag and forced the three of us to jackknife ourselves in the back.

The journey to Samdrup Jongkhar would take anywhere from five to six hours, winding as it did, provided there were no landslides or the road was not washed out. The narrow road kept to nosebleed elevations, following contourlines and ridgetops, and always to one side there was a precipitous drop of hundreds of metres to a young river kicking its way through fallen rock with coltish energy. We stopped several times for tea at little bamboo stalls and once bought tangerines from a woman walking along the road with a shallow basket of the fruit balanced on her head. It had to be nerve-wracking for the driver, and he leaned on the horn constantly to warn oncoming traffic on the blind curves. More often than not, though, it was cattle, not vehicles that we encountered when rounding a sharp corner. In a country with so little level terrain, a roadway, however narrow, made an excellent footpath from one mountain pasture to another. As we travelled southward, we moved into lower elevations and the temperature grew warmer. Once, we surprised an old man trying to cool off by flapping the skirt of his gho in the sultry breeze, exposing his naked buttocks with each undulation. Knut cried, "My goodness, look at that fellow," and the back of his neck burned red in embarrassment, but the rest of us, I'm sorry to say, burst out laughing. The driver slowed the truck and honked his horn, but the old man paid him no heed, just continued to rhythmically expose himself to our view. We crept to within yards of him before he was aware of our presence. He must have been as deaf as a post, for when he finally did turn around, his expression was more of terror than embarrassment.

As you get lower and closer to Assam, the scenery changes dramatically. Temperate forests give way to black gorges of actual jungle. You feel like you might have strayed onto the set of a Tarzan movie, and you expect that at any moment a tiger might step out from behind a palm frond and onto the road (as indeed it might). But the most dramatic thing we saw that day was not the jungle, but its absence.

After several hours of driving, we rounded yet another corner and gasped. The hillside was suddenly bare of vegetation. A corrugated scab of chestnut soil was all that remained. Hardened rivulets of earth ran across the road like blood, leaving behind deep parched gulleys on the mountain face. Charred stumps covered the slope and stalks of harvested corn bristled in the dry mud. Above the road and partway up the mountain we could see the perpetrator's simple home: a bamboo hut with veranda, erected on stilts, itself threatening to slide down the hillside.

Sights like this were becoming more and more common. Even in Khaling, all of the arable land was in use and several small farms like this had been started, eating away at the mountain's green coat like mange. The slope was much too steep and there was no attempt to terrace the hillside. In next year's monsoon this whole mountainside could slide into the river. Then the family would be forced to move and start again if they were to grow enough food to survive. Bhutan was land poor and beginning to feel the stress of overpopulation. One only had to look next door, to Nepal, to see the future: denuded hillsides, severe soil erosion, flash floods, and sterile rivers.

Twenty-five years ago Bhutan had the highest rate of infant mortality in the world. It was also the poorest country in the world by our standards, but it was self-sufficient. A delicate balance had been struck between man and nature. What had upset the balance? Well, we had, of course. With the introduction of modern health care the population had boomed. In Khaling it was not unusual for families to have seven or eight children, but there was no farm to will to such a large family. And what were these children to do when they left school? Many drifted to the growing urban centres and, for the first time in Bhutanese history, there is unemployment and juvenile delinquency. I said something along these lines to Karin as we gazed out the window.

"Would you have us let the babies die, then," said Karin, "when it is so easy to save them? People have better health now—no more goitres, no more tuberculosis, and what of the lepers?"

I had difficulty answering her, especially her last point.

Sangye intervened. "With all respect, Mr. Ken, you are being foolish. Our government invited foreigners to build us schools and hospitals. We want these things. I do not want to go back to the farm. My life is better now."

"Yes, I know. But what of my students? They do not want to go back to the farm either, but will there be jobs for them when they graduate? It used to be that a highschool graduate in this country was guaranteed a position in the civil service, but that is no longer the case. What will they do?"

"Become businessmen," said Sangye. "One day I would like to run trekking tours for foreigners—take them to places like Jhomo Lhari, Laya, or Sakteng."

"Perhaps," I reluctantly agreed, having private reservations about the benefits of tourism.

"The Lord will provide," pronounced Knut piously.

"If Allah wills," whispered Sangye, winking at Karin and me.

The final stretch of road dropped swiftly from the sky to the plain below. The jungle closed in. Brilliant tropical flowers bloomed by the roadside, and orchids hung from caches of humus in the cleft rock. Bright waterfalls sparkled in quiet glades and troupes of rhesus macaques climbed liana vines and screeched in alarm at our passage through their world. We touched down where the young river burst from its mountain confinement and spread itself out over a wide gravel bed, where, energy spent, it began to wind in huge oxbow bends through palm plantations, orange groves, cardamom plots, and rice paddies. This delta was one of Bhutan's *duars* into the mountains, where lushly forested hills fell away on either side, like a crowd parting for royalty, to reveal with sudden unexpectedness a sweeping view of the billiard table plains of Assam.

The immigration check post was here where the road left the mountains, and a blue-bereted policeman checked my documents. A check post in town would have been useless, as the town sprawled on both sides of the border, separated only by a low brick wall. This wall had numerous gates through which the residents of both countries passed back and forth at will. Some type of settlement must have always existed here, where Indian merchants had set up a bazaar to trade with the Bhutanese of the Himalayan interior. It was from here that the British had invaded in 1865 in the Anglo-Bhutanese conflict.

Samdrup Jongkhar must have been just a small dusty village back then, but recent political developments have led to its prosperity. The Chinese invasion of Tibet closed northern borders and forced more trade to come south. Nineteenth-century transmigration in the Himalayas saw large numbers of economic refugees from Nepal come to these malarial foothills and carve out farms. But ironically, the greatest prosperity has come indirectly from development projects. Huge infusions of foreign capital into Bhutan's economy by development agencies and loans from the World Bank have seen Samdrup merchants grow rich.

The town, despite its location, is Indian in character. It is hot, dusty, and humid. The shops and blocks of flats are constructed of whitewashed brick and concrete with flat rooflines. There is a functional simplicity about the main street. Everything runs in straight lines, both horizontal and vertical, as if the chief architect of the place had been an unimaginative child of three with a set of building blocks. The paint on the buildings was faded, peeling, and stained by the monsoon rains. The façades were crumbling, and rusting steel reinforcement rods still protruded optimistically from the flat rooftops, waiting for that third or fourth storey to be added. The fashions one saw were Indian, too: white singlets and dhotis; poorly made Western-style clothing in synthetic fabrics; saris, nose-rings, and bangles. Even the Bhutanese seemed a minority here, a curiosity.

We parked on the dusty street outside the concrete steps that led up to the Shambala Hotel. *Shambala* is another name for the Buddhist paradise. If so, I expect paradise will look a lot like a college dorm. Karin and Knut booked their own rooms, but Sangye asked if he could share a room with me to save money. It was late afternoon, but Karin wanted to get a head start on her shopping. Knut disappeared mysteriously down the street with his blue vinyl carryall tucked protectively under his arm. Sangye had schoolmates he wanted to catch up with, so he abandoned me, as well. I sat at a table in the lobby restaurant under the ceiling fan and tried to unwind.

"Hi, Ken. What'll it be?"

I turned in my chair. "Hello, Danny. It's good to see you. How's business?" I extended my hand to the dapper man whose neatly trimmed beard framed a broad smile.

"Not bad. How are you surviving in Khaling?" Danny was an Indian from Kerala who had originally come to Bhutan to teach high-school science. He had been lured by the excitement and the promise of a relatively high salary but had quit when a fundraising effort went sour. He and his students had raised thousands of rupees to outfit new science labs at his school, but when his principal heard that His Majesty was paying a visit, he spent the money on paint instead to spruce up the institution's appearance. It was, of course, the principal's call, but Danny felt betrayed and did not renew his contract. Instead, he came south and became the manager of this hotel. Like many businesses in Samdrup Jongkhar the absentee owner was Bhutanese, the staff Indian.

"Can I get you a drink? Perhaps a gin? You're in malaria country now, my friend."

"No, I'm off the hard stuff for a while, Danny. *Tsetchu*, you know. I need a vacation from alcohol."

"Ah hah!" laughed Danny. "I remember that feeling well enough. How about a soda—a Limca or a Thums Up?"

"Limca would hit the spot, thanks."

When he returned with a glass and the unstopped bottle of lime soda, I asked him, "Why are there so many monks in the hotel? Some sort of convention?" I had noticed an unusual number of red-robed clerics in the halls and in the lobby.

"You wouldn't believe me if I told you."

"Try me."

"They're trading on the black market."

"You're kidding!"

"No. They meet buyers here, middlemen, and flog Buddhist relics: paintings, statues, books, masks, musical instruments, that kind of thing. There's a big market out there for Buddhist artifacts. Collectors in Japan, Europe, and North America pay top dollar, I'm told."

"I don't believe it."

Danny shrugged. "Believe it, buddy."

I had trouble picturing these benign men, young and old, with shaved pates and swaddled in wine-red robes, as accomplices in the spiritual rape of their own country. Nevertheless, it was true. Enormous numbers of cultural relics were leaving Bhutan. The newspapers blamed tourists, but it was clear that there must be some collusion to facilitate such a vacuuming of the cultural treasure houses. Barbara Crossette, a correspondent for the New York Times, writing in 1995, said that there were virtually no chortens in the entire country that had not been vandalized in the search for saleable treasure. She also reported on a violent attack on a monastic site by young thugs intent on thievery that had ended in murder and had shocked the country.[14] I think it is safe to say that if you purchase a Bhutanese relic in an antique store outside of Bhutan, it has been stolen from a temple site somewhere. The only bright note in this entire picture is that the skills required to replace these artifacts have not been lost, unlike (for example) some of the damage done in China in the twentieth century, which can never be repaired because the knowledge required has not been passed on.

I finished my soda and stepped outside. Danny was engaged with another customer. I was starved for something to read. I had read nearly everything in our school library. I had even read all of the back issues of National Geographic magazine. I remembered seeing a small bookstall in town on a previous trip and decided to pay it a visit. Dusk was falling in a soft orange glow across the plains. Shopkeepers were lighting candles and lamps, and the open storefronts took on the cosy aspects of caves, their Neanderthal occupants casting long flickering shadows. I walked down the main street and then turned left, down a dark narrow alley, careful to avoid the open sewers, the rotting vegetables underfoot, and the roaming pye-dogs.

I found the bookstall jammed between two blocks of flats. It was a wooden shanty, hardly bigger than a garden shed. It was really more of a newsstand than a bookstall. Stacks of newspapers and magazines in Hindi, Nepali, English, and Dzongkha sat weighted down under heavy lug nuts that also functioned as candle-holders. The books were found at the back of the stall and most had passed through the hands of more than one reader. Most were lurid romances or improbable adventure thrillers in Hindi, judging by the covers, but there was also one sagging shelf of English books at the very back, and you had to wriggle your way past stacks of books, browsing customers, and open flames to see it. I entered the stall, careful not to upset any of the candles perched precariously on unstable piles of reading material and careful, too, not to jar the elbows of any of the meditative customers who were deeply involved in a book or magazine. I moved to the back of the shop and ran my finger over the spines of the cheaply bound paperbacks. These were the sort you saw flogged on any Indian railway platform: Sidney Sheldon, Robert Ludlum, Ian Fleming, Erle Stanley Gardner, and every book with a photograph of a scantily-clad blonde on the cover regardless of the content. At the end of the shelf, however, in the deepest corner of the shop, there were some hardcover books bound in series. I removed one from the shelf and held it up to the weak candlelight. I had to smile. Progress Publishers, Moscow. I flipped through the titles. Most were Soviet Socialist–Realist stuff that I didn't recognize, cheaply bound and printed on poor quality paper, with titles like *How the Iron Was Forged* or *The Young Idealists*. Many, I noticed, had been awarded the Stalin Prize. One title caught my eye, *Gogol: The Collected Stories*. Tales of the macabre. That was the ticket. I pulled it from the shelf.

Suddenly, the municipal diesel generator kicked in and the lights came on all over town. The single naked bulb hanging in the centre of the shop glowed unevenly. The customers looked around with pained expressions as their eyes adjusted to the brightness. Without leaving his seat or his cashbox, the shopkeeper reached out and began snuffing candles with moistened fingertips. I turned, squinting, and found myself face to face with the mysterious European stranger from the Dantek Canteen in the Khaling Bazaar.

"Hey!" I started involuntarily. His face went long in surprise, and he turned quickly and left the shop, spilling a stack of newspapers to the ground. The tiny shop-keeper hopped off his stool and shouted in protest. I started out of the shop, too, in pursuit and the proprietor's protestations followed me in Bengali. I found my arms firmly pinned, and I struggled to free myself. "What? What?" I shouted. In desperation, I tried a little Sharchopkha, "Hang tshaspe-mo?" Then I realized it was the book. I had forgotten it was still in my hand. Hurriedly, I pulled a fifty-rupee note from my pocket, wrapped the shopkeeper's fingers around it and twisted out of his grasp, shouting, "Sorry, sorry," as I dashed off into the night.

I entered the main street at a run, but it was too late. My mysterious stranger had eluded me once again.

When I returned to the hotel, I found Karin and Danny seated on wicker armchairs on the porch under a row of coloured lanterns.

"Hei, Ken. Come sit with us."

"Thanks. Let me get something to drink first."

I entered the lobby and returned with a Limca and another chair. Somewhere in the night, firecrackers went off. We turned and looked up the street. A procession of lights was wending its way toward us. A line of brightly dressed women in their gold-embroidered saris, the tail of each drawn discreetly around their heads and held across their mouths, walked, gently swaying down the middle of the dusty street, their soft musical voices rippling like wind chimes on the cooling breeze. Men padded after them with baskets of fruit balanced on their heads, each basket illuminated by a small candle in a copper dish. Across the street in the gloom, I was sure I saw once again the saddened eyes of the unknown road worker reflected in the glow of the candles. I rubbed my eyes and the vision was gone.

"Ghosts," I murmured.

"What is that you are saying?" asked Danny.

"Nothing, Danny," I said. "I've just been imagining things."

"Things?" he inquired gently, "what things?"

"Oh, it's nothing." To change the subject, I asked, "What is this procession for? A wedding?"

"Probably Diwali. This is the last day. Today is the day young men visit their sisters to have tika put on their foreheads."

Diwali, of course, I thought. "It is the festival of the return of the god, Rama, right?" The lights were to guide Rama on his journey home after his period of exile.

"Yes, but also of Lakshmi, consort of Vishnu, and, if you live in Calcutta, of Kali." Kali, fiercest of the gods, with her garland of skulls. Kali, the destroyer.

"You must feel sad that you are far from your family," commiserated Karin. "Your sisters will be thinking of you this night. You must wish you were home with them." Danny just nodded and looked thoughtful. I knew that he, like many Keralans, was a Roman Catholic, but it must have been painful all the same to watch these happy families pass by. Karin patted him delicately on the back of his hand.

I felt things were getting a bit too morbid, so I slapped the arm of my chair and said, "Hey, how about that peg you promised me earlier?"

Danny grinned wryly. "Sure." He disappeared into the hotel lobby and returned a minute later with a bottle of Bhutan Mist and two glass tumblers. (Karin didn't drink alcohol.) Danny poured a generous dollop in each glass. Then I raised mine in a toast.

"Cheers."

"Here's mud in your eye," he replied with a cock-eyed grin, and we all laughed.

That night I fell asleep over Gogol's stories. I had been reading "The Overcoat" and I dreamt that I, like Akaky Akakyevich in the story, wrestled for my overcoat with two unknown assailants in a dark street. The little Bengali bookseller was in my dream, too. He was clasped tightly about my right ankle, and he was screaming, "You cannot have that item until you pay for it with your life! I am afraid it is most impossible!" I awoke in a sweat and discovered that someone had covered me in a rough woolen blanket. I could hear snoring from the other bed, and I realized that

Sangye must have returned from the Hindi film palace where he had gone with his friends. I got out of bed to wash my face. I noticed that Sangye, though heedful of my welfare had neglected his own. I let down the mosquito net and tucked it in under his mattress. I crawled back under my own and lay awake. You know how it is when you have had a nightmare; you need a few moments to sort out what is real and what is not before you can go back to sleep. I tossed and turned in the narrow cot and could not get comfortable. There was a hard lump in the small of my back and I reached down and found poor Gogol. I had rolled over on him in my sleep and he was in a horrible state. I tried to straighten his crimped pages.

When I had first come to Bhutan I had no way of knowing how much, if any, reading material would be available. There had been severe weight restrictions imposed on our journey from Canada, so I had carefully chosen five titles I thought I could read again and again, and stuffed them in my backpack. I have already mentioned the Tolkien anthology given to me by my sister, but I also took a copy of the King James Bible, a Viking anthology of Henry David Thoreau, and two collections of poetry, one by William Butler Yeats and the other by Gerard Manley Hopkins. It was curious to reflect on the authors I had chosen. Was it a coincidence that the last three were failed hermits? Thoreau living his Walden Pond fantasy a stone's throw from Emerson's back door; Yeats, the failed man of action and failed lover, living in his Norman keep at Thor Ballylee; and Hopkins, perhaps the only true hermit among them, forced by his Jesuit vows into contact with a people he felt inadequate to help. All of these men were torn between the life of action and contemplation, working out that tension in their writing. Why did I love these writings? What was it I found so sympathetic in them? Was it their authors' contact with the countryside, or was it their dislike of the civilized communities of men? I came back repeatedly to Walden Pond, Innisfree, and Penmaen Pool, and dreamt of finding my own hermitage. But that night, I fell asleep once again, a victim of fearful premonitions and dreams.

The next morning, I awoke to the sounds of more firecrackers and by a chorus of roosters and human yowls of delight—perhaps the hangers-on of last night's celebrations. I crawled from beneath the mosquito netting and stumbled into the bathroom for a shower. The "shower" was a faucet fixed in the wall at waist height. I filled a bucket with cold water—the only temperature available—and scooped dipperful after dipperful over my retracting flesh. I wrapped a towel around my waist and returned to the room. I pushed open the hinged window and gazed out. The rising sun cast its light, rose-golden, over the dusty Indian plain. From my window, I looked across the river, which was mostly gravel channels at this time of year, to a flat tableland upon which sat the residential district of Samdrup Jongkhar, little one-storey bungalows of mud and wattle, white with red-corrugated roofs, set amid palm groves, behind which rose the lofty Himalayas, pale blue in the soft light of early morning, like a stage backdrop.

Sangye stirred in his bed. "What is the time?"

"Breakfast time. I'll see you down in the restaurant."

He muttered something, rolled over and went back to sleep.

In the lobby restaurant, I greeted Danny at the front desk-cum-bar and looked for a place to sit down. I was surprised to see Knut at the far end of the restaurant already up and dressed and talking to two Indian gentlemen. He was passing them a sheet of white paper that he had extracted from his ever-present blue carryall. I noticed then that the other diners also had these pieces of paper in their hands. The expressions on the diners' faces ranged from polite interest to extreme annoyance. I walked to the nearest table and asked a bearded Sikh if I could read his copy. He wagged his turban from side to side and handed me the paper. It was closely printed in Hindi, or perhaps Bengali, so I could not read it, but the title was also printed in English: "Good News," it said, "He Is Risen Indeed." I was floored. They were religious tracts.

I quickly went from table to table, gathering the pages from hotel patrons. There was no argument; many had already been discarded and lay on the floor. "Knut, Knut," I hissed and beckoned him over. "Take a seat"—he did—"and put these back in your bag." He left them untouched on the table between us and regarded me benignly with an innocent smile.

"What the hell are you doing?" I whispered.

"Goodness, what can you mean?" he asked in poorly pantomimed surprise.

"These!" I stabbed the pile with my forefinger.

"I am giving these people Good News."

"You can't do that!"

He raised his eyebrows in mock reproach. "I can see nothing wrong—"

"It's against the law in this country," I reminded him, trying to keep my voice under control.

"I can see no harm—"

"Damn it, Knut. Don't play the innocent with me. It was in our contracts when we signed on: 'No Proselytizing.' And I don't have to translate that for you. I'm sure it was made quite clear."

"I am only asking them to read, not—"

"You are breaking the law!" Curious faces turned in our direction.

"The Lord will protect me. I am doing his work."

"Worse still, you are breaking a trust."

There was a pause. He continued to smile guilelessly, but there was a sea change behind his eyes, like black oil spilling over water. "I have a higher trust. The Lord has called me to bring His Heavenly Jesus to these people. They must learn of his great love for them. I am following the example of Our Lord, who said, 'No man can serve two masters.' I have a greater trust, yes, a calling that is higher than any law of man. 'Go ye into all the world, preach the Gospel to every creature,' he commanded me—Mark, chapter 16, verse 15—and this also He spoke: 'Bring light into the darkness'—Second Corinthians, chapter 4, verse 6."

"I know where it comes from!" I shouted in annoyance. "Don't quote chapter and verse to me." Relax, I told myself, take a deep breath and count to ten. I tried a different tack. "Do you realize that you could end up in jail for this?"

"It is written: 'The very hairs of your head are numbered.' Also: 'The Lord is my strength. He is my refuge and my fortress: in him will I trust.' It is also written: 'If God is for us, who can be against us?' The Lord has promised to protect me, Ken, and so I put my trust in the Lord."

"Sure, he'll protect you," I snarled. "He'll protect you all the way back to Sweden. What of the mission, Knut? By openly bandying these about," I indicated the tracts, "you could endanger their work. You could get the whole lot of them kicked out."

A cloud darkened his face, and I supposed this had been a bone of contention between him and his colleagues already. "The Lord has made my duty clear," he stated emphatically, meaning, I suppose, that he knew better; so I tried another angle of approach.

"How closely have you looked into Buddhism, Knut, or Hinduism for that matter? Do you really believe that by turning these people into your brand of Christian you can make them better people? You must agree with me that the most important thing we can do, as human beings, is to try and love one another."

He smiled piously. "I do love my fellow man, as you put it. That is why I give them this Good News to read. I want them to know God. For unless a man knows Jesus Christ, Our Saviour, who is Love, he cannot love, not truly."

I was caught off guard, surprised to find Thomist logic coming from this man's mouth. Nevertheless, I persisted, trying to explain Mahayana Buddhism to Knut, and to convince him that the people he was trying to save were already generous, kind, and loving. "Converting them to Christianity won't make them more so. You should look into other religions, Knut, before you begin pushing your own. You owe them that much."

He said that all he read was God's Word and that was enough. He had been called to spread the Gospel and so he would. It was not his job to second guess God's commandment. Then his voice took on a tone of fatherly condescension.

"There is no use arguing, you know. You have your opinions and I have mine. You should recognize my right to my own opinions." He excused himself politely and left the hotel, the airline bag tucked up under his arm. I gathered up the tracts and took them to the front desk.

"Danny, can you get rid of these for me?" Danny tipped his head to one side and secreted them behind the counter. "I'm really sorry. I had no idea he was up to this."

He waved away my apologies. "No problem. I am a businessman and it comes with the territory. I have had to humour worse cases than his."

Later that day, Karin offered to take Sangye and me to the Mela Bazaar.

Mela Bazaar. The words conjured up visions of sin. The place was the Sodom and Gomorrah of the East, where every shop was a tavern and where the sullen-faced girls of many faiths and nations hung listlessly over windowsills beckoning the unwary. I, of course, had never been; not because I had never wanted to but because the Mela Bazaar was several kilometres over the border and so off limits to foreigners like me. I could not imagine why Karin would want to go.

"The prices are cheaper there, naturally."

I thought about that for a moment. "How will we get past the check post?"

"Oh, I am sure that will not be a problem. They must be reasonable when we tell them we are only going shopping."

I was not so sure, but I agreed to participate in the experiment. After all, what was the worst they could do? Send us back to Samdrup Jongkhar?

We all piled into the Hi-Lux and, as we drove, I reviewed all of the stories I had heard of the Mela Bazaar. Each year it was customary for the graduating class at Jigme Sherubling to take a tour to some other region of Bhutan and to visit some of the cultural and economic highlights of the area. The previous year the Class 10 students had made a trip to south-central Bhutan and had spent the first night boarding at the primary school in Samdrup Jongkhar. That night the Class 10 boys had made a surreptitious visit to the Mela Bazaar. Several weeks after their return some of the boys started walking like cowboys, with a peculiar rolling gait. Eventually when they couldn't take the pain anymore, they shamefully admitted they were in need of some medical attention. We sent them to the mission doctor and half a dozen or so were diagnosed with gonorrhea.

I also heard the tale of a volunteer teacher, who, returning, after a night in Mela, made the dire miscalculation of trying to leap across a stream only to learn that it was, in fact, a river. He fell fifteen feet down a slippery clay bank into the icy torrent, breaking his hip. It was all he could do to hold his head above the water and cry for help. Eventually, two good Samaritans came to his aid, loaded his carcass into a wheelbarrow and carried him to his cottage. They stripped off his wet clothing and made him comfortable on the cold concrete floor—the hard floor being more suitable than a soft bed in his condition. It wasn't until several hours had passed that the unfortunate realized that his rescuers weren't coming back and that they hadn't thought to send for a doctor either. He lay on the floor for three days, passing in and out of consciousness, and feebly crying for help. On the third day he heard voices outside his door and decided that if he didn't make an effort and stir himself he might lay there forever. He dragged himself across the floor, hauled himself to his feet using the handle of the door, and rested his weight against the doorframe. When he wrenched the door open, he saw a party of monks engaged in earnest conversation. He must have looked a sight, half-naked and half-dead, but the monks quickly recovered their composure when he, to the best of his linguistic ability, explained his predicament. A senior monk barked an order and a young novice hitched up his skirts and ran out of sight. Imagine our young teacher's alarm when the novice returned, not with a doctor, but with a cup of tea.

My thoughts continued along these lines as we drove across the dusty plain, through fields fallow with dry grass, and made a great bend toward a smudge of green in the distance that must have been the willows and neem trees along the bank of the river. To my surprise, the Indian border guard succumbed to Karin's charm and waved us through. When we finally reached the fabled bazaar, the Mother of Afflictions, my disappointment could not have been more complete. To begin with, everything seemed new. The streets were broad and dusty and laid out in a neat grid pattern. Most of the shops were one-storey cubicles of brick, open to the street, like so many automobile garages. I had expected something seedier, more atmospheric. I began to wonder if the driver had taken a wrong turn. This was not the Kasbah, it was the Asian equivalent of a North American strip mall.

The driver pulled over and parked in front of a row of shops. When the engine stopped, it was perfectly silent. We stepped out of the Hi-Lux. A lone emaciated cow strolled down the middle of a street in a scene straight from the last reel of a Spaghetti Western. There was no one around. Even the shops looked hollow and empty. I looked around in vain for some evidence of Mela's lurid reputation. The proprietor of one shop advertised that he was the purveyor of "pantings," but a closer inspection revealed that he was only a men's tailor.

Karin, however, seemed pleased with what she saw and hurried off in high spirits with her lists and her shopping baskets. Sangye, too, seemed happy enough to wander off and browse. I entered a brick cavern that advertised itself as the "Lakshmi Hotel: Fooding-Cum-Lodgings"; though, as it only had one floor, I could not imagine where the lodgings might be. Circular tables covered in linoleum were scattered about, surrounded by straight-backed wooden chairs with seats of plastic caning. Two ceiling fans turned slowly in the heat. A Mickey Mouse clock with moving eyes tocked the seconds. The walls were decorated with posters of Hindi and American film stars. I recognized Rambo, Bruce Lee, and the ubiquitous Phoebe Cates. There were plastic carnations in empty pop bottles in the centre of each table. The room was empty but for a gangly lad in singlet and sarong who was leaning against a doorframe at the back of the room and taking long drags on his bidi, the poor man's hand-rolled dart-shaped cigarette. I took a seat at one of the vacant tables and beckoned to him.

He approached the table, bobbed his head and smiled. "Would Sir be wanting somethings to eat?"

"Yes, what do you have?"

"I am sorry; there is no fooding at this time, please."

I digested this. "Perhaps, you have something to drink?"

"Sir is very kind, but I am not drinking somethings at this time also, please."

"Ah, then perhaps I could have something to drink."

He smiled again. "Most assuredly, Sir. I would be most pleased to bring Sir a something to drink. What would Sir's ah-pleasure be?" I asked him what he had and he began to list the various brands of soda pop and squash he carried, and of course he could always make Sir some tea or Nescafé instant coffee.

"Do you not have any alcoholic beverages?" I asked.

He seemed surprised at the question. "No, Sir."

"This is the Mela Bazaar, is it not?"

"Most assuredly, Sir."

I hummed and hawed a bit while I tried to think of how I would frame my next question. "Are there no, well, you know, *girls* in the bazaar."

The young man wagged his eyebrows in surprise and leaned forward. "Sir is looking for girls?"

"Well, no. I was just, you know, wondering if there were any."

"Yes Sir, there is many girls in Mela Bazaar." He wagged his eyebrows again and leered. "Many, many girls."

I looked around the empty room and out into the deserted street. "Then where are they?" I asked.

He leaned in close as if imparting a great secret. "Sir, they are shleeping."

"Sleeping?"

"Yes, this time of day, all girls shleeping."

So I ordered a Limca and sat alone at my table and tried to imagine the place full of desperate characters and scarlet women. But it was no use. It was impossible to feel seedy while sipping lime soda through a plastic straw in a clean restaurant with plastic carnations on the table and Mickey Mouse keeping time on the wall, when you knew darned well that all the girls were sleeping.

TWENTY-TWO

CHRISTMAS IN SAKTENG

CHRISTMAS IN 1988 PROMISED to be a bleak affair. School closed in mid-December, and we sent the children home. Because the school and dormitories were unheated, this was the best time of year for an annual holiday. Also, it was easy for the children to travel in winter, as the roads and trails were in good repair. Closing at this time, however, did mean that our school year did not match that of children in India and, as our Class 10 students had to write the Indian Central School Examinations to pass out of high school, the whole graduating class had to return in February for a study camp and then sit for their final examinations in March. This meant, in effect, that even though my contract was officially over, I still had to hang around for a couple of months and coach my senior students through their exams. In the meantime, I had a month and a half with nothing to do. I had moved out of my house in Khaling Gompa and into one of the empty teaching quarters at the school. It was a cold drafty concrete box with a metal roof, impossible to heat. The school was empty. I was at loose ends.

I was rescued from my melancholy isolation by a telegram. Ann, one of the Canadian teachers in Tashigang, had persuaded the local Dasho Dzongdag to grant her a travel pass to Sakteng Valley.[15] She could take four other teachers with her. Did I want to come? Did she need to ask? For two years I had dreamed of doing this very trip and now it was a possibility.

Sakteng Valley lay north and east of Khaling, in a corner of Bhutan that was on the border of the Indian territory of Arunachal Pradesh. The northern border of Arunachal Pradesh is called the McMahon Line after Sir Arthur Henry McMahon who had drawn this dotted line on a map in 1914 based on the highest watershed dividing

India and Tibet. China had never recognized this border, and after the Chinese take-over of Tibet, the McMahon Line became a bone of contention between India and China. There was sporadic fighting in the area in 1959, and, in 1962, a major battle was fought in which thousands died. There was a renewal of hostilities in 1975, and in 1988 the issue was still unresolved. As a result, Arunachal Pradesh was heavily garri-soned with Indian troops. Because Sakteng was so close to this disputed boundary, a special permit was required to visit the valley and these permits were rarely issued to foreigners; so when Anne said that she had received permission to travel to this little-visited part of the world, I jumped at the chance to be one of her party.

I caught the bus to Tashigang where I met with Anne and two other teachers, Sarah and Lily. Dasho Dzongdag himself gave us a ride into Radhi Valley, to the end of the vehicle road at Phongmey. The *dasho* was going to Phongmey to witness the swearing in of a new *gapu*, or village headman. Nancy, the fifth member of our party, was a teacher at Phongmey Primary School, and so we slept that night on the floor of her residence.

At Phongmey, we picked up two additional members for our party, Karma Yeshey, a senior student at Tashigang Middle School, whose father was the chief of police in Sakteng, and Pema Wangdi, a young student of Nancy's in Phongmey, whose home village was halfway to Sakteng. Both were heading home for the holidays and so it made sense to include them in our party. Pema Wangdi asked to be included in our trek to Sakteng. He seemed curious to witness our Christmas *chutsi* and to see Sakteng, as well. He was quite willing to work as a porter in exchange for room and board. Nancy found him an old sleeping bag for the journey. Unlike Karma Yeshey, who was touted out in track suit, sneakers, baseball cap, and powder- blue, quilted, down vest, Pema had only his school uniform and a pair of *chappals*. His *gho* was so old and worn, and had been washed so many times, that the navy blue had turned to bronzy-green. He did, however, own an old-fashioned aviator's cap with earflaps of which he was immensely proud and that he never took off.

That night, after the swearing-in ceremony was over and most of the people had gone home, our little expedition sat around a dying bonfire in a dry paddy below the school and chatted with the Dasho Dzongdag. The *dasho* was the chief administrator of Tashigang District and a very important man, but he was very friendly and humble and easy to speak with. He entertained us with stories of the Brokpa.

As we sat around the fire, someone jokingly said, "Maybe we'll see a yeti on our trip," for tales of the snowman are common in this corner of Bhutan. The *dasho* looked uneasy, hugged himself, and said, "I'm feeling cold. Is anyone else cold? Why don't we move inside?" We moved into the agricultural office, where the dasho was spending the night, and the dasho sent an assistant to rustle up six bottles of beer. As we left the fire, Karma Yeshey whispered, "It is bad luck to speak of the yeti out-of-doors. If you do, you may meet one. And no one wants to do that."

When we had settled ourselves on hard-backed chairs around the agricultural officer's desk and when enough cups were found for the party and the beer passed around, the dasho began to speak.

"Do you believe in the yeti?" he asked us.

We looked at each other uneasily, not willing to offend. Someone, I think it was Nancy, gave a very diplomatic answer, "We are skeptical, but since all of our Bhutanese friends believe in the creature, we cannot dismiss the tale. What do you believe, Dasho?"

He seemed pleased with Nancy's candour, for he continued. "Oh, of course, I believe in the yeti—His Majesty, himself, is a firm believer in the yeti—though 'yeti' is the Sherpa word for the creature; in Bhutan we call it migoi." He took a sip of his beer. "Actually," he said, "there are two separate creatures: the lesser known is called the mirgola, it is the smaller of the two, and maybe a metre (three feet) in height, with long arms. It is found deep in the forests at lower elevations. The migoi is much larger, more than two metres (6 feet) tall and larger than a yak; some say larger than two yaks. The migoi walks like a man on two legs and his body is covered in reddish-brown hair, though his face is generally hairless. The female migoi have large sagging breasts, otherwise male and female look much alike. They communicate by whistling, and it is said that they smell very strongly—something like ammonia. They are solitary creatures and live at high elevations so are rarely seen."

"Have you seen one, Sir?"

"No, but I have spoken with people who have. There are a number of Brokpa who have seen the migoi."

"Wouldn't that be neat!"

"No, you would not want to meet a migoi. They are dangerous when startled and it is generally agreed that seeing a migoi is bad luck—that illness and death can follow. Besides," the dasho grinned, "it is also said that lonely migoi carry off beautiful young women to be their brides and keep them captive in their caves in the mountains. I would hate to have to send out a search party should one of you be carried off.

"However," he continued, "should one of you be carried off, you must look for the creature's *dipshing*. The *dipshing* is a charm located under the *migoi*'s right arm that allows it to become visible or invisible at will. Such a charm would be very useful.

"The Brokpa have several interesting beliefs about the *migoi*," he said. "To begin with, they believe that the *migoi*'s feet are on backwards. This explains why no foreign expedition has ever tracked one with success. A Brokpa, of course, would never go looking for a *migoi*, but chance encounters are fairly common. The Brokpa believe that the *migoi* are supernatural beings who serve the local god and who are the guardians of certain sacred places. Most of the time, they are not seen because they can make themselves invisible. They are not dangerous, but they must still be shown the proper respect. Brokpa children are taught that if they meet a *migoi* they must bow down before it and remain silent and still. They must never anger the *migoi* by behaving disrespectfully." He paused and leaned forward dramatically. "So, who knows, you may meet a yeti, but it is not something to wish for. Even the Brokpa, who see the *migoi* as helpful creatures, regard such encounters as ill omens."

Dasho Dzongdag's final kindness to us was to organize two pack ponies for our party. We had been prepared to pack our own things on our backs, but Lily had recently been very ill with amoebic dysentery and was still quite weak, so the sturdy mountain ponies and their Brokpa owner, a man called Yeshi, were very welcome. The ponies also solved another problem. Since we suspected that we would not be able to buy food in Sakteng, we needed to pack in all of our supplies, and in this country that meant sacks of rice, lentils, potatoes, chilis, tea, milk powder, sugar, and salt—nothing freeze-dried or dehydrated—and since the bulk of it would probably have ended up on my shoulders, I was therefore doubly grateful.

Seen from above, Radhi Valley resembled a deep-bellied fishing dory—the river, its glittering keel, and its sides fashioned clinker-style in narrow strips of rice paddy. The prow was the narrow gap where the Gamri and Kulong Rivers joined beneath the watchful eyes of Tashigang Dzong; and its sternpost, Phongmey. East of Phongmey, the valley narrowed to a deep gorge. We were to follow the Gamri upstream through forest and rocky defile to the alpine valley of Sakteng, home of the Brokpa.

We left Phongmey the next morning. We passed above farmsteads for the most part—roofs bright red with drying chilies. We could hear the clack of shuttles as weavers wove cloth for the elegant *kiras* and *ghos* for which the valley was famed. Children scampered in the dry dusty paddies playing *korla* or football. Cows were staked on long tethers, one to a terrace, chewing contentedly on sheaves of banana leaves or willow shoots lefts by their owners. Women with towel headscarves pounded dry corn in tandem in large wooden mortars, reducing it to tengma. We passed above them, out of sight. Far below us, a shepherd played a haunting melody on a bamboo flute. The trail followed the folds of the hills as it descended, and several times we were forced to cross tributary streams on wire suspension bridges. The ponies baulked a little at this, and the ponyman threw stones at them until they skittered across the swaying planks in a burst of panic.

At one point, Pema Wangdi pointed out his village. It was across the chasm in a small green hanging valley cradled in the clouds. The path up from the river was a zigzag stitched straight up the cliff. There were few places in the world as isolated as Pema's home, I realized, and I wondered what it might be like to live there.

The trail slowly descended, and the river rose to meet us as the canyon walls closed in tightly on either side. We followed the south bank of the river where cold water went leaping over stones. The air grew chill and damp. We had once more left settlement behind and the vegetation became quite lush and thick. Orchids clung to the boles of moss-covered trees and ferns abounded. Azure water plashed and leaped between enormous grey boulders, many ribboned with crystalline intrusions. In time we emerged into a small clearing where there was a timbered cantilever bridge and, beside it, a small gristmill. In the clearing were numerous open-sided bamboo pavilions. Several Brokpa families had set up camp here for the night. Campfires flared in the dusk. Small family groups huddled around the blazing logs and eyed us suspiciously. There were yaks spread out and tethered across the meadow, resting, their burdens stacked neatly at their sides.

This was the closest I had been to the shaggy beasts, so I examined the yaks with interest. They were enormous, much larger than the scrawny cattle of Khaling, and as they breathed in and out, they swayed with a peculiar rocking-horse rhythm I had never seen in an animal before. To compare them to cows would be to say that mastodons were like elephants; they were altogether more primeval, like the muskox of the Canadian Arctic. These animals were the Brokpa's wealth. They provided him with milk, cheese, butter, meat, and hides. They were also his beasts of burden, though our ponyman assured us that they were very slow and had to be rested every five or six kilometres (three or four miles). As we passed through the meadow, Yeshi called out a greeting to several shepherds he knew, a greeting that was returned with curious questions. We crossed over the river on the timbered bridge, which had no guardrails. We could hear the creak of the horizontal waterwheel at the mill. Yeshi said that our destination for the evening was not much farther.

On the other side of the river we found ourselves in shadow, as the wall of the canyon towered over us, leaning over the river. We gained height on a couple of narrow switchbacks until we reached a broad stone shelf that extended so far under the overhang as to be almost a cave. There was a second smaller shelf farther up. The place reminded me of pictures I'd seen of abandoned cliff dwellings in the American Southwest. It was obviously a place much favoured by travellers; there was old straw bedding lying around and blackened rings on the rock, the evidence of past campfires.

After we unloaded the ponies, Yeshi led them back down to the river meadow and tethered them. The boys busied themselves with dinner preparations. Later we lay in our sleeping bags, just outside the circle of firelight and stared up at the stars.

From somewhere in the darkness, deeper in the cave, Karma Yeshey's voice interrupted the silence. "Look, Miss Nancy. We are just like cavemen"—a subject he had studied at school. He found this tremendously funny.

I lay awake for a long time that night, watching the fire-lit shadows cast against the cave wall, seeing the sparks from the campfire shoot out into the darkness like dying stars, and listening to the voice of the river. Yeshi continued to sit motionless by the fire long after the rest of us had retired to our beds, like a figure carved in ivory. His shadow, many times life-size, loomed and rippled over us. Stretched out on a mattress of rhododendron leaves, I fell asleep under his benevolent shade and a canopy of stars.

The next morning, we continued. As the canyon walls closed in, we had to leave the river and the path became steeper. We passed more pasture and began to enter bamboo groves with tufts of snow blooming amid the green shoots like flowers. Just below the pass, the trail cut into the side of a chalky cliff, with the river hundreds of metres below. Here, we met a yak caravan coming down and we, ponies and all, had to make ourselves very small against the cliff face to allow them to pass single-file along the cliff edge. One smaller yak, a young one (later, I heard its owner tell Yeshi it was shingmoo, that is, "new") grew frightened. It showed the whites of its eyes, baulked, tried to reverse, ran into the yak behind it and then bucked its load into the abyss. Yeshi reacted quickly. He ran forward and grasped the young beast's sharp upthrust horns and spoke soothing words to calm it down. The owner sidled up carefully and looked down the cliff face. Two large sacks tied at the throat and linked together hung draped across a bonsai-like pine growing in a cleft in the chalky cliff. There was a quick consultation, Yeshi locked wrists with the other man and then dropped over the edge out of sight. I gasped in alarm, but before I could say anything, there he was back on the ledge with the bags over his shoulder. I was astounded. I couldn't have done that. I would have thought myself into paralysis, wasting time conceiving fancy rope belays and other safety measures; but these men had no such doubts. They simply acted. After the yak was loaded and the pack train shuffled forward, we were released from our claustrophobic position and continued to the pass.

The pass was a broad grassy saddle, graced with a line of prayer flags. As we climbed onto the grassy verge, the valley beyond was slowly revealed: first, the circle of jagged snow-covered peaks, like sawteeth; then, the steep upland pastures; then, the forested lower slopes; and then, the broad flat valley floor, with a quilt pattern of fallow buckwheat fields and numerous grey stone *chortens* scattered like pawns on an irregular chess board. Sweeping around the right side of the valley was a broad alluvial plain of gravel and lichen, like Arctic tundra, threaded with innumerable streams that joined and separated like a vast shimmering silvery root system. In the centre of the valley, tight against the base of the rising mountains, was a tiny village, brown and grey and congested, very medieval in appearance: Sakteng. We had arrived.

As I read over these last few pages, I realize that I have not given you a very clear picture of the wonder of Sakteng Valley and of our journey. Words are, at best, a poor approximation. What is really needed is a movie taken from a helicopter, sweeping down from the pass, with music—something like William Byrd's "Kyrie" in his *Mass for Four Voices*—ringing in your ears, or, at the very least, a photograph. As it happens, I do have a photograph. I am looking at it right now. It was taken from the pass, looking down into the valley. It is the picture of an arch, a large, highly decorated stone-and-timber arch, which crowned the mountain pass. I framed the picture rather artistically, so that the arch fills the foreground and you have to look through it to see the valley beyond. There is a blurred figure in the lower right who is passing through the arch, which I believe to be Sarah, but you can only see her back and she remains anonymous and disquieting.

Looking at the photograph, I realize, too, that the camera can lie, for it can be very selective in what it shows us. The photo makes the arch look very grand and imposing, a necessary gateway, but in fact, it was a little ridiculous. For you see, it served no real purpose. It was linked to no wall or palisade. It defined no boundary that I could see. You could just as easily have walked around it as through it. So why was it there? I asked this question later to Françoise, and she told me that such archways were common in the old days and marked the old borders of different feudal

Entrance to Sakteng.

demesnes before unification. They were signals to travellers on the trail that they were entering a new place. Riders were expected to dismount and walk their horses as a sign of respect to the local authority. Today, they are anachronisms, memories of a feudal past, and served much more practical functions, such as temporary shelters in a downpour, like a bus shelter back home or one of those massive covered lych-gates you see in English country churchyards. Looking at the picture now, I am a little ashamed, for I realize that I was trying for an effect. I wanted the arch to become a magic portal, like the cave in Frank Capra's film version of Lost Horizon. It was this cave that led to Shangri-La. Outside, the storms of war were raging (symbolically shown by the terrible blizzard that the actors had to struggle through to reach the cave); while inside, in the valley of Shangri-La, the sun was shining and everyone was living in peaceful coexistence. But that was a work of fiction; this was real life, and in real life, as we all know, there are no Shangri-Las. Still, in coming to Sakteng, a real place, I was looking for something extraordinary, too.

Looking back on it now, I think it is highly ironic that, when we first arrived in Sakteng, we were made the guests of the border police. Between the pass and the town and close to the river were four newer buildings that represented the first forays of progress into this remote valley: a basic health unit, a small primary school, a wireless station, and the police post. Because it was the winter season, the valley was largely depopulated. Most houses in the village had only one or two occupants, usually the young or very old, those unable to travel. The other residents were in lower elevations, tending the herds that represented the valley's wealth, trading with the Sharchopa or with the residents of Arunachal Pradesh, or working for wages. The government presence was also limited. The school and clinic were closed. The wireless station was manned by a young man from Mongar, Kezang, who lived there with his parents. He was a Sharchop speaker and therefore as much an exile as I among the Brokpa. There was only one policeman at the station with his family, the chief of police (and Karma Yeshey's father), and he invited us to occupy two of the many empty rooms in his staff quarters, as his constables were either on vacation or out on patrol.

The police post was rather Spartan. It was long and rectangular, one storey with stone walls and a shake roof. It had twelve rooms of equal size, six to a side, all opening to the outside under an ample overhang. We were allotted two rooms facing the river. Each room was divided from the others with rough-hewn plank walls and had wooden flooring worn smooth by the passing of many feet. There was a small clay chula in each room for cooking, but no chimney, so that when you stood, you were invisible from the waist up, cloaked by thick smoke. The ceiling beams were festooned with black tarry cobwebs. There were two layers of windows, upper and lower, so that you could see out sitting or standing, but no window glass, only sliding shutters. A low roughcast wall surrounded the compound to keep out the yaks, sheep, and other beasts. The close-cropped lawn within this enclosure made it a pleasant place to recline in the bright December sun. In one corner of the yard, where a small stream undercut the wall, there was a latrine—a little stone-built hut, cold as a meat locker, whose facilities consisted of a springy plank stretched over the running brook.

The next morning we explored the valley. A short walk of a few hundred yards, along a dusty track, across the barren fields of harvested buckwheat, brought us to the village of Sakteng. At first glance it appeared to be deserted. The narrow, crooked, mucky lanes were all bounded by high roughcast walls. The walls were punctuated at regular intervals with heavy wooden doors, many of which were padlocked. Each led to a separate household. One of the doors stood open, and we peered inside. An elderly Brokpa man in his distinctive spider cap and wearing a yak-skin vest, hair-side in, was sitting cross-legged in the courtyard. He was bent over a long block-printed prayer flag to which he was affixing a cloth reinforcement tape along one long edge with a needle and thread. The banner was stretched across his knees, which were encased in leather leggings. On his feet he wore traditional felt-and-leather mukluks. He smiled and bade us enter.

We ducked through the low doorway and walked into the flagged the courtyard. The contrast could not have been more complete. The lane outside was rocky and uneven, covered in animal dung, and probably a river of mud in the rainy season; but the courtyard was level and clean, carefully flagged with flat stone, and already warm from the thin morning sun. The courtyard fronted the house and you could see that in good weather it acted as another living room for the family. Several cords of firewood were carefully stacked against the walls. An elaborate timber-framed loom was set up in the sun, much more sophisticated than the simple back-strap looms that the Sharchopa used. The Sharchopa sat on the ground to weave, but this loom was mounted on legs and the weaver sat on a bench. Silas Marner would have felt comfortable working on this loom and nothing about it would have been unfamiliar to him. A broad band of coarse black cloth was under construction on this particular loom. This waterproof cloth was woven of yak hair, we knew, and was used for bags, women's capes, and tents.

Brokpa man sewing prayer flag.

We were facing the front of the house. A small prayer wheel was spinning in a niche beside the door. The house was two storeys high and rectangular in shape, with a shallow pitched roof. We were facing the narrow end. The roof was covered in hand-split wooden shingles, held down with withes of bamboo cane and large stones. The rafters were supported by three tree trunks, trimmed hexagonally, which protruded out through the end gables—one served as rooftree, defining the peak of the roof, and the other two rested lengthwise along the top of the side walls. The attic was enclosed at either end by a screen of bamboo mat. These attics were shallower than those found in Sharchopa homes, so presumably there was less need for a granary in Sakteng, as Brokpa livestock spent most of their year out in pasture. The home was entirely built of undressed roughcast stone and, unlike other Bhutanese homes I had seen, was not painted with whitewash, but left plain. The front of the house had a cantilever extension on the second floor made of rough unpainted planks, which sheltered the front door. Into this second-storey façade were cut two small gothic windows. These were sealed from the inside by wooden shutters. It was a very simple sturdy design, constructed to withstand the strong winds that whistled down the valley.

Our attempts at conversation with our host were frustratingly inconclusive, but we left as cheerfully as we had arrived, his and our curiosity satisfied.

We walked through Sakteng village and out the other side. In all, there were probably no more than fifty to sixty households in the valley. There may have been an equal number in the valley of Mera to the southeast and a few cousins in the Tawang region of Arunachal Pradesh, but in total there could not have been more than a few thousand Brokpa in the whole world. A frightening thought. How long, I wondered, will their culture survive? How long will the Brokpa continue to speak their distinctive language, now that their splendid isolation has been penetrated?

We walked out over the harvested fields of buckwheat and barley toward the river. The river bed was a very broad plain of gravel. The river split into many shallow channels, sparkling in the sun. Built into the bank of the river, where a small rivulet spilled over to join the confusion below, was a small gristmill. The stream was contained between two stone walls and a small wooden hut housing the millstones bridged the walls. Two horizontal wheels with wooden paddles hung below the hut on vertical wooden axels, turning continuously in the foaming water.

We turned downstream, walking along the high bank on our way back to the police post for lunch. We came to a kind of Brokpa Golgotha, a place where the remains of slaughtered animals were pitched. The rendered bones of sheep, yak, and horse were mingled in a great heap below our feet. Suddenly, to our alarm, the bones begin to stir and rattle. Then a great horse's head, half-decomposed, rose from the pile, looked in our direction and growled.

We yelled in alarm.

The head began to shake menacingly and to move in our direction. Something about the picture was not quite right (I mean, other than the fact that a dead horse's head was moving of its own volition). The body that supported the head was disproportionately small. Then we realized what was wrong.

"Yuck," said Sarah.

"That's grotesque," I added, for we realized that what we were seeing was not a zombie, but a large dog that had been feasting on the horse's brain and had got his head stuck inside the skull. Several more vigorous shakes freed the startled dog and he ran off.

Walking along the river, we met several yak trains heading upstream to Arunachal Pradesh. We spoke with one man who was just beginning a fifteen-day journey with his entire family and about twenty heavily laden yaks. He told us that while yaks are very strong, they do not travel very far each day, so the journey has to be made in short stages. When we returned to the police post, we cooked a lunch of goulash, made with egg noodles, smoked yak meat, and some well-aged and very smelly yak cheese. After lunch, Sarah and I decided to cross the river and explore. It was cold and bright in the sun. The snow-capped peaks were oddly flat, like a photograph cut out of some magazine and pasted against the blue of the sky. The skin across the bridge of my nose felt dry and very tight. The broad alluvial plain through which the river threaded its many-channelled way was dotted with islands composed primarily of moss, lichen, and short grass. It was damp underneath this groundcover and boggy in places, and I felt like I was walking across the barrenlands of the Arctic. We crossed the main channel on a simple bridge constructed of a single tree trunk, split lengthwise, with the halves laid side-to-side, flat sides up. We walked up a snow-covered path to the rim of the valley. Here, we rested atop a low pass and looked down upon a long broad valley that ended at a much higher pass in a snow-covered saddle. This was the road to Mera, the other Brokpa settlement in Eastern Bhutan. While Sarah sat in the sun and sketched the scene, I deliberated the ethics of continuing my journey, but decided against it. It was tempting. I could travel up over the pass ahead and into the valley of Mera, then turn west, climb up to Brangzung-La, and down into Khaling, completing the circle. But the fact that I did not have permission to make such a journey, and the probable repercussions for Howard and our volunteer organization if I did, stilled my ambition. As Sarah packed up her sketchpad and charcoal, I took one last look down the forbidden path and sighed. Sarah asked me what was wrong. I told her. "Cheer up," she said. "I have a surprise." And out of her *jola* she drew a neatly folded sheet of plastic. We cut the plastic in half and then, like the children we had once been, slid down the snowy slope, back into Sakteng, on our makeshift toboggans.

On our return, we plucked some holly to decorate our accommodations. It was Christmas Eve. When the others saw our holly, they said, "Why not do up the thing properly?" and sent Pema Wangdi and I out into the forest to get a tree. As Pema and I stumbled around in the dusk, I tried to explain to him about Christmas trees and their significance. I'm not sure I was very successful. Nevertheless, he found me a little fir, about a metre (three feet) in height, with a nice shape, and we dispatched it with my *kukri*. Then, back in Sakteng, we visited the town's only shop (a small closet with about four shelves of trinkets, bubble gum, and tinned goods) and bought all of the shopkeeper's red ribbon and a few plastic bangles to stand in as tree ornaments. From scraps of cardboard torn from an empty detergent box, I also cut some reindeer, bells, and angels. And for the top of our tree, I made a cardboard star and covered it in the foil wrapping taken from a chocolate bar. We decorated our little tree, sucking on chunks of undissolvable Indian chocolate, and tried to remember the words to "O Tannenbaum."

We were invited to the wireless station for dinner that evening. The wireless station was a small stone cottage with three rooms. The large front room was both bedroom and sitting room, and in the centre of this room was a large barrel stove on a tray of smooth river pebbles. There was a tiny smoke-blackened kitchen in one back corner of the cottage and in the other corner, a room that housed the wireless equipment. I was intrigued to see that the station was run by solar energy that was stored in old car batteries. There was quite a crowd of us that night: our party, the wireless officer, his mother and father, the chief of police, and the assistant headman, or *chupen*, of Sakteng Village. We sat around the glowing stove on the floor, eating red rice, dhal, smoked yak meat, shredded radish, and a curry made from bones, rawhide, and yak innards. The curry contained some chamois-textured stuff that I later learned was yak intestine. After the meal, we sat around the fire, warming our fingers on enamelled mugs of hot *ara*.

It was a warm comfortable evening despite the language barrier—Sharchopkha was the *lingua franca*. A feeling of hearty good fellowship prevailed. With much coaxing, the old woman of the house was prevailed upon to sing, and I gathered from her half-pleased refusals that she was a singer of some repute and that while she was pleased to be asked, she liked to be coaxed into a performance.

When she began to sing, her voice belied her years; it was the voice of a young woman, liquid, true as a bell. She sang a song in Dzongkha, which I did not understand but was led to believe was their version of "Auld Lang Syne." She sang in true Bhutanese fashion, in a wavering nasally style, employing numerous glottal stops, as if she were trying to make the human voice sound like a bagpipe. I realized that I was privileged. I was hearing a singer of rare quality, though the style was foreign to my tastes—as Italian *bel canto* would be to theirs. There was an appreciative silence when the long lyric was finished. We sipped our liquor, lost in thoughts of those who were parted from us by years or distance or death. The village *chupen*, a gregarious fellow, would not let us sink into melancholy. He prevailed upon his hostess to sing something more upbeat. She obliged with a lively song about a girl who yearns to have a dress made of beautiful cloth. I knew the song and joined in with the others on the chorus. Then each member of the company was called upon to do an item. I sang "Good King Wenceslas" in my squeaky tenor.

At one point, the young wireless officer excused himself. He had to monitor his station. He asked if we would like to send any messages. As it was Christmas Eve, we decided it would be fun to send Christmas greetings to our colleagues who were still in Bhutan over the holidays and to Dasho Dzongdag. To the *dasho*'s note we appended: "No yeti as yet."

We thanked our hosts and stumbled home to bed. As we curled up in our cold sleeping bags in the pitch blackness, most of us wearing toques and long underwear for warmth, we sang ourselves to sleep with more carols. We even invented our own version of "The Twelve Days of Christmas" with Bhutanese references.

I awoke at six and stepped outside to use the meat locker. The ground was covered in silver frost. The sun was not yet up, but a full moon lay cradled in the mountain pass like an agate in a sling. Yaks stood about the compound, tethered to posts, their backs silvered, panting as yaks do, and great flumes of steam issued from their nostrils. When I returned, the others were not yet up; so I went into one of the empty rooms, stuffed my red wool union suit with sweaters to produce a suitable belly, put on Sarah's red Brokpa jacket and topped the ensemble with Anne's red beret. Then I burst into the room, *jola* over my shoulder, shouting, "Ho, ho, ho, Merry Christmas," and passed out oranges, chocolate bars, and small Canadian flag pins. The boys loved it. The others had also brought small gifts and had wrapped them in cloth or newspaper and tied them up in ribbon. My gifts were two chocolate bars, a bar of OM soap, a tube of tooth-paste, a small "gold" ring, and a red exercise book to write my stories in.

Many people stopped in to see us and we served them coffee, rum, and orange squash. We gave the children small parcels of candy and Canada pins. We invited everyone back that evening for Christmas dinner.

We spent the afternoon preparing: chopping, slicing, standing over smoky fires with eyes smarting, and stirring glutinous cauldrons of rice and curry. We found a huge rattan mat and spread it out on the lawn. We had invited everyone we could think of and twenty-three guests arrived: Karma Yeshey's family, the wireless officer and his family, the *chupen*, the *dungpa*'s clerks, Yeshi and his son, a local *gomchen*, and others. They sat in a circle on the mat, and we bustled in and out of the smoky kitchen, carrying pots of food and spooning out smoked yak meat, rice, and radish curry onto a strange collection of platters: wooden bowls, tin plates, and straw *bung-chus* (in fact, whatever we had been able to scrounge for the feast). The food was kept lubricated by a plentiful supply of *ara* and rum poured into a similar hodge-podge of drinking vessels: wooden *gorbus*, tin mugs, coffee cups. We had singing and dancing afterwards, where everyone was expected to contribute an item, followed by a wild volleyball game. It was a hilarious game. Everyone, even the most august

Christmas feast, Sakteng.

amongst us, let their hair down and got their knees dirty diving for stray balls. The only English word our Brokpa guests knew was "Ready," which they always said twice—"ready-ready"—and which they shouted indiscriminately throughout the game. "Ready-ready" could mean "serve the ball" or "pass the ball to me" or "look out!" Later, we retired to the fireside and Kezang's *ama* regaled us with more songs. I fell asleep. It had been quite a busy day.

The next morning, we resolved to climb to the plateau above the village and visit the monastery. The first part of the climb was very steep, straight up the crest of a ridge for the most part. We emerged from a scrubby hardwood forest onto a grassy slope. Eventually, knees aching from so much climbing, we crested the plateau in cluster of snapping prayer flags. From this point it was a much gentler slope up to the monastery. The monastery was much larger than the one in Khaling, but as we drew close we could see that it was in a bad state of repair. To one side of the temple was a two-storey set of apartments. The upper floor was reached by an outside set of steps and a covered verandah, which looked ready to collapse at any moment. There was supposed to be a caretaker, but everything was locked up and no one appeared to be about. We shouted, but the wind whistling through the rafters mocked us. While Sarah took the time to make a few sketches, the others sat on the temple steps to catch their breath. I examined the murals on the walls of the porch. They were quite good, if faded. They were also the first temple paintings I had seen that featured Brokpa figures in the narrative. As we turned to leave, I thought to myself that even in the bright sunlight, the old monastery was a bit spooky.

It had not always been so deserted. In the early part of the twentieth century a famous lama had resided here and had attracted a number of novices from outside the valley to study with him. He was called Lama Wookpa, or "Lama Owl," because of his strange habit of sleeping during the day and praying at night. Over the years Lama Wookpa became a prominent figure in the local folklore, and many fantastic stories attached themselves to his name.

One of the folktales collected by Kunzang Choden, the first Bhutanese to trans-late the folktales of her homeland into English, concerns Lama Wookpa and his new novice, a young man who was far too sophisticated to believe the tales people told him about his teacher or about Sakteng Valley.[16] When the other novices told him the story of a ghostly caretaker who was seen occasionally prowling about the grounds of the monastery at night, rattling a large bunch of keys, the new novice rolled his eyes and replied, "Some people will believe anything."

Lama Wookpa's monastery, Sakteng.

One night Lama Wookpa asked the new novice to go to the temple and fetch a large vessel in which incense was burned. It was dark. The only lights in the temple were the flickering butter lamps on the altar. The novice quickly entered the gloomy chapel, prostrated himself three times before the altar, grabbed the censer, and turned to leave. As he was closing the door, he heard a jangling sound, like someone shaking a ring of keys. He looked toward the altar and thought he saw a large shadowy figure standing in the gloom. He rubbed his eyes and looked again. The figure was gone. He smiled at his own gullibility and put his vision down to nerves and to the power of suggestion.

Time passed and the novice put the vision from his mind. One day, Lama Wookpa was invited down to the village to perform a special *pujah* in honour of the valley's guardian deity, Penden Lhamo. The lama asked several novices, including the young skeptic, to accompany him. The prayers continued all day and into the early evening. The patrons of the *pujah* begged the lama to stay in their home for the night rather than make the long journey up the mountain in the dark, but the lama laughed at their concern and said, "Am I not Lama Owl? Why should I be frightened of the dark?" He had the novices saddle his horse and gather up all of the prayer books and ritual instruments. Then they began the long climb up the mountain with only starlight to guide them. It was hard going, for, in addition to the bundles they had carried down

Brokpa shepherds visiting a shrine.

the mountain that morning, the young novices were also burdened with the many gifts that the grateful people of Sakteng had given them as payment for the *pujah*. The novices took a rest when they reached the edge of the plateau. They stood and caught their breath in the great forest of prayer masts. There was no wind. The prayer flags hung limp and silent. Suddenly, the new novice had the disquieting feeling that, all around him, the night was full of movement and that shadowy figures were pushing past him in the darkness. Lama Wookpa calmed the novices and bade them continue their journey to the monastery.

"I will be along in a minute," he reassured them.

Then they heard him begin speaking to the darkness as one might address an old friend. But the conversation was one-sided. After a while, the lama bid the darkness farewell, turned the horse's head and caught up to the trembling novices.

"Oh Guru," asked the frightened skeptic, "what passed us in the darkness? To whom were you speaking?"

"Did you not see them?" Lama Owl smiled. "Why, it was the *migoi*, the servants of Penden Lhamo."

For lunch that day, we all reached deep into our packs and brought out the treasures we had been hoarding for this special occasion. Sarah had saved a can of tinned ham, Anne, a box of dehydrated scalloped potatoes, and Lily and I both reached into our bags and produced identical bottles of California Chardonnay. We were taken aback at the coincidence, until we realized that we had both been given the bottles by the young lady from the Canadian High Commission as she passed through in November.

While we had been exploring the monastery, a note had arrived at the police post, inviting us to have dinner that evening with the chupen and his family. The chupen lived across the river. There were three or four houses set apart from the main village on a narrow strip of cultivated land at the base of the mountain. We set out in the late afternoon, with the sun creating subtle horizontal bands of colour across the face of the mountains. We crossed the river on the split-trunk bridge and turned northwest toward Tawang and the little village of Pusak where the chupen lived.

We entered the courtyard of the chupen's house and stooped to enter the front door, which stood open. The door, typical for Bhutanese homes, had a high sill and a low lintel, forcing us to both step up and bend over to enter. This, we had been told, was deliberate. The Bhutanese believe that ghosts and demons cannot bend over and therefore such an arrangement protects the home from evil influences. We proceeded down a dark and smoky corridor. There were several openings off to our right, which I presumed were storage rooms of some kind. The kitchen was at the back of the house. It was immensely gloomy. Only one window, cut into the thick stone wall, allowed any light or fresh air to enter. It was almost impossible to breathe and my eyes smarted from the smoke. A wizened old crone rose from the gloom and beckoned us forward, grasping my hand in her horny paw and pushing me to a scrap of a mat on the stone floor. An open fire blazed in the middle of the room and a tarry cauldron was suspended above it, supported by an iron ring with three peg legs. Down here, in these lower elevations, it was suddenly easier to breathe. I found myself in a circle of acquaintances: Yeshi was already there, as were the chupen and the wireless officer and his parents. Against the blackened stone walls of the room were piled yak-skin bags, barrels, and beautifully carved trunks the size of bathtubs. There were also blanket rolls piled on the trunks, so I assumed that in the cold winter months, the household slept here by the kitchen fire. There were other people in the room, too, moving in the smoke, vague shapes visible only from the waist down.

My companions seated themselves around the fire. The old woman sat herself by my side, still holding my hand, and gazed up at my whiskers with interest. She was old, perhaps the oldest human being I had ever met. Her skin was so deeply wrinkled and blackened it was like scrimshaw on old ivory. I found myself the spokesman for our party. Yes, we had a good climb. Yes, it was a shame the temple was not open at this time of year. Yes, we were very tired. And, yes, we were very thirsty. Glasses of hot *bangchhang*, barley beer, were placed in our hands. When the conversation stalled, I leaned forward and peered into the somewhat gluey contents of the cauldron. I asked my hostess what she was cooking. She tried to explain, but since she knew no English and I knew none of the Brokpa dialect, we tried to converse in Sharchopkha, a second language to us both. I could not understand what she was saying. She turned to the young wireless officer for help.

"Lopen, this woman say pot contains skin of yak and she is cooking to make soft. The skin is from making shoes. These are, unh, that is to say, these are...sorry, these are—"

"The scraps?"

"La!"

"But why is she cooking them?"

"They are for dinner."

Throughout this exchange the toothless old woman was following our conversation with her eyes and nodding encouragingly. When we paused, she asked, via the young man, what leather was used for in my country. I tried to explain, in Sharchopkha, that in my country, leather was used for making shoes, but that we did not, as a rule, eat it. There was a gasp of surprise at this statement, all of the Brokpa were shocked to silence, and then the old woman began to cackle hysterically and roll on the floor in mirth. She was soon followed by most everyone in the room. The wireless officer, clearly embarrassed, began a sharp two-way conversation with the old woman and then he, too, began to sputter. Between spurts of laughter like a badly tuned outboard motor, he explained that the old woman understood me to say that "in my country, we eat our shoes." I had to grin sheepishly at this, and soon I, too, was laughing. The mirth was infectious. The ice was broken and after that, the party went smoothly. We enjoyed a soup of bone marrow, hide, and intestines, eaten with *keptang*, a flat loaf made of buckwheat, Tibetan style. It was actually tastier than it sounds, though a bit chewy.

After the meal, our Brokpa host asked if we had an automatic camera. When I asked him to explain, he reached into this filthy tunic and produced a snapshot that he passed to me. It was a Polaroid of him, much handled and wrinkled, so that the layers of colour were beginning to separate. I asked him where it had come from. He replied that some German tourists had passed through earlier in the year and had given it to him. I passed the photo back apologizing that I did not have an automatic camera. I could take a picture of him with my old-fashioned camera, develop it at home and mail him a copy. He was a bit disappointed but agreed.

We returned to our quarters at dusk under a pink mackerel sky. There was a telegram from Dasho Dzongdag, saying that he had sent a yeti to us at 3:00 A.M. on Christmas Eve. Had we seen it? We had to laugh at that. It was a nice way to end our visit to Sakteng. Tomorrow we would have to leave, and we were all reluctant to go.

I ventured out alone after dark to watch the full moon rise over the valley. But for the chuckling of the river, it was perfectly silent as I walked to a pasture above the police station. The moon came up over a ridge, first a glow, a false dawn, then a quick spark of light like a star, and then the rim rose slowly over the knife-edge of the mountain. I was startled. I had not expected it to appear so quickly. It loomed so large and bright that I could make out all of the features on its surface, the mountains, the plateaus and craters. When the moon finally cleared the ridge, the valley lit up brightly, the field of grass turned silver, and the mountains loomed two-dimensionally, like the cardboard scenery in a child's pop-up book, and to my surprise and horror I discovered that I was standing in the middle of a circle of sleeping dogs. The moon had aroused them, as well, and they discovered my presence at about the same time as I detected theirs. They rose stiffly to their feet, hackles rising, and began to bay and snarl. I knew I was in trouble if I ran—these Brokpa mastiffs are bred to guard the livestock and are wild, half-starved, and big as horses—so I faced them down, disregarded them with a scornful, "ssht," and pretended interest in the moon. It worked. Slowly, they turned from me and stared up at the moon with rapt wise expressions. Then they lay down, curled up in husky-like balls of fur, and feigned sleep. I tiptoed through their perimeter to leave, and a dozen pairs of watchful hooded eyes followed my retreat.

That last morning was a confusion of packing with many partings. We had to return many things—cooking utensils, mostly—to the people from whom we had borrowed them. Our caravan set out with many hangers-on—our party had grown to thirteen—and a bottle of *ara* was passed around. A number of elderly people had decided to accompany us over the pass to lower elevations to join other family members for the balance of the winter season. A small controversy arose when one old man arrived and began loading a large amount of luggage onto the two ponies we had hired. Our ponyman had some harsh words with him, but in the end it did not matter much, since we had eaten most of our food and so we had less baggage to carry out. We said goodbye to Karma Yeshey and his family and thanked them for their hospitality. We stopped at Yeshi's for more *ara* and *sujah* and some last minute trading—Ann was determined to have a Brokpa jacket. Then, at long last, we set out to climb out of Sakteng, the "plain of bamboo," and return to lower elevations and the world of the Sharchopa.

I sat on a grassy bank at the top of the pass and took a long last lingering view of the valley, reluctant to leave. Heavy clouds had moved in at our parting. There was some new snow in the rocky peaks and high passes, and despite the grey light, the mountains had taken on a luminous quality. Farewell, Sakteng, farewell. *Tashi delek.*

As I walked from the pass, the last to leave and loath to say goodbye, I heard cheering and shrill whistling and the chanting of a single word from my companions up ahead: "*Namdrung, namdrung*," they were shouting.

"*Hang gotcha-mo?*" I thought. Two years in Bhutan had conditioned me to think in simple Sharchop phrases. What were they looking at?

Then I heard it. A roaring filled my ears like the apocalypse, and I looked to the leaden clouds. A black cross was scored across the grey sky. Airplane, airplane, they were chanting. An army transport, props drumming, was heading into Arunachal Pradesh with supplies and reinforcements. The twentieth century re-entered my consciousness with shrill violence.

TWENTY-THREE

THEREfORE OUR EVERLASTING fAREWELL TAKE

WHEN I RETURNED TO THE SCHOOL at the end of January, it was empty, but for a few of the support staff. I was the only teacher on the premises. It was cold, and for the first time I actually used my small barrel stove, or bukhari, on a regular basis and contracted for firewood to be delivered to my backdoor by a little elf of a man named Meme Tombola. In English, this would have translated into "Grandfather Bingo," so it had obviously started as a nickname and then stuck. His original name seemed to have been forgotten. Perhaps he had outlived all those who could remember what he had been called before; for Meme Tombola was old, a gnarled walnut of a man, about 152 centimetres (five feet) tall, dressed in a robe so tattered and dirty that the original pattern was unrecognizable. When he showed up each week, bare-legged, with a mountain of split rhododendron on his back, he would take his few rupees and wipe his furrowed brow with the back of his soiled sleeve in an exaggerated expression of exhaustion, pant in mock thirst and grin with a mouth devoid of teeth. I always gave him a drink of rum. It became our ritual. He always brought me more firewood than I had asked for and then pleaded ignorance. I knew I was being conned, but I did not care.

There was a kind of winter rhythm in Khaling, like that in a Breughel painting. The hills were softly textured browns and oranges, with splashes of green here and there. The grass was yellow like parchment. Sounds carried across the valley: the clank, clank, clank of a cowbell; the sharp chock of the woodcutter's axe somewhere in the forest, like the echoing report of a rifle; the ploughman's "hup" and "haw" to his oxen as they inscribed crooked rows in a small walled terrace. It was a time of mending fences, fetching firewood, thatching roofs, and building houses. There were grey wintry days when the laundry did not come clean in the icy water and then would not dry on the line because there was no sun, no heat. The silhouettes of barren trees stood out starkly along the ridge against the grey featureless canopy. Dumb, anguished, knotted limbs spindled against a melancholy sky, fit repose for crows. And there were lots of crows at that time of year, or at least they were more noticeable. "In the bleak midwinter" summed it up beautifully.

Class 10 students drifted back to the school in threes and fours each day that month. Some came on the bus; some cadged rides; some walked. We started classes again. They had a month to relearn everything I had taught them over the course of two years to prepare them to write the Indian Central School Examinations, the dreaded ICSE, which would decide their futures both as students and as adult wage earners. Good results would send them to the university college at Kanglung. Fair results would send them to a training college, perhaps to become primary school teachers or rural health-care workers. Poor results would send them back to the farm, and nobody wanted to do that. In actual fact, rather than go back to the farm, students whose education ended after Class 10 most probably drifted into one of the larger urban centres and looked for employment there, where their education might get them work as a desk clerk or as the ticket collector on the local bus. A great deal hung on the results of these exams.

In the evenings, I pulled up my table beside the roaring bukhari, marked essays and listened to the BBC on shortwave. The Ayatolah Khomeini had condemned Salman Rushdie to death for writing a book called The Satanic Verses. It was hard to imagine a world where this could happen.

I went for walks when I could find the time. The beauty of my surroundings helped to lift my spirits. And they needed frequent lifting, for thoughts of leaving Bhutan increasingly occupied my mind.

One day in early February, I took a walk to a lovely promontory overlooking Bramang from which I could see most of the valley. From my perch I could see an old woman at the edge of the forest gathering firewood with the aid of a billhook and packing the sticks in a great wicker basket that hung on her back from a tumpline across her forehead. The basket was almost as big as she was. I had repeatedly cautioned myself not to romanticize the life of the peasant—it was mostly toil, dirt, hunger in winter, insufficient clothing, illness, ignorance, poverty, and alcoholism—and yet, I could not help myself. I could see all that—I could delude myself no longer—but the incredible beauty of this mountain valley overwhelmed me. I knew that soon I would have

Sun breaking though the clouds over Khaling Valley.

to leave this all behind, perhaps forever. From my Olympian perspective, I could also
see a man ploughing a tiny field, followed closely by his family who were sowing corn
in the furrows he carved. The sound of his voice, as he talked to his wife or grunted
encouragement to his team, came faint but clear across an incredible distance. I saw a
tiny file of girls in headscarves with bundles of firewood on their backs wending their
way home along the river. There were children playing korla in the stubble fields, and
a woman was mucking out a pigsty with a wooden spade. I saw coarse bristly pigs—
almost feral—rooting in the earth for those of last year's potatoes that had escaped
the hoe, and I saw tendrils of smoke rising from the little huddles of whitewashed
houses with roofs of bamboo thatch. I saw the newly thatched roofs as bright yellow
squares, contrasting strongly with the weathered slate-grey squares of the unregen-
erate. I saw mist in the hills, lying in the hollows, hiding from the sun. This valley had
been my home for two years and I loved it as I had not loved anywhere else. From here,
I could see it all: the villages strung along the river like pearls on a thread of silver, the
missionaries' school for the blind, the two-storey primary school, the small bazaar
clustered near the bridge where the road bent back upon itself, the high school and
its dormitories, the tiny hydro-electric project and, above it all, on a little plateau at
the head of the valley, the Buddhist temple with its giant cypress standing sentry over

everything and the little village that clustered around it that had been my home.

Just when I was starting to feel a little too maudlin, a chatter of childish voices disturbed my reverie. Four small boys rounded the corner dressed in the rejects from a church rumble sale. One wore nylon track pants, another had on a wool toque, and another was wearing a Nike baseball cap. Only one was dressed in his school uniform. Clearly this was a special occasion. They were carrying a large *jola* stretched between them, full to bursting, and they were having a great time. "Sir!" they shouted when they saw me and ran to my side.

They bowed and grinned. "Good morning, Sir!"

I laughed and corrected them. "Good afternoon, boys. Where are you going on this fine day?"

"Picnic, Sir. Would Sir like to see?" They displayed the contents of their bag: *bangchungs* full of cooked rice, chili paste, and jerked beef.

"What is the special occasion?"

They looked surprised. "*Losar*, Sir."

Of course, in my melancholy I had forgotten. It was the Bhutanese New Year, my third in Bhutan. First Rabbit, then Dragon, and now Snake. The boys arranged themselves around me and started distributing food. I dug into my knapsack and found a bar of chocolate and package of biscuits, which quickly disappeared.

"Tell us a story, Sir."

I thought for a moment and then told them an adaptation of Anatole France's story, "Our Lady's Juggler." When I finished, I asked them for a story. The oldest boy—with a great deal of help from the others—began to tell me a story he had heard from one of his uncles. It was a little frustrating. We communicated in a patois of English and Sharchopkha, but the story went something like this.

Once, an old man and woman go out in the jungle to find food. ("They were very starving, Sir.") They meet a *deeptu* [Sharchop for yeti] who lures them to his cave with the promise of food only to threaten to eat them. ("I, too, was hungry, but now I have found a meal—you!") They are saved by the arrival of a mysterious stranger brandishing a torch. The stranger throws the torch at the yeti, rendering him unconscious, and leads the old couple from the cave.

When he hears of their predicament, the stranger leads them to an enormous peach tree. He ascends the peach tree and calls to the old man to climb up, as well. The stranger tosses down several peaches to the woman on the ground and encourages them both to eat their fill. The peaches have the property to induce sleep, and as the old man gets drowsy, the stranger, who is really a demon in disguise, devours him. The old woman on the ground sees none of this.

The old woman grows impatient, drifts away from the tree, and finds herself in a field of round stones arranged in a geometrical pattern. She fetches water from the river in a pot, builds a fire, and, for some reason, begins boiling one of these stones. She bites into the first of her peaches and falls asleep. She is woken by the sound of a voice calling to her from the pot. "Woman, woman, you are boiling me. Get some cold water from the river." When the woman looks in the pot, very frightened, she sees one finger extending above the water. She runs to the tree and screams for help. The demon throws her another peach, which she eats and falls asleep. When she awakes she runs back to the pot and sees an arm extending above the boiling water. Before her eyes a headless torso emerges. She runs again to the peach tree, but this time there is no response to her summons, so she runs to the village and fetches the local magician—a fat man who carries a mighty sword.

When they return, the headless body is emerging to its knees. They run to a nearby tree and with a mighty blow, the magician cleaves the trunk. Inside is a slender wand. When the wand touches the grass, it shrivels and dies. When it touches a bush, the leaves dry up and fall to the ground. It starts to rain and the magician holds the wand above their heads, and they remain miraculously dry. The magician touches the peach tree, the leaves fall and the demon is exposed, feasting on the bleeding carcass of the old man. The woman is horrified. The demon leaps to the ground and devours them both.

I cannot help but feel that the story contained the germ of one or possibly more folktales and that the ending was awkward and somewhat abrupt. It struck me, as I listened to the boys tell their tale, that someone should travel through this country with a tape recorder and make a record of these stories before they are lost. Bhutan needs a Brothers Grimm.[17]

One evening, a week before I left Khaling, Tashi Dorje and his daughter, Sonam Choeden, came to visit me. It was late. I was marking essays when they knocked on the door. I invited them in and offered Tashi a glass of rum. He accepted, but it was clear that he had been drinking already, and there was something artificial in his manner.

He was overly friendly and very nervous, and it seemed to me as if he were trying to say something, but couldn't quite bring himself to do it. One drink led to another, until finally, he asked me, in a pained voice, if I would have anything to give away.

I knew what was going on here. I had sensed it coming for weeks. I had sensed it in the many dinner invitations I had been receiving lately, some from complete strangers who had protested undying friendship for me before inquiring what I would be leaving behind when I returned to Canada. Poor Tashi was caught between his feelings of genuine and unselfish affection for me and the increasing pressure put on him from well-meaning friends who urged, "The lopen will be leaving soon. Don't waste time. Ask him what he will be leaving behind before someone else claims the booty."

"Sure," I reassured him. "Not to worry." Relieved and embarrassed and perhaps even a little humiliated, he did not bring up the subject again, but things had changed irrevocably between us. Now the real drinking began. That night, the two of us polished off a bottle of rum and two bottles of ara. Sonam had spent most of the time poking around the cottage, quietly casing the joint, as I am sure she had been directed to do. When Tashi finally passed out, Sonam shook him a couple of times, snorted in exasperation, and then left by the back door. I made Tashi comfortable on the sofa, covered him with a blanket, and fell into my own bed. In the morning I made him some breakfast, he thanked me and rose to take his leave. As he turned at the door to say goodbye, he clasped my hands. There were tears in his sad eyes, but he could not find the words to say. He shook his head and left. Something had broken between us and could not be repaired. As I returned to the kitchen and was washing up the breakfast dishes, I began to notice a few things were missing—some silverware, a bunch of bananas, a Tupperware container—not much, nothing valuable, but I was dismayed. Damn, I thought, I would have given you those things. I meant to give you those things, those and so much more.

February continued cold and clear. On the eighteenth, it was very windy. The zinc-plated sheets on the gymnasium roof clattered like a pickup truck on a corduroy road. Prayer flags snapped tautly in the breeze. There was blue sky but for some thin cloud over Dunglingtso stretched across the empyrean like the white ribs of a great beast. The forest shimmered under a bright sun that left me squinting like an Inuit hunter on the spring sea ice. A newspaper did a fandango in a dust devil. I had to cover my tea to keep the dust out. A fine, fine day.

But it ended badly. By mid-afternoon the sky had clouded over and the tempera-ture dropped. Meme brought me some firewood and I stoked the *bukhari*. As we were chatting, we watched the aerial acrobatics of a flock of migratory birds from Tibet. They were small with compact bodies, short wings and tails. They flew like schools of minnows in perfect uniform formation, flitting like wind-tossed aspen leaves—black, white, black, white—up and down, riding currents of air in a display of consummate, yet seemingly senseless artistry.

I went to sleep amidst a violent thunderstorm that rattled the roof and awoke in the morning to the sound of water dripping from the eaves. I threw open the curtains and was astonished to see snow everywhere. The windstorm had developed into a gale that uprooted two of the prayer flags on campus and blew the roof off the haunted house far up on the mountain. As the sun rose, dogs all over the valley began to bark. I think they were as surprised as the rest of us at the transformation, and the dogs were about the only ones not happy with the arrival of the snow. The morning sky was pure blue without a hint of cloud. The sun was bright and the air had a tang of freshness. There were animal tracks around my back door and across the woodpile, which wore a cap of snow. The boys made a snow *chorten* in front of the hostel.

I got caught in the middle of a snowball fight in the bazaar that morning. One group of boys had snuck up on their rivals by entering a herd of cows being driven through the village. The assassins had arrived unseen, in their moving Trojan horse, and then, with a wild yell, had pummelled their classmates with snowballs. Soon the bazaar was a melee of flying snow as everyone—students, shopkeepers, and teachers—pitched snow with hilarious abandon.

Later, as I was entering the exam hall to supervise a geography exam, Wangpo handed me the letter. I glanced quickly at the return address—my mother's—and stuffed it in my pocket. I settled the students in their desks, distributed the papers and exam booklets face down, and went over the rules. Were there any questions? There were none. I checked the clock on the wall and told them to begin. The students were not allowed to speak once the exam began. If they needed more paper, they tapped their desks with their pencils.

Once the students had settled down to their papers, I remembered the letter and opened it.

I have some bad news. We did not want to burden you with it earlier, since there was nothing you could really do. Your grandfather has been very ill this past winter and has spent much of it in the hospital. He died last Thursday in his sleep...

I looked at the date on the top of the page. It was three weeks old. My grandfather had been dead for a month and I had not known. I returned to the letter.

Richard did the eulogy at his service. He did a wonderful job...

The eulogy should have been my job—would have been, if I had been home. I wondered what other burdens my younger brother had had to shoulder in my absence.

I cast my mind back to the day of departure from Canada. The whole family had assembled at my mother's house to see me off. They gathered on the icy curb as I slung my bags in the airport taxi. I was too excited to pay much attention to nuances of feeling. I hugged everyone, my grandfather last of all. I remember thinking how frail he had become, but my impending departure pushed all other worries aside. As I waved goodbye in the departing cab, I noticed he was leaning heavily on his cane and looking completely forlorn. Tears were running down his face. It frightened me, but in the days ahead I pushed the picture out of my mind. I think he knew that he was dying even then and that he would never see me again. But family is like that. We always leave the important things unsaid.

"Tap, tap, tap." The sound was constant, angry, and insistent. I looked up from the page upon which the tears were beginning to flow. The tapping hesitated for a moment. The students were unused to seeing their teachers cry.

"Sorry," I said. "Very sorry." Wiping my face with my sleeve, I began to distribute extra exam booklets as quickly as I could, walking up and down the rows of desks, muttering, "Sorry. I'm so very sorry."

For two years I had worked on my student's grammar skills and spelling, but more important I had honed their essay writing skills. I had taught them how to write an expository essay, how to organize their thoughts and produce a coherent argument. Some had been amazed to discover that they even had thoughts of their own. Some had complained that their brains hurt. In the four weeks before the final exam, I had prepped them each day by giving them a practise exam question toward the end of the lesson. We would discuss the question briefly and then they would write a response. I would collect all of their answers at the end of the class, mark them, and return them the following day for review.

On my last day of classes, I entered the room and noticed that someone had neatly copied a passage from *Julius Caesar* on the chalkboard. It was Brutus's parting speech to Cassius:

But this same day

Must end that work the Ides of March begun;

And whether we shall meet again I know not.

Therefore our everlasting farewell take.

For ever, and for ever, farewell, Cassius!

If we do meet again, why, we shall smile;

If not, why then this parting was well made.

I turned and looked at my pupils. They were all grinning, but no one would own up.

"We do not know *how* that got there, Sir."

The day of the English exam arrived, and I was, if anything, more anxious than my pupils. After all, I had promised them that they would be ready for this when the time came, but there was always the nagging doubt that I might have let them down. I had arranged to see one of the exam papers as soon as the doors to the gymnasium were closed. I quickly tore open the sealed envelope and scanned the contents. I could have leapt for joy. As impossible as it seemed, I had anticipated every single question the examiners had set. There was not one question on the exam that the students had not seen before in rehearsal. If they had studied as I had asked them to, I did not see how they could go wrong. I was exultant, and I was sad. My job was finished. It was time to go home.

But let me tell you one last story before we go.

On my last day in Khaling I took a walk. I left the school campus, walked through the bazaar and headed down the valley, past the primary school, past the school for the blind, and started down the path that wound between the small irregularly shaped fields. I trod like a phantom, unseen by the busy people ploughing, planting potatoes, and spreading baskets of manure on the earth. Sometimes the path seemed almost subterranean, the pounding of so many feet and hooves during the rainy season having eroded it below the level of the surrounding fields, and I had the eerie feeling of passing by busy family groups unremarked. It was as if I had already left. Life in this valley would carry on without me. I would soon be forgotten. But I realized that I would carry a piece of this place in my heart, wherever I went, for the rest of my days. It would be a source of great contentment, but also of loss. I would mourn for Khaling (and I did: this book is the result).

I followed the path down the valley, through villages, past walled orchards and pit-like pig enclosures. I traversed dry streambeds and forest glades. I was rewarded with the rare sight of a muntjac, a lesser panda, a family troupe of common langurs, and

Me and my class 10 students on my last day in Khaling.

numerous colourful birds. I passed small copses of *yadong metho*, splashes of vermilion on the dry mountainside where the rhododendrons bloomed like daubs of fresh paint on an old palette, and before I knew it I was in the old cremation grounds at the bottom of the valley. I sat on a low stone wall, feeling as grey as the old grass-grown monuments. I couldn't help reflecting that I had wasted so much time. I had spent two years in the most beautiful and remarkable place in the world and it was not long enough. There was so much more to learn, so much I hadn't done, so many wasted opportunities.

I pushed on and came to the junction with the old north–south road. I turned south and headed down a steep wooded path to the river and the old covered bridge. I stood for a long time on the bridge looking down at the clear rushing water. My depression lessened somewhat. Walking always cheered me up, and it was impossible to feel sorry for myself in such beautiful surroundings. I told myself: remember this moment, this perfect moment. The time may come when you will have need of it. I gazed around at the surrounding hills and drank it all in. Then with a shock of recognition, I realized that the little cone-shaped hill on the other side of the river was the one Ray and I had stumbled all over on that memorable drunken hike two years before, when we had been searching for King Dewa's Palace. I had to laugh at myself. It had seemed so important at the time to find the ruins of the old *khar*.

UNDER THE HOLY LAKE

Me on the bridge in Khaling Valley near the cremation grounds.

As I stood there, it occurred to me that, while I had many photographs of my friends and students, I had none of myself; so I balanced my camera on a boulder at the side of the river, set the timer and ran to take of a picture of myself standing on the old covered bridge spanning the Jeri Chhu. Even today when I look at that picture I can see how downcast I must have been.

I knew that if I crossed this bridge and followed a winding trail up the mountain spur it would eventually take me up to the modern vehicle road and from there it was an easy hike back to Khaling Bazaar. It was the same route Ray and I had used two years before, the same route I had followed many times on weekend walks with my students. I started up the steep trail and had been walking about fifteen minutes or so when I was startled by the sudden apparition of a satyr-like face appearing above a hedge. The creature had a goat-like beard and short black horns. It lumbered to its feet, and I was startled to see a great cow-like body attached to the Pan-like countenance. The creature had a shaggy bronze coat and a darker ridge of hair on its heavy shoulders. It fled with surprising speed up the hill and disappeared into the underbrush. As soon as I got over my fright I set off in pursuit, camera in hand, because I realized I had just seen a takin, a rare sight indeed in this part of the Himalayas. It soon out-distanced me and so I circled around to find the place where I had first spotted it. I found the circular depression where it had been lying in the grass and tried to estimate its size.

As I was pacing the takin's depression, I noticed that the hedge was, in fact, an overgrown stone wall. I traced the path of this wall through the forest and came to an acute angle where it joined another wall. Then an amazing thing happened: the proverbial scales dropped from my eyes and I realized that here, in the twilight of the forest understory, there were not two walls, but a whole maze of walls. I also realized that these were not paddocks, but the foundations for a very large and ancient structure. I had stumbled upon the ruins of King Dewa's khar. Sometimes, you spend a lifetime looking for something and never find it. At other times, that something finds you. And then it is gone.

It has been twenty years since I left Khaling, but it still feels like an open wound. The two years I lived there changed me irrevocably, made me the person I am today. I have never been able to look around me since with the same contentment I once had. I miss Bhutan; I miss it every day. I miss the copper sunsets, the graceful folk dances, the cheerful faces and easy laughter. I miss the mountains and their wildlife, the misty mornings, the splash of water on stone, the cough of the muntjac, the manic impersonations of the hill mynah. I miss simple things like reading by candlelight, barley beer, and living without glass in the windows. I miss the sounds of the prayer hall, the clatter of butter churns, the bawl of cattle waiting to be milked, the rhythmic clack of watermills, the drip of water from the eaves, the snap of prayer flags on the ridge in a gale, and the clicking of bamboo groves in a light wind. I miss the smell of burning rhododendron, the gentle insinuation of incense, even the smell of rancid butter in the glittering temple lamps. And the brightness; I miss the light in all its subtle shades on the folds of the mountains. But most of all, I miss the sense of being fully alive and of being fully a part of life for every hour of every day. In Canada, I so rarely exercise my sense of wonder, but it in Bhutan it was exercised daily, so that it became toned and muscular, receptive to the subtle changes in the natural world. And wonder brought joy. "I will look unto the hills from whence cometh my help," wrote the psalmist. Can the dwellers of the plains know this joy?

For many people, there are landscapes that obsess the memory: The white cone of Fuji rising from the sea, the cloud-shadow-dappled plains of the Serengeti, the morning's sunrise over the Ganga at Benares, the blue shadows and green ice of the

Baffinlands, Ayers Rock, rose-tinted in the tangerine of dawn. And yet for me, there is only one place: a green narrow valley in the eastern Himalayas, resting under the influence of a holy lake and an ancient tree, a place that was once my home and is no longer.

AFTERWORD AND
ACKNOWLEDGEMENTS

TO THE QUESTION "WHY WRITE A BOOK?" I think I can supply at least one answer: Because it won't leave you alone until you do. Some people have asked me: Why did you wait so long? Why begin now, after all this time? The truth is that I started writing this book twenty years ago, but I just couldn't get it right. The manuscript went through numerous incarnations. At one point, it was even a very bad spy thriller. For many years, it smouldered at the back of my filing cabinet while my life and career took the front seat. It started in a spiral-bound notebook in Karin's kitchen in Norway a few weeks after I had left Bhutan and, over the years, it progressed through as many drafts as it did computers and software upgrades. In the writing, my book actually became shorter, as episodes were dropped or compressed and characters disappeared from its pages entirely. Most of my careful research was cut or turned into endnotes. I won't say that the final result is good, but it is better, and I can't take all the credit for this.

Credit must go first of all to the many friends and family members who read this book in an earlier draft and offered their encouragement and advice. Special thanks go to my father-in-law, Bob Sherwin, to my sister, Kerry, and to my friend, Kay Percival, who took the time to go through the manuscript with an editor's eye and to make many helpful suggestions. My best, first, and most tireless reader has always been my wife, Nancy. Without her faith, this book would never have been finished. Thanks also to my children, who don't think it's odd that their father is a writer.

I must also thank the excellent people at The University of Alberta Press. Working with them has been a pleasurable and rewarding experience. Because of them, this book is better than I ever could have hoped. Thanks too, to Ann Percival for re-drawing my sketch map, and to the staff at the L.E. Shore Memorial Library for their patience with my many inter-library loan requests.

Time is the great editor. This book, the book you hold in your hands, couldn't have been written twenty years ago. The material was still too fresh; the ache of separation, too raw. But time brings perspective. The Bhutan I wrote about in my first attempts was too perfect. I see this tendency in travel writers all the time when they write of Bhutan. They cannot resist the dreaded S-word: Shangri-La. The book I would have written in 1989 would not have been a completely honest book. For while Bhutan is to be lauded for its cautious development policy, its determination to put Gross National Happiness before Gross Domestic Product, its forward-looking environmental policies, and its tentative but brave steps toward parliamentary democracy, Bhutan harbours a dirty little secret: more than a hundred thousand of its citizens, about one-eighth of its total population, mostly Lhotsampa, live in exile. I witnessed the beginnings of this policy of cultural hegemony in 1988. Since then things have only gotten worse. Many of the Nepali minority had to leave because they did not have the required bits of paper to prove their residency; many left because they no longer felt safe in southern Bhutan. By the 1990s, the trickle of refugees had become a flood. Schools were closed across the southern districts. There were violent acts on both sides. The situation is summed up admirably in Michael Hutt's, *Unbecoming Citizens* (see "Suggested Readings").

Today most of these refugees live in camps in eastern Nepal administered by the office of the United Nations High Commissioner for Refugees (UNHCR). Amnesty International has called the situation "one of the most protracted and neglected refugee crises in the world."[18] Bhutan has not made any serious attempt to resolve the crisis and there has been little international support for the plight of the refugees. The UNHCR has thrown up its hands in despair, asking Western countries to accept Bhutanese refugees for resettlement, as there is little hope for their future in Nepal and little hope of their repatriation to Bhutan.[19]

The government of Bhutan has defended its actions by saying that theirs is a culture under threat. Where there were once many Buddhist kingdoms in the Himalayas, there is now only one. "If we were spotted owls," the foreign minister of Bhutan once remarked, "the world would care about us. Can't you see that we're an endangered species too?"[20] The government's case is put most sympathetically in Barbara Crossette's *So Close To Heaven* (see "Suggested Readings"). There are obviously two sides to any story. I know where I stand. I will leave the reader to make up his or her own mind.

NOTES

1   This figure is taken from Raymond G., Jr. Gordon, ed., *Ethnologue: Languages of the World*, *Fifteenth Edition* (Dallas, Tex.: SIL International, 2005). Online version: http://www.ethnologue. com/(September 5, 2007). Sadly, with the advent of modern communication routes and schools, some of Bhutan's languages are in danger of disappearing.

2   From Michael Aris's *The Raven Crown* (London: Serindia Publications, 1994), 24.

3   *Gharry*, or *gari*, is the Hindi word for "cart" or "carriage."

4   Both of the manuscripts containing Dewa's story were stored in Tashigang Dzong. They were discovered by Michael Aris in 1971, and he made English translations of them. Aris attributed both works to the same hand, a Drukpa monk named Nawang of the Byar Clan, working in Tashigang Dzong. The first, called *The Lamp which Illuminates the Origins of Royal Families*, is a kind of royal genealogy, listing the clans that claimed descent from Prince Tsangma of Tibet. King Dewa is mentioned and placed in context. The second, more interesting text (at least from my perspective), is called *The Clear Mirror*, a narrative account of the Drukpa subjugation of Eastern Bhutan. Both texts were written in the early part of the eighteenth century, but they narrate events that happened at least eighty years earlier. The author seems curiously two-faced. *The Lamp* praises and legitimizes the rule of the eastern clan kings, while *The Clear Mirror* glorifies the Drukpa conquest. Aris explains this contradiction by noting that the author is a member of the ancient Byar clan, mentioned in the *The Lamp*, but also a monk of the Drukpa order.

    The Clear Mirror begins with a land dispute. King Dewa of Khaling and another claimant both claim the same piece of land in the Indian *duars*. Two envoys are sent from Tibet to adjudicate the dispute and Dewa loses. Because the envoys do not speak the local languages, interpreters are needed and, for some reason, Dewa takes a dislike to his rival's interpreter, Lama Namsay. Dewa's revenge is Machiavellian. He invites the envoys to his home, plies them with delicious food and liquor, and then, when they are inebriated, hints that Lama Namsay has kept all of the best-looking girls for his own service. The drunken envoys reel off to confront Namsay over the truth of this statement. A fatal scuffle breaks out. Two men are killed and one is wounded. Lama Namsay has to flee for his life. He can't return to Tibet, so instead he escapes to Tongsa where he enlists in the service of the powerful Tongsa *penlop*, a man who would later become the first temporal ruler of Bhutan after the death of Shabdrung Nawang Namgyal. Three years later, Lama Namsay marches back to Eastern Bhutan at the head of the Drukpa army and, step-by-step, starting in Bumthang, begins the conquest of Eastern Bhutan for the Shabdrung to whom he had sworn allegiance. Eventually, he faces his last opponent, King Dewa, and Dewa's allies at the Weng-li Bridge. When Dewa's allies see Lama Namsay's victorious army, they capitulate without a fight and Dewa has no option but to eat crow and submit to the rule of the Shabdrung (who, in all likelihood, is probably dead by this time, but this remains a state secret for many years). The author of *The Clear Mirror* makes it clear that Dewa's allegiance is pragmatic rather than heartfelt and that he is only biding his time before he can openly declare his independence once again. As it happens, when the *Khaling-pa* do rise up in revolt some years later, they have a new king named Chand-lo-dpal. Nothing more is mentioned of the cunning Dewa and he disappears from history. Chand-lo-dpal allies himself with the King of Kanglung and they are soundly and easily defeated by Lama Namsay. The kings and their sons are marched off to prison in Punakha Dzong and Prince Tsangma's dynasty comes to an end. There will be one last uprising in Eastern Bhutan, but this time it is led by an invading Tibetan army in 1657. Disgruntled *Khaling-pa* join forces with the Tibetans and besiege Lama Namsay at Bengkhar (the old name for Tashigang Dzong). Lama Namsay is captured and taken to Lhasa as a prisoner where he later dies trying to escape. Drukpa forces quickly march in, expel the Tibetans, and restore order. And so the independent kingdom of Khaling becomes a memory.

5   Michael Hutt, *Unbecoming Citizens. Culture, Nationhood, and the Flight of Refugees from Bhutan.* (New Delhi: Oxford University Press, 2003), 165.

6   *Shing* is Bhutanese for "stick" or "wood." "Lopen Shing" was the nickname for the bamboo staff teachers used to beat their pupils.

7   If he had mailed it to me in a parcel labeled "video," it would never have arrived. Our mail was frequented purloined. My favourite story was of a volunteer who received a parcel from home with some new music cassettes. She could see that her parcel had been opened and then resealed, but everything appeared to have arrived in one piece. However, when she opened the plastic cases containing the cassettes, she found that the thief, in a strangely honorable gesture, had replaced each of her rock-and-roll cassettes with a tape of Hindi film music.

8   Most of the statistics quoted in this chapter are taken from the Renewable Natural Resources Statistics 2000 published by the Ministry of Agriculture, Royal Government of Bhutan. This can be found online at http://www.moa.gov.bt/ (accessed February 26, 2008).

9   Food and Agricultural Organization of the United Nations, "Table 1. Land Use in 1998" and "Table 3. Agricultural Population" from *Selected Indicators of Food and Agricultural Development in Asia-Pacific Region, 1989-99*(2000).

10   Writing of the black-necked crane in Gantey, Peter Matthiessen notes: "In winter, the black-necked crane seeks valleys wide enough to provide waste barley in the harvested, unplowed fields and a stream broad enough to ensure safe roosting. Since most of these high valleys lack wetlands for foraging, the winter cranes depend almost entirely on harvest gleanings, as they have for centuries. (One wonders how they managed before man.) Such dependence is dangerous, since agricultural practices may change[.]" Matthiessen also notes that, were it not for the Buddhist prescription against taking life, the vulnerable crane would surely have been hunted to extinction by now. From Peter Matthiessen's *The Birds of Heaven* (Vancouver: Greystone Books, 2001), 128, 137–38. Travelling the same route in 2004, Michael Palin noted that an attempt to substitute the cultivation of barley in Gantey Valley with more profitable seed potatoes was blocked by no less an authority than the king himself on the grounds that a shift in agricultural practices would signal the demise of the black-necked crane. From Michael Palin's *Himalaya* (London: Weidenfeld & Nicolson, 2004), 241.

11   Bhola did not return to the school until seven months had passed (long after I had returned to Canada), and had not communicated with the school during that whole period of time. This left things a bit awkward, since he was just one payment short of owning my shortwave radio/cassette player. When he returned and found that I was gone and had not left the radio for him, he was understandably furious. Fortunately, Grant wrote and told me the situation and I was able to reimburse Bhola, though I still feel guilty about not being able to honour our original bargain.

12   Not all of these visitors were foreign travellers. Many were volunteers, like me, seeking a weekend away in the sybaritic pleasures of the district capital. Still, it must have been hell to play host every single weekend.

13   The rift between the two families goes back to the founding of Bhutan and to the failure of Shabdrung Ngawang Namgyel to provide an acceptable heir. Following his death, the Shabdrung returned in a triple incarnation: body, mind, and speech. The line of the body incarnation quickly died out, but the speech and mind incarnations continued to be reborn and hold an importance in the religious life of Bhutan. Of particular importance was the mind incarnation, who held the seat at Talo Monastery and who functioned, at least in British eyes, as the ceremonial head of state.

     The sixth mind incarnation, Shabdrung Jigme Dorji, became involved in some political intrigue during the reign of the second king of Bhutan. It is difficult to say at this point what his degree of culpability was. Was he a traitor or simply a naïve pawn in the game of other ambitious men? At any rate, a delegation from the Shabdrung went to India to seek the aid of, of all people, Mahatma Gandhi in the restoration of some of his ancient rights, privileges, lands, and honours. It wasn't the first time that the young lama had trespassed on the king's prerogative. When this action came to the ears of the king, he ordered the Shabdrung's family and followers arrested and brought to Tongsa for questioning. Troops loyal to the king laid siege to Talo Monastery, but for two weeks they left the Shabdrung in peace under house arrest, unsure of their next step, since the Shabdrung was such a revered person in Bhutan. As Michael Aris notes, it was a situation that called to mind the conflict between Henry II and Thomas Becket, and one could almost imagine the King of Bhutan muttering, "Who will rid me of this troublesome priest?" (Michael Aris, *Raven Crown*, 120). In any case, on November 12, 1931, the Shabdrung died under mysterious circumstances at the young age of twenty-six. The official version was that he died in his sleep. Some said that he had ingested poison to avoid punishment, but most suspected that he had been assassinated. The truth finally came to light in 1999 when the eldest Queen of Bhutan, Ashi Dorji Wangmo Wangchuck, published a biography of her father in which it was stated that Shabdrung Jigme Dorji was choked to death by men loyal to the king. The Shabdrung had been her father's uncle. Her father's brother was also the last speech incarnation of the Shabdrung. Thus, in one powerful family, the last two incarnations of the Shabdrung had come to be joined and a second royal family had been created, something the Wangchucks saw as potentially dangerous to the stability of the realm; but, it should be noted, something they were willing to overlook until Shabdrung Jigme Dorji began to make a nuisance of himself. The Shabdrung's family was dispossessed of many of its lands and possessions by the Paro *penlop* and they fled first to Tibet and then to India for safety and lived for a time under house arrest in Ha Valley. In time, their fortunes were rehabilitated, lands were restored, and the royal marriage in 1988 signalled that old grudges were at last forgotten. The last speech incarnation of the Shabdrung died in 1949 and the last incumbent indicated before his death that there will not be another. There have been several candidates for the line of mind incarnation, but none that have been officially recognized by the government of Bhutan and none live within the boundaries of its rule. In 1995, the King of Bhutan sponsored a gold statue of Shabdrung Jigme Dorji to be installed in Talo. His Majesty the King of Bhutan, attended the installation on the anniversary of the Shabdrung's death and his son, the crown prince, assisted with the ritual. The second king had acted through agents when punishing the Shabdrung and his family, but the present monarch publicly participated in the rehabilitation of Shabdrung Jigme Dorji's reputation and that of his family. In the words of the queen's father, "No monarch had visited Talo before and the gift of the golden statue was an exceptional act of faith, nobility and requital." (Ashi Dorji Wangchuck. *Of Rainbows and Clouds*, 118). After sixty-four years, the ghosts of enmity had finally been laid to rest.

14 Barbara Crossette. *So Close to Heaven: The Vanishing Buddhist Kingdoms of the Himalayas*. (New York: Vintage Books, 1996), 9.

15 *Dzongdag* is a title, meaning "district chief." The *dzongdags*, all eighteen of them, are appointed by the king and responsible to the minister of home affairs. They replace the old system of district governors or *penlops* established by Shabdrung Ngawang Namgyel in the seventeenth century.

16   See Kunzang Choden, *Bhutanese Tales of the Yeti* (Bangkok: White Lotus Press, 1997), 137–39.

17   "The documentation of folk tales in Bhutan is still in its infancy," wrote Tandin Dorji in the *Journal of Bhutan Studies* in 2002. The first collection of folk tales was by Dasho Sherab Thaye in 1984, and several others have followed, most notably by Kunzang Choden, Kinley Wangmo, and Françoise Pommaret, but "the collections made until today [are] just a drop considering the vast reservoir of folktales that [lie] recorded in the memories of the Bhutanese." (Tandin Dorji, "Folktale Narration: A Retreating Tradition" in *Journal of Bhutan Studies*, 6 (Summer 2002): 5–6). See also the article by Françoise Pommaret, "Recent Bhutanese Scholarship in History and Anthropology," in *Journal of Bhutan Studies*, 2:2 (Winter 2000): 128–50 for a list of folktale sources. Most of these collections of ballads, proverbs, and folk tales, however, are not available in English. Notable exceptions are the collections by Kunzang Choden: *Folk Tales of Bhutan* (1993) and *Bhutanese Tales of the Yeti* (1997), both published by White Lotus of Bangkok.

18   "Amnesty International's concerns at the 55th Session of the Executive Committee of the United Nations High Commissioner for Refugees, October 2004," http://archive.amnesty. org/library/Index/ENGIOR410312004?open&of=ENG-BTN (accessed February 27, 2008).

19   http://www.unhcr.org/news/NEWS/43c7a5505.html (accessed February 27, 2008). http://www.unhcr.org/news/NEWS/45262b462.html (accessed February 27, 2008).

20   Quoted in Michael Hutt, *Unbecoming Citizens*, 272.

GLOSSARY

Glossary of Dzongkha, Hindi, and Sharchopkha words used in this book
Key: (d) Dzongkha; (h) Hindi; (s) Sharchopkha

abi (s) grandmother
ama (s) mother
apa (s) father
ara (d) alcohol made from distilled corn mash
bidi (h) small hand-rolled cigarette
bangchung (s) flat, round baskets sold in pairs; can be used as a plate or as a storage
    container if one basket is used as a lid on the other
chappals (h) sandals, usually refers to plastic beach sandals in Bhutan.
chhang (d) beer made from grain; sometimes "bangchhang" in Eastern Bhutan
    if made with barley
chhowang (s) large straight knife, like a machete
chhu (d) water or river
chorten (d) Buddhist funerary monument
chula (h) clay stove
chutsi (s) holiday
dacoit (h) bandit
dani (s) cat
Dasho (d) title of high rank conferred by the king, as royalty in English confer
    the title of "Sir" in England
Dasho Dzongdag (d) district administrator

dekor (s) a game similar to horseshoes played with flat stones

dungchen (s) long telescoping brass horns played in religious ceremonies, similar in size to Swiss alpenhorns

dzong (d) fortress

galing (d) oboe-like instrument played in religious ceremonies

gapu (s) village headman

gasha (d) barking deer

gharry (h) truck

gho (d) traditional robe for men

go-down warehouse

gomchen (s) a lay priest, usually Nyingmapa, who is allowed to marry

gompa (d) monastery that is not a teaching establishment

Guru Rinpoche "Precious Master," the title applied to Padmasambhava

imadatsi (d) a dish made of fried cheese and hot chilies

jola (s) large shoulder bag carried by men and women

kading-chhe (d) thank you

kemar (d) a broad red horizontal stripe decorating the outside wall of a religious building

khalasi (h) helper, ticket-taker for the driver of a bus or truck

khar (d) ancient fortified tower

kira (d) traditional dress for women

korla (s) a game like horseshoes played with large darts

kota (s) brother

kuzu zangpo (d) hello; literally translated, it means "you are well."

lam (d) road or pathway

lha-kang (s) temple

Lhotsampa (d) people of southern Bhutan

lopen (d) teacher

meme (s) grandfather

mo-mo a Tibetan dumpling

Ngawang Namgyel first Drukpa ruler of a united Bhutan in the seventeenth century; also known as the Shabdrung

ngultrum (d) unit of currency in Bhutan, on par with the Indian rupee

o jonme (s) where are you going? (a polite form of address, as opposed to "o dele" in the common speech)

odo (s) come here

Om Mani Padme Hum the mantra of the deity Avalokiteshvara, translated as
"The Jewel in the Lotus"; L. Austine Waddell says that each syllable represents
a different Buddhist realm and that by chanting the mantra, one helps to break
the cycle of rebirth.

Padmasambhava eighth-century Buddhist missionary from Swat in Pakistan,
founder of the Nyingmapa School

pan (h) betel nut

philing-pa (s) foreigner

pujah (h) religious ceremony

sari (s) in Bhutan this refers to a broad sash used to carry firewood or children
on one's back

Shabdrung (d) title meaning "at whose feet one submits," typically used for
Ngawang Namgyel and his mind incarnations

shedra (d) monastery where young monks are educated; *dratshang* in Sharchopkha

sujah (s) butter tea

tengma (s) pounded corn

thanka (d) large wall-hanging of a religious subject

tsetchu (d) religious festival honouring Guru Rinpoche, usually held over three days

tukpa noodle soup with meat

tulku the reincarnation of a lama

usen (s) sister

Yallah or Yallama (d) common exclamation, like "Oh my God!" in English

zhugcho-la (s) please sit down (in polite speech)

SUGGESTED READINGS

Aris, Michael. *Bhutan: The Early History of a Himalayan Kingdom*. Warminster, England: Aris & Phillips Ltd., 1979.

Aris, Michael. *Hidden Treasures and Secret Lives: A Study of Pemalingpa (1450–1521) and The Sixth Dalai Lama (1683–1706)*. London: Kegan Paul International, 1989.

Aris, Michael. *The Raven Crown: The Origins of Buddhist Monarchy in Bhutan*. London: Serindia Publications, 1994.

Aris, Michael, ed. *Sources for the History of Bhutan*. Wien: Arbeitskreis Fur Tibetische und Buddhistische Studien Universitat Wien, 1986.

Choden, Kunzang. *Bhutanese Tales of the Yeti*. Bangkok: White Lotus Press, 1997.

Collister, Peter. *Bhutan and the British*. London: Serindia Publications, 1987.

Crossette, Barbara. *So Close to Heaven: The Vanishing Buddhist Kingdoms of the Himalayas*. New York: Random House, 1995.

Davis, Samuel. *Views of Medieval Bhutan: The Diary and Drawings of Samuel Davis, 1783*. Edited by Michael Aris. London: Serindia Publications, 1982.

The Divine Madman: The Sublime Life and Songs of Drukpa Kunley. Translated into English by Keith Dowman and Sonam Paljor. London: Rider and Company, 1980.

Dorji, Tandin. "Folktale Narration: A Retreating Tradition." *Journal of Bhutan Studies*, 6 (Summer 2002): 5–23.

Eden, Ashley, et al. *Political Missions to Bootan: Comprising the reports of The Hon'ble Ashley Eden, 1864; Capt. R. B. Pemberton, 1837, 1838 with Dr. W. Griffiths's Journal and the Account by Baboo Kishen Kant Bose*. New Delhi: Munshiram Manoharlal Publishers Pvt. Ltd., 2000.

Hellum, A. K. *A Painter's Year in the Forests of Bhutan*. Edmonton: The University of Alberta Press, 2001.

Hutt, Michael. *Unbecoming Citizens: Culture, Nationhood, and the Flight of Refugees from Bhutan*. New Delhi: Oxford University Press, 2003.

Matthiessen, Peter. *The Birds of Heaven: Travels with Cranes*. Vancouver: Greystone Books, 2001.

Palin, Michael. *Himalaya*. London: Weidenfeld & Nicolson, 2004.

Pommaret, Françoise. *Bhutan: The Himalayan Kingdom*. Lincolnwood, Illinois: Passport Books, 1990.

Pommaret, Françoise. "Recent Bhutanese Scholarship in History and Anthropology." *Journal of Bhutan Studies*, 2:2 (Winter 2000): 128–50.

Sarin, V. I. K. *India's North-East in Flames*. New Delhi: Vikas, 1980.

Solverson, Howard. *The Jesuit and the Dragon: The Life of Father William Mackey in the Himalayan Kingdom of Bhutan*. Toronto: Robert Davies Publishing, 1995.

Waddell, L. Austine. *Tibetan Buddhism, With its Mystic Cults, Symbolism and Mythology, and in its Relation to Indian Buddhism*. New York: Dover Publications, Inc., 1972 (reprint of the 1895 edition).

Wangchuck, Ashi Dorji Wangmo. *Of Rainbows and Clouds: The Life of Yab Ugyen Dorji as told to his daughter, Her Majesty the Queen of Bhutan Ashi Dorji Wangmo Wangchuck*. London: Serindia Publications, 1999.

Zeppa, Jamie. *Beyond the Sky and the Earth: A Journey into Bhutan*. Toronto: Doubleday Canada Limited, 1999.